RV Education 101 Presents

The RV Book

Your Personal Guide to Understanding and Enjoying your RV

Take an RV tour with Mark Polk and get all of your questions answered

- ➤ What is an RV?
- ➤ RV Terminology
- ➤ Selecting your RV
- ➤ Buying your RV
- ➤ Using your RV
- ➤ Maintaining your RV
- ➤ Weighing your RV
- ➤ Winterizing your RV
- ➤ Storing your RV
- ➤ RV Insurance
- ➤ RV Towing
- ➤ RV Safety

…and everything in between

By Mark J. Polk

Mark J. Polk

RV Education 101
3969 Stedman Cedar Creek Rd.
Fayetteville, NC 28312

The RV Book, Copyright © 2007, By Mark J. Polk

Second Paperback Edition

First printing 2006
Second printing 2006
Third printing 2007, revised and expanded

All rights reserved. No part of this book may be reproduced or transmitted in any form or by any means, be it electronic, mechanical, photocopying, recording, digital scanning or information storage and retrieval system without written permission from the author. Copying this book or any portion of this book is in violation of copyright laws.

There are numerous RVs and RV product and equipment manufacturers. The details provided in this book are generic and may not be applicable on certain tow vehicles or Recreation Vehicles, equipment and products. RV Education 101 is not liable for the information covered, or not covered in this book. Always consult your owner's manuals, equipment manuals, towing manuals and specific product installation and operating manuals prior to using any RV products, equipment or appliances on your RV. If you do not feel comfortable or if you have questions regarding a specific system, product, or product installation you should consult a professional RV technician prior to using any system, product, or equipment on your RV.

Cover designed by Cary Hyodo, www.gnuink.com

Opening page photograph by Stephanie Bruce/Fayetteville Observer

Library of Congress Control Number 2005909412

ISBN 0-9776025-1-6

www.rveducation101.com
www.rvuniversity.com

This book is dedicated to my wife Dawn and our two boys Josh & Tyler

Mark J. Polk

C ontents

Mark J. Polk

Acknowledgements

For many years, I have been writing RV related articles for RV magazines, RV newsletters, RV websites and other publications. I wrote these articles in an effort to help RVers learn how to properly use and maintain their RV's. One day, a while back, I was sitting at my desk and the thought occurred to me if I could organize all of this writing I had enough information to fill a book. "The RV Book"

And so it was done. To reach this point required a great deal of time, research and help from other people along the way. I am grateful to own a business, RV Education 101, which allowed me the time to work on and eventually make "The RV Book" a reality.

Our primary business is to produce RV training videos on how to use and maintain RV's. In addition to actually producing the videos, day to day business operations require processing, packaging and shipping orders, answering phone calls, responding to e-mails, running errands and more. If I had to do all of this by myself there would be no book. I would like to thank my wife, Dawn, for handling the day to day business operations, to include the sales and marketing of our various products.

Writing this book also required input from other people and organizations at times. I would like to thank John Anderson and the Recreation Vehicle Safety Education Foundation (RVSEF) for their input. John is the former Executive Director of RVSEF. RVSEF is dedicated to the improvement of Recreation Vehicle Safety, with a focus on education. Their goal is to provide safety education resources to everyone who operates a Recreation Vehicle. RVSEF offers a comprehensive RV Safety Education program that includes both written manuals and video instruction. More information about RVSEF is available at **www.rvsafety.org**

Mark J. Polk

In no particular order I would also like to thank:

The Recreation Vehicle Industry Association (RVIA) **www.rvia.org** for their contributions. RVIA represents the RV industry and works to promote RV travel by providing information to the media and the general public.

The Recreation Vehicle Dealers Association (RVDA) **www.rvda.org** for their contributions. RVDA represents RV dealers and provides educational programs, products and services to its members. RV Education 101 is proud to be an associate member of RVDA.

The Go RVing Coalition **www.gorving.com** for working to provide the public with pertinent information about the benefits of RV travel and to foster customer satisfaction with the RV experience.

The Recreational Park Trailer Industry Association (RPTIA) **www.rptia.org** for their contributions. RPTIA represents the manufacturers of RPTs and provides industry specific information for consumers.

Bridgestone/Firestone North American Tire, **www.tiresafety.com** & **www.trucktires.com** for their contributions on increased RV consumer tire safety awareness.

Peggi McDonald, author of *RV Living in the 21st Century* and webmaster of **www.rvliving.net,** for helping to edit and proofread my book.

Bob Zagami, former editor for RV News magazine, current editor for RV Enthusiast magazine at **www.popuptimes.com**, and industry consultant, for helping to edit and proofread my book.

Without the help of these organizations and individuals certain portions of this book would not be possible.

For photographs and charts used in "The RV Book" I would like to thank:

The Recreation Vehicle Industry Association RVIA, **www.rvia.org**

The Recreation Vehicle Safety Education Foundation RVSEF, **www.rvsafety.org**

Blue Ox Towing Products, **www.blueox.us**

Roadmaster, Inc., **www.roadmasterinc.com**

Reese Products, **www.reeseproducts.com**

Equalizer Hitch, **www.equalizerhitch.com**

RV Education 101 Endorsed Partners:
RV Education 101 is a proud co-founder of the Circle of Trust RV Family (COT), **www.circleoftrustrvfamily.org.** COT is a group of independently owned RV related companies who proudly serve the RV consumer. Anne Pierson, a fellow COT co-founder, owns the Happy Camper Half Price RV Club. As a member of the Happy Camper RV Club you can enjoy camping for half price at over 1,000 campgrounds. For more information go to **www.camphalfprice.com** or call 1-866-677-6453. Anne also owns **www.rvscrapbook.com**, a fun, social network for RV camping.

RV Education 101 is proud to partner with KOA (Kampgrounds of America) where you can enjoy great people and great camping, www.koa.com. With 450 campgrounds in their North American network you can always find a KOA close by.

RV Education 101 is proud to partner with National Interstate Insurance Company and Explorer RV Insurance Agency, Inc., www.exlorerrv.com. Be sure and read the specialty RV insurance content provided by National Interstate Insurance Company and Explorer RV Insurance Agency, Inc., in Chapter 5.

Mark J. Polk

Introduction

I was first introduced to RV's as a teenager in the seventies. A good friend of mine, whose father was the General Manager for an RV dealership, would take us camping all of the time. Before long I was working for the dealership. I started out washing RV's, and soon I was working as an apprentice RV technician.

Not long after graduating from high school I joined the Army and was a wheeled vehicle and power generation mechanic. Six years later I graduated from Warrant Officer School, as an automotive maintenance technician, and was in charge of some very large maintenance operations throughout my military career. I retired from the Army in 1996 as a Chief Warrant Officer Three.

After retiring, I got back into the industry I had a passion for. I started out selling RVs for a dealership in North Carolina and was soon promoted to the sales manager. When we sold a unit we would give the new owners a walk through orientation of the RV. I quickly realized it was too much information, in a short period of time, for them to retain everything. I was concerned about the lack of education and safety awareness available to the RV consumer and started my own company, RV Education 101, in 2000. We produce and sell RV training videos on how to use and maintain RV's.

RV Education 101 started with orientation videos for the different types of RV's and eventually expanded into more specialized videos and e-books on all types of RV related subjects. I found myself writing for RV trade and RV consumer magazines, RV newsletters and various RV websites. In 2004 I started doing a television segment, called RV Savvy, for an RV television program that airs in the United States and Canada. The only thing left to do was write a book about RV's. So here it is, "The RV Book." I hope you enjoy it and more importantly, I hope you will benefit from reading it.

Happy Camping,
Mark

Mark J. Polk

Chapter 1

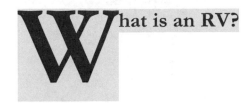

What is an RV?

Before we talk about the types of Recreation Vehicles (RVs) let's talk about what an RV is. The Recreation Vehicle Industry Association (RVIA) describes an RV as a vehicle that combines transportation and temporary living quarters for travel, recreation and camping. RVs come in many different types, sizes and price ranges. Some are very basic starting around $5,000, which provide basic sleeping arrangements and cooking facilities. On the other end of the spectrum there are luxury land yachts on wheels costing more than $1,000,000.

RVs are categorized as either towable or motorized. Towable RVs are towed behind a vehicle, then disconnected and set up when you arrive at your destination. This allows you the benefit of using the tow vehicle to make a trip to the store, or go sight seeing while you are camping. Towable RVs include folding camping trailers (pop-ups), truck campers, travel trailers, hybrid trailers, sport utility trailers (toy haulers) and 5th wheel trailers. Motorized RVs are built on a special vehicle chassis and powered by either a gasoline or diesel engine. There are three classifications for motorized RVs: Type A, B, and C. Another type of RV is the Recreational Park Trailer (RPT). RPTs are basically designed to be set up at a vacation destination and left there. Let's take a look at each type. Understanding more about each type of RV can help you decide which type is right for you.

Types of RV's

Folding Camping Trailers often referred to as pop-ups are the least expensive RVs. They are designed to be lightweight and for the most part inexpensive while still providing many of the comforts and conveniences found in a travel trailer. Pop-ups incorporate a lift system to raise the roof. When the roof is raised there is a tent fabric, either one piece or several sections, that is attached to the roof and the box, and expands out to accommodate the pull out bed ends.

RV photos courtesy of RVIA
www.rvia.org

The beds come in different sizes and along with the box size determine the overall open length of the pop-up. Sizes range from 15 feet to 24 feet when open. The ends and sides collapse for towing and storage, and therefore take up little space when not being used. Most pop-ups provide standard equipment or features like a sink, stove, icebox, fresh water storage tank, table, pull out beds, an LP gas supply, and a separate 12-volt DC and 120-volt AC electrical system. Many of today's pop-ups have small slide out sections on the sides, designed to give you additional living space inside.

Most pop-up manufacturers offer what I refer to as an entry-level line and a deluxe line. Some of the differences are in construction such as the roof and lift system, the size, and in how they are equipped. Options available for some pop-ups are air conditioning, refrigerator, water heater, furnace, dual LP gas bottles, inside or outside shower, upgraded interiors, awning, screen room and electric brakes. Top-of-the-line units may also include an interior bathroom for maximum privacy while camping.

Pop-ups are commonly referred to by their box size. What this means is the length of the box that is mounted to the frame of the trailer. For years, manufacturers offered 8-foot, 10-foot and 12-foot boxes for their pop-ups. Now innovative manufacturers are coming out with even larger versions, 14-foot boxes, and off road models for campers that really want to explore America's back roads. The closed length of a pop-up is measured from the front of the tongue to the rear bumper. Pop-ups can sleep up to eight people depending on the model and prices can range from $5,000 to over $13,000.

> **Note:** All prices mentioned in this book are in US currency.

Pros	Pop-Up	Cons
Lightweight		Set-up & take-down
Doesn't require a special tow vehicle		Limited security
Fairly inexpensive		Limited protection in bad weather
Compact & versatile		Limited storage space

Truck Campers are campers loaded onto the bed of a pickup truck. This makes for a very versatile RV that can access back roads and remote areas other RVs can't get to. Truck campers are often times the choice for avid outdoorsmen and women.
It provides all the benefits of other RVs and still allows you to tow a boat, motorcycle trailer or horse trailer behind the truck.

Today's truck campers comes available in many different sizes and floor plans. They are built in 8, 9, 10 and 11 foot plus models. They come equipped with kitchen facilities, dining areas, bathrooms, and sleeping arrangements. Many manufacturers are making these campers more spacious by extending the cab-over area and adding small slide-outs. Slide-outs are designed to provide more living space inside an RV. Numerous options are available to include air conditioners and generators making the truck camper fully self-contained. You need to have a truck that is capable of carrying the weight of the camper. When you're not using the camper it can be removed from the truck.

Like most other RV types there are entry level models and deluxe models. There are also light weight versions available. Construction methods vary from wood frame with corrugated aluminum sides to welded aluminum framing with fiberglass sides. Some manufacturers offer fold down versions of truck campers that are low profile and lighter for traveling. When you arrive at your destination you raise the roof for additional head room. A tent fabric similar to what is used on a pop-up attaches the roof to the hard sides of the trailer when it's in the raised position. Truck campers can sleep up to six people depending on the model, and prices range from $6,000 to over 23,000.

Pros	Truck Camper	Cons
Access remote areas	Most require heavy duty truck
Still able to tow a boat or trailer	Limited space inside
With a generator you're fully self-contained	Limited storage
No extra license plate or inspection	Loading & Unloading from vehicle

Travel Trailers are a popular choice among RVers because of the wide variety of floor plans available. Whether it's for two people or eight you can find a model that will suit your needs. As with other towables they can be disconnected and set  up when you arrive at your destination. This allows you the benefit of using the tow vehicle to make a trip to the store, or to go sight seeing.

Travel trailers range in size from 15 to 37 feet and offer all the comforts of home. Most travel trailer manufacturers offer what I refer to as entry level models, mid-line models and high end models. Think of it in terms like a Chevrolet, a Buick or a Cadillac. With today's lighter weight tow vehicles almost all manufacturers offer lightweight and ultra-lightweight versions too.

Construction techniques vary from wood frame with aluminum siding to welded aluminum frame with fiberglass siding. Many travel trailers offer slide-outs designed to provide more living space inside an RV. You press a button and the slide-out extends outward giving you additional living space inside. It's not uncommon to see units with multiple slide-out sections in the living room, kitchen and bedroom areas. Travel trailers like most other RVs offer cooking facilities, dining areas, living rooms, bathrooms and sleeping arrangements. Travel trailers can sleep up to eight people depending on the model and prices range from $8,000 to more than $50,000.

Another version of the travel trailer is the **Hybrid Travel Trailer**. The concept is a small, light weight trailer with pull-out or drop-down bed ends similar to a pop-up. These hard-sided trailers can be easily  towed with today's smaller SUV's and provide much more space inside when they are set-up, without having to raise and lower the roof. Hybrids are equipped with most of the same amenities found in conventional travel trailers. Hybrid trailers can sleep up to six people and prices range from $8,000 to over $ 25,000.

Another addition to towable trailers is the **Sport Utility Trailer (SUT)**, also referred to as toy haulers and Sport Utility RV (SURV). These trailers have living quarters in the front and cargo space in the back. There is a rear ramp door that  lowers so you can load your motorcycles, ATV's or other toys that you want to take with you. They offer cooking facilities, dining areas, bathrooms, slide outs and sleeping arrangements like conventional travel trailers. There are lots of options available including generators, making the SUT fully self-contained so you can enjoy out of the way places. SUT's come in a variety of sizes to accommodate what the outdoor enthusiasts want to take along. The popularity of toy haulers lead manufacturers to build these in fifth wheel and motorhome models too, so prices can range anywhere from $15,000 to over $100,000.

Pros	Travel Trailer	Cons
Good selection of floor plans & sizes		Hitching & unhitching
At campground you have a vehicle to use for transportation		Requires specialized tow vehicle
More security & protection than a pop-up		No access to amenities while in route
Doubles as a guest house		Requires towing & backing skills

Fifth-Wheel Trailers are the ones you see that extend over the bed of the pickup or custom tow vehicle. Because of the bi-level design, fifth-wheels offer the most living space of any towable RV. They range in size from 21 to 40 feet. Fifth

wheels require a special type of hitch to be installed in the bed of a truck. The truck must be properly equipped and capable of handling the weight; this includes the weight placed directly over the rear axle.

Fifth wheels tow and handle better than conventional travel trailers and combined with spacious living quarters are often times the choice for fulltime RVers. Fifth wheels, like other towables, are available in entry level, mid-line and high-end models. Fifth-wheel manufacturer's offer many different floor plans. Two-thirds of all fifth-wheels built today offer at least one slide-out and most have multiple slide-outs, increasing the already spacious interiors. Lightweight versions that can be towed by smaller trucks are also very popular.

Construction techniques vary from wood frame with aluminum siding to welded aluminum frame with fiberglass siding. Like most other RVs, fifth-wheels offer kitchen facilities, dining areas, living rooms, bathrooms and sleeping arrangements. Optional equipment like generators, make fifth-wheels fully self-contained. Fifth-wheel trailers can sleep up to eight people depending on the model and prices range from $12,000 to $120,000.

Pros	Fifth Wheel	Cons
Extremely spacious		Requires specialized tow vehicle
Tows and handles better than travel trailers		More expensive than travel trailers
More storage than travel trailers		Weight concerns
Still have a vehicle to use		Hitching and unhitching

Type A Motorhomes are the largest and most luxurious, ranging from 25 to 45 feet. They are the ones you see that look similar to a bus, and depending on the price they can be equipped with features like washers and dryers, back-up cameras, hydraulic leveling jacks, multiple slide-out rooms, satellite dishes, home entertainment systems and much more.

Type A motorhomes are built on a specially designed vehicle chassis and are powered by either a gasoline or diesel engine. Many people think it would be difficult to drive a Type A motorhome, but with power steering, automatic transmissions and great visibility any experienced driver can quickly adapt. No special driver's license was required at the time this book was written. You have access to all of the amenities while you are traveling, including the bathroom. Type A motorhomes are fully self-contained with an onboard generator. Type A motorhomes, like other RV's, are available in entry level, mid line and high end models. They can sleep from six to eight people and prices range from $50,000 to $500,000. Some higher end luxury bus conversions can cost more than $1,000,000. If you want economical transportation when you arrive at your destination you can tow a small vehicle behind the motorhome.

Pros	Type A Motorhome	Cons
Extremely spacious		Added expense of towing a vehicle
Access to amenities while traveling		More expensive than other RV's
Most offer more storage than other types of RV's		Requires more maintenance & upkeep
Fully self-contained		

Mark J. Polk

Type B Motorhomes are the smallest of the three motorized RV's ranging from 16 to 20 plus feet. They are conversion vans that have been modified and equipped with all of the comforts and amenities found in other RVs, in a compact size.

They are easier to maneuver and park, more fuel efficient, and can be used as a second vehicle. Type B motorhomes are popular among all types of consumers. They work well for one and two travelers, or they can make a great family vehicle. Some models can sleep up to four people and come equipped with toilets, showers, kitchen facilities, water heater, furnace and a generator making them fully self-contained. Lots of people use Type B motorhomes to tow horse trailers and boats. They can range in price from $30,000 to over $80,000.

Pros	Type B Motorhome	Cons
Easy to drive	Limited interior space
Access to amenities while traveling	Limited storage space
More fuel efficient than other RV's	Not as convenient for long trips
Good for travel and everyday use	

Type C Motorhomes, also referred to as mini-motorhomes, are built on a cutaway van chassis. With larger and heavier models being built some manufacturers are using truck chassis' with higher weight

capacities. Type C motorhomes range in size from 20 to 37 feet. They are the type you see with the sleeping area extending over the vehicle cab. This additional sleeping space makes the Type C a good choice for a family. Some models can sleep 6 to 8 people. They are equipped with all of the amenities found in Type A motorhomes, and you have use of the amenities while you are traveling. The generator makes the motorhome fully self-contained. Like other RV's they are available in entry level, mid line and high end models ranging in price from $50,000 to $150,000. If you want economical transportation when you arrive at your destination you can tow a small vehicle behind the motorhome.

Pros   **Type C Motorhome**   **Cons**

Pros	Cons
Access to amenities while traveling	Added expense of towing a vehicle
Good motorhome for families	Requires more maintenance & upkeep
Most are fully self-contained	Many have limited outside storage

Recreational Park Trailers (RPTs) are designed to be used as temporary living quarters for recreation, camping, or seasonal use. In most cases these seasonal cottages are taken to a vacation spot,  set up and left there. This may be in an RV park, resort area, or a tranquil location in the mountains, or at the coast, usually within a few hours drive from the owner's residence. RPTs come in various designs but are normally one of two types. There are 12 foot wide models that are usually around 36 to 40 feet in length. This type has a peaked, shingled roof and siding like on a house or cottage. 12 foot wide models need to be moved by professionals with the proper type of equipment. The other type is slightly less than 8' 6" in width and up to 39 feet in length. This type looks more like a travel trailer and can be transported by the owner with a proper tow vehicle. They have slide outs to give additional living space when they are set up. Most park model trailers do not exceed 400 square feet and they are equipped with full bathrooms, kitchens, living room, bedrooms, heat and air, appliances and they are fully furnished. Because they are designed to be stationary for the most part many RPTs have full size appliances like you would find in your home, rather than RV type appliances. Prices can range from $15,000 to over $60,000.

Pros   **RTP**   **Cons**

Pros	Cons
Vacation home at favorite location	Less mobility
No towing or driving RV	Added expense of leasing a lot
More spacious	More maintenance & upkeep

9

Chapter 2

RV Terminology

When you work in the RV Industry and around RVs almost everyday you take some things for granted. One of those things is RV terminology. When you hear these terms everyday you just assume that everybody else understands them. Before we go any further there are some RV terms that you should be familiar with. If you hear or read an RV term that you don't understand you can come back here and find out exactly what it means. It would not be uncommon for a typical conversation between two RVers at a campground to go something like this:

"Hi my name's Fred. Nice rig you got there." "Thanks Fred, I'm Joe. It's a new pusher my wife and I just got. This is our maiden voyage with it." Fred replied "We still have our Type C; it works better for us with the kids. I told my wife we'd upgrade when we're empty nesters and can go fulltiming." Joe said, "Well I've seen some Type A's that aren't as nice as your Type C, you have two slides and a full basement." "We don't have any complaints, it's 29 feet long and with the Triton V10 it has plenty of power. I do wish the holding tanks were bigger, it seems like I'm dumping them all the time." Joe said, "We had the same problem with our fiver we traded in. I told the wife this time we're getting bigger holding tanks; pass through storage, 50-amp service and fiberglass with aluminum frame construction. No more stick and tin for us."

"Hey Joe is that the dinghy you tow behind your motorhome?" "Yes, we just got that too." Fred said, "I didn't know you could tow that model with all four wheels down." Joe replied, "That's why we got it. I didn't want to use a dolly and it only weighs 2,800 pounds. With the motorhome fully loaded we can tow it and not worry about exceeding our Gross Combined Weight Rating." Fred asked, "Did you have to make any driveline modifications to tow it with all four wheels on the ground? "No, and there are no speed or distance restrictions either." "Well Joe it was nice meeting you, I better finish with the campground hook ups." "Nice meeting you Fred. Why don't you and your wife stop by later." "We'll do that."

Now, for an RVer with a little experience this conversation makes perfectly good sense, but for the new RVer it may be a bit confusing. To help clear things up here are some common RV terms that you will encounter during your RVing experiences.

30 Amp, 120-volt Electrical System – Most RVs are designed with 30 amp, 120-volt electrical systems, and some of the larger RVs with more appliances and two roof A/Cs use a 50 amp, 120-volt electrical system. What this basically means is, for everything to operate properly the manufacturer intends the RV to have a 30 or 50 amp electrical service supplied to the RV. This subject is covered in depth in Chapter 6.

(A)

Aluminum Frame Construction – When the RV framing is made of aluminum as opposed to wood.

Artic Package – An RV that is equipped with additional insulation and heated holding tanks for cold weather camping.

Awning – An acrylic or vinyl covering mounted to the side of an RV that provides shade. Some awnings are retractable and use a spring-loaded roller tube. Other awnings must be rolled out by hand and are supported by poles, rope tie downs and stakes.

Axle Ratio – The number of times the drive shaft must turn to turn the axle one time. If you have a 3.73:1 axle ratio, the drive shaft turns 3.73 times for each full turn of the axle. The higher the numeric value of the axle ratio, the better the vehicle will tow; and the higher the numeric value the more gas you will use.

(B)

Backup Monitor – A monitor located in the driver's view that is attached to a small camera on the back of a motorhome. It is used to assist in backing the motorhome and to monitor what is happening behind you while traveling.

Ball & Ball Mount – Hitch balls have three basic measurements, the ball diameter, the shank diameter and the shank length. Ball diameter sizes come in 1 7/8", 2" and 2 5/16". The ball size must be the right size for the coupler on the trailer you are towing, and be rated to tow the trailers GVWR. The ball mount is the removable portion of the hitch that slides into the hitch receiver. For Weight Carrying (WC) hitches it may be necessary to find a ball mount with a drop or rise to help level the trailer when its hooked up to the tow vehicle. An adjustable ball mount is used for heavier trailer applications. Adjustable ball mounts allow the ball to be raised, lowered or tilted to compensate for trailer tongue weight and to attain proper height adjustments. Adjustable ball mounts are normally used with Weight Distributing (WD) hitches.

Basement Storage – Storage compartments or storage area located below the floor of the RV. You access the storage from outside. Some storage areas are referred to as pass through storage, which means it goes from one side of the RV to the other with no dividers, and can be accessed from either side.

Black Water Holding Tank – A tank mounted under the RV that collects water and waste from the toilet. When the tank is ¾ or more full it is emptied or dumped into an approved dump station or campground sewer. The black water tank is treated with chemicals to control odor and assist in breaking down waste.

Brake Controller – An electronic controller that is normally mounted under the dashboard of the tow vehicle, but within hands reach of the driver. The controller is designed to activate the trailer brakes when the tow vehicle brakes are applied. It also has a manual over ride that can be used to activate the trailer brakes without using the vehicle brakes.

Break-away Switch – A switch that is wired into the trailers brake system. It is attached from the trailer to the tow vehicle by a cable lanyard. In the event that the trailer and vehicle separate, the cable pulls a pin from the switch and the trailer brakes are activated. The switch must have a 12-volt source to operate.

Bumper Pull – A term used to describe towing a travel trailer or pop-up, also referred to as a pull behind.

(C)

Cab Over – The portion of a Type C motorhome that extends over the vehicle cab. It is usually outfitted with a bed or entertainment center.

Campground Hook-Ups – When you hook-up or connect your RV to the campground electric, water and sewer utilities. This would be considered a full hook-up. Some campgrounds may only offer one or two of these utility connections.

Cargo Carrying Capacity (CCC) is the maximum permissible weight of personal belongings and cargo that can be added to the RV. CCC is equal or less than GVWR minus UVW, full fresh water weight, and full LP gas weight.

City Water Connection – A water connection on the outside of the RV, used when you have an external water supply, such as at a campground. A potable water hose is used to connect the water supply to the city water connection on the RV.

Converter – An electrical device that converts 120-volt AC power into 12-volt DC power. With the exception of the roof air conditioner, microwave, TV and the electric mode of the refrigerator almost everything in an RV operates on 12-volt DC power supplied by a battery. When you're plugged into a 120-volt electrical source, the converter changes the 120-volts AC to 12-volts DC so everything can operate without draining the battery(s). The converter also has a battery charger that will keep the battery(s) topped off when you are plugged in to a 120-volt power source.

Coupler – Located on the front of the trailer A-frame, the coupler attaches the trailer to the ball on the hitch.

(D)

Deep Cycle Battery – Often referred to as the auxiliary battery(s) or house battery, it is used to supply 12-volt DC power to the appliances and accessories in the RV. Unlike an automotive starting battery they are designed to hold a charge longer and be discharged repeatedly. The RV battery(s) is charged when the motorhome is running, or in the case of a trailer, when the tow vehicle is running, if a charge line was wired in to the trailer plug. It is also charged when the RV is plugged into a 120-volt power source and by an onboard generator when it is running.

Delaminating – When the fiberglass panel separates from the luan backing used to construct fiberglass sidewalls on an RV. This is usually caused by water damage.

Demand Water Pump – The onboard water system that operates with a 12-volt demand pump. When you have potable water in your fresh water holding tank, and the pump is turned on, it pressurizes the onboard water system. When you open a faucet and the water pressure drops, the pump cycles on and off to maintain a constant pressure.

Diesel Pusher – A motorhome with a rear mounted diesel engine, often times referred to as a pusher.

Dinghy – A term used for the vehicle you are towing behind a motorhome.

Dry Camping – Camping in an RV without any utility hook-ups (water, electric, and sewer). You can still use all 12-volt appliances and accessories as long as the deep cycle battery(s) has a charge. You can also use the onboard water system with the 12-volt demand pump and if you have a generator you can use the 120-volt appliances and recharge the auxiliary battery(s). This is what makes an RV fully self-contained.

Dry Weight – Dry Weight (DW) or Unloaded Vehicle Weight (UVW) is the actual weight of the RV as built at the factory. The DW does not include passengers, cargo, fresh water, LP gas, fuel or after market accessories.

DSI- Direct Spark Ignition (DSI) is a system used to ignite the burner on a propane appliance with the touch of a button. It is commonly used on RV refrigerators, furnaces and on some water heaters.

Ducted A/C and Heat - When the A/C and heat is supplied throughout the RV using a ducting system. A/C is ducted in the ceiling and the heat is ducted in the floor.

Dually- A pickup truck that has two tires on each side of the rear axle.

Dump Outlet - Where both holding tanks terminate into one main outlet. This is where you connect the RV sewer hose to dump or empty the gray and black water holding tanks.

Dump Station – An area designated and approved for dumping or emptying your gray and black water holding tanks.

Electric brakes – Trailer brakes are electric and are activated when the tow vehicle brakes are applied by means of a brake controller installed in the tow vehicle.

Empty Nester – When all of the children are finally out of the house.

Equalizing Hitch – An equalizing hitch, or weight distributing hitch, uses additional hardware (spring bars and brackets) to distribute a percentage of the trailer's tongue weight to the axles on the tow vehicle and the axles on the trailer. Trailer tongue weight should be 10 to 15 percent of the loaded trailer weight.

Fifth Wheel Trailer – A trailer with a raised front end, that extends over the bed of a pickup truck, or custom tow vehicle. A special hitch is mounted in the bed of the truck, over the rear axle, to tow a fifth wheel trailer. Fifth wheels are frequently referred to as a fiver.

Filon® – A type of fiberglass sheeting made by Kemlite Company, Inc. used on RVs with fiberglass sidewall construction.

Fiver – Another term used for a fifth wheel trailer.

Folding Camping Trailer – Also known as a pop-up or tent trailer. They are the smallest of RV's with collapsible ends and sides for ease of towing and storage.

Fresh Water Fill – An opening on the outside of the RV where you can fill the fresh water holding tank with potable water to use when you are traveling or dry camping.

Fresh Water Holding Tank – A tank mounted under or in the RV that stores potable water for use while traveling or dry camping. To pressurize the system and use the water in the holding tank you turn the 12-volt demand pump on.

Full Hook-Up – A full hook-up means you connect the RV to the campground electric, water and sewer facilities. In addition to this it may also include cable TV and phone line connections.

Fulltimers / Fulltiming – Terms used for RVers that live and travel in their RV fulltime.

(G)

Generator – Commonly used on motorhomes, a generator produces 120-volt AC power. A generator allows you to use 120-volt appliances when you are not plugged into an external electrical source. Generators are rated in kilowatts. For example a 5 KW generator is 5,000 watts.

Genset – A short term for a generator set.

Gray Water Holding Tank – A tank mounted under the RV that collects wastewater from the sinks and shower. When you dump or empty your holding tanks you should always dump the black tank first, and then dump the gray tank. This will assist in rinsing out the flexible sewer hose.

Gross Axle Weight Rating (GAWR) - The maximum allowable weight that an axle is designed to support. The tow vehicle and trailer each have a GAWR.

Gross Combined Weight Rating (GCWR) - The maximum permissible weight of the tow vehicle and trailer **combined** when both are fully loaded for travel.

Gross Vehicle Weight Rating (GVWR) - The maximum permissible weight of the vehicle when fully loaded for travel. The tow vehicle and the trailer each have a GVWR.

Gross Vehicle Weight or Gross Trailer Weight (GVW), (GTW) - This is not a rating; this is the actual weight of the tow vehicle or trailer when they are fully loaded for travel.

(H)

Heat Strip – An electric heating element in a roof mounted air conditioner. A heat strip will take the chill off, but is not designed to actually heat the RV.

Hitch Receiver – The hitch receiver is mounted to the frame of the tow vehicle. The ball mount slides into the receiver. There are five classes of hitch receivers based on the maximum amount of weight the receiver can handle.

Hitch Weight – Hitch weight or Tongue Weight (TW) is the amount of weight pressing down on the vehicle's hitch from the coupler of the trailer when the trailer is fully loaded for travel. For trailers that weigh over 2,000 pounds TW should be 10 to 15 percent of the loaded trailer weight. For fifth wheel trailers hitch weight should be 15 to 20 percent of the loaded trailer weight.

Hydraulic Leveling Jacks – Used for leveling an RV, typically a Type A motorhome, they are leveling jacks that operate using hydraulics and are controlled by levers or a touch pad normally located near the drivers seat.

(I)

Inverter – An electrical device that changes 12-volt DC power into 120-volt AC power. It is used to power 120-volt appliances or electronics such as a microwave or TV when you don't have access to an external 120-volt power source. The amount of power that is available depends on the storage capacity of your battery(s) and the wattage rating for the inverter.

(K)

Kilowatts – Power generators are rated in kilowatts. Each kilowatt equals 1,000 watts.

(L)

LP Gas – Liquid propane or liquefied petroleum is the gas used for RV appliances. Typically it is used for the range burners, oven, water heater, furnace and the LP gas mode of the refrigerator. LP gas is stored in cylinders or bottles on trailers and in tanks mounted to the frame of motorhomes.

LP Gas Leak detector – LP gas leak detectors are audible alarms that warn you of a potential gas leak. They are normally located close to the floor level of the RV because LP gas is heavier than air and will settle towards the floor.

(M)

MH – Abbreviation for motorhome.

Monitor Panel – Allows you to check or monitor the fluid levels in the gray, black and fresh water holding tanks. You can also check the condition of the auxiliary battery(s) and on some monitor panels the propane level.

NADA Book – The RV edition of the National Automobile Dealers Association (NADA) book is used by RV dealers to determine used RV values.

OEM – Abbreviation for Original Equipment Manufacturer

Overhang – The portion of the motorhome that extends from the rear axle to the rear of the motorhome.

Pilot Flame- The pilot flame is a small flame used to light the main burner of an LP gas fired appliance. The pilot flame heats a thermocouple control that opens the flow of gas to the burner.

Porpoising – A term used to describe the up and down movement of an RV when traveling.

Portable Toilet /Porta-Potti – A portable RV toilet with a small water tank and holding tank. When the holding tank is full it can be removed and emptied at a dump station.

Pull Through Site – A campground site that requires no backing. The site is designed for you to drive or pull through.

Recreational Park Trailer (RPT) – An RV trailer designed to be taken to a location such as a campground or resort area and set up permanently. A park model trailer has more household type features and amenities than a travel trailer.

Refer – A short term for your RV refrigerator.

Regulator – LP gas regulators control or regulate the LP gas flow through all appliances, and maintain the proper operating pressure in the LP gas system.

Rig – A term RVers use for their RV.

RPTIA – Recreational Park Trailer Industry Association

RV – Abbreviation for Recreation Vehicle. A Recreation Vehicle combines transportation and living quarters for recreation, camping, and

travel. They can be classified in two basic groups, motorized RVs and towable RVs. Motorized RVs include Type A, B and C motorhomes. Towables include pop-ups, travel trailers, fifth wheels and truck campers.

RVDA – Recreation Vehicle Dealers Association

RVIA – Recreation Vehicle Industry Association

(S)

Safety Chains or Safety Cables – These are used on trailers in case of a hitch failure. One end of the chain is attached to the trailers A-frame, and the other end to a permanent fixture on the tow vehicle, normally the receiver. The chains are crossed to form a saddle that would prevent the coupler from contacting the road surface in the event of an accidental separation. Safety cables are also used on vehicles being towed behind a motorhome.

Screen Room – A screened-in enclosure that attaches to the exterior of an RV. They provide protection from insects and rain.

Sewer hose – A flexible hose that attaches to the RV sewer outlet and the campground sewer used to dump or empty holding tanks. You should have a 10' and 20' hose available with necessary sewer hose attachments.

Sewer hose donut – A plastic or rubber ring used to get a good seal between the sewer hose and the campground sewer connection. Sewer hose donuts are required at many campgrounds.

Shore Power – Shore power is a term used for plugging the RV in to an external 120-volt power source such as at a campground.

Slide-In – A truck camper that slides into the bed of a pickup truck.

Slide-Out – A section of the RV that slides out to provide you with additional living space. Some RVs have multiple slide outs.

Slider Hitch – A 5th wheel hitch used with short wheel base pickup trucks. With short wheel base trucks the front of the 5th wheel trailer can make contact with the cab of the truck when turning to sharp. A slider hitch has two positions. One for normal driving conditions and one for maneuvering where turns are required.

Snowbird – RVers that head to warmer climates for the winter.

Stabilizer Jacks – Jacks that are used on the corners of an RV to stabilize it when it is set up at the campground. Some are mounted to the frame of the RV and others are portable. Stabilizer jacks are not designed to level the trailer, just to stabilize it.

Stick and Tin – An RV with wood framing and corrugated aluminum exterior.

Surge Brakes – A hydraulic braking system used on some lightweight trailers. Surge brakes activate when the trailer surges or pushes against the hitch ball when slowing down.

Sway Control – A device used to help control trailer sway when traveling. There are two basic types of add-on sway control, friction and cam action.

(T)

Tag Axle – A non-drive axle located behind the rear drive axle that is used to support the weight of the RVs overhang.

Three Way Refrigerator – An RV refrigerator that operates on 12-volt DC, 120-volt AC and LP gas.

Toad – Another term used for the vehicle being towed behind a motorhome, also called a dinghy.

Tongue Jack – The jack mounted on the A frame of the trailer that supports the front of the trailer and is used to raise and lower the trailer when hitching and unhitching.

Tongue Weight –Tongue Weight or Hitch Weight is the amount of weight pressing down on the vehicle's hitch from the coupler of the trailer when the trailer is fully loaded for travel. For trailers that weigh over 2,000 pounds TW should be 10 to 15 percent of the loaded trailer weight.

Tote tank – A portable tank used to dump the contents of a holding tank into, and then transport it to a dump station to be emptied.

Tow Bar – Tow bars are used to tow a vehicle behind a motorhome when the vehicle is towed with all four wheels on the ground.

Tow Dolly – A trailer used to tow a vehicle behind a motorhome when the vehicle cannot be towed with all four wheels on the ground. Two of the vehicles wheels are on the tow dolly and two are on the road surface.

Toy Hauler – An RV that has a ramp door on the back and cargo space to load motorcycles, ATVs or other toys inside.

Transmission Oil Cooler – A small heat exchanger or radiator designed to protect your transmission from overheating. Automatic transmission fluid circulates through the oil cooler and is cooled by the airflow.

Travel Trailer – An RV that is towed by a vehicle, by means of a hitch. Travel Trailers are a popular choice among RVers because of the wide variety of floor plans available. Whether it's for two people or eight, you can find a model that will suit your needs. They range in size from 15 to 37 feet and offer all the comforts of home. They are unhitched from the tow vehicle when you arrive at your destination.

Truck Camper – Truck campers are campers loaded onto the bed of a pickup truck. The tailgate is removed and the truck camper is attached to the truck with tie-downs. This makes for a very versatile RV that can access back roads and remote areas other RVs can't get to.

TT – Abbreviation for travel trailer.

TV – Abbreviation for tow vehicle.

Type A motorhome – They are the largest of the motorized RV's ranging in size from 25 to 45 feet. Commonly referred to as a conventional motorhome they are the ones you see that look similar to a bus, and depending on the price they can be equipped with features like washers and dryers, multiple slide out rooms, satellite dishes, home entertainment systems and much more.

Type B motorhome – They are the smallest of motorized RV's ranging in size from 16 to 20 feet. They are conversion vans that have been modified and equipped with sleeping, eating and bathroom facilities and amenities found in other RVs in a compact size.

Type C motorhome – They are also referred to as mini-motorhomes and are built on a cutaway van chassis. With larger and heavier models being built some manufacturers are using truck chassis' with higher weight capacities. They range in size from 20 to 37 feet.

Mark J. Polk

Water Pressure Regulator – A water pressure regulator is used to prevent too much water pressure from entering the RV and damaging the plumbing system. You attach the pressure regulator to the campground water supply and then attach one end of your drinking hose to the regulator and the other end to the city water inlet on the RV.

Weight Carrying Hitch – When all of the tongue weight of the trailer is supported by the hitch itself. WC hitches are normally used for lighter trailer applications. Too much weight directly on the hitch can affect the steering and handling of the tow vehicle.

Weight Distributing Hitch – when additional hardware is used to distribute a percentage of the trailers tongue weight to the axles of the tow vehicle and the axles of the trailer. WD hitches are used to tow heavier trailers and allow the tow vehicle to handle better, also referred to as an equalizing hitch.

Wheelbase – The distance between the centerlines of the primary axles of a vehicle.

Wide Body – An RV that is wider than 8 feet. The majority of RVs are 8 feet wide. A wide body RV is usually 8 feet 6 inches wide.

Well that about does it. This list is not all-inclusive, but if you learn these terms you will soon be talking "RV talk."

Chapter 3

Before you Buy

Before you go out and purchase an RV, there are many things to consider and many things to learn. This section covers everything you need to know if you are thinking about buying a towable RV.

Precious Cargo

Just the thought of towing a thirty foot long, three ton trailer down the Interstate can be somewhat intimidating, not to mention dangerous if it's not done properly. The last thing we want to do is to put anybody in harms way. So, whether you have already purchased an RV, or you are thinking about it, let's talk about some things you need to know before you tow.

Tow Vehicle Capacity

If you already have the vehicle that you plan to tow with, you need to find a trailer that is within the weight range of your vehicle. This was a common problem I ran into during my days as an RV Sales Manager. Customers would come in to purchase a travel trailer only to find out that their tow vehicle did not have a very good tow rating. It can be extremely frustrating to go out and find the perfect travel trailer or fifth wheel and then be told that you can't tow it. On the other hand it can be worse if you go to a less reputable RV dealer and the sales person tells you that you can tow it! This happens every day, and this is why you need to be armed with the right information before you buy.

It is not my intention to upset any RV dealers, but if you go to a dealership and they don't ask you for information about the tow vehicle it would be wise to go elsewhere. The first question my salespeople were required to ask was if you already had a tow vehicle. If so, they would

Mark J. Polk

look in our towing book and identify the tow capacity for your particular vehicle. Then we would inform you of your options. We lost many sales because the customer could not safely pull the camper they wanted, but we did not allow them to jeopardize themselves or their family.

If you don't already have the tow vehicle, it's a good idea to find the camper you want first and then buy a vehicle that is capable of safely towing it. I will caution you again, be careful if you listen to the salesperson at the auto dealership. They are only interested in selling you a vehicle, and a large percentage of salespeople do not understand vehicle tow ratings. Call a reputable RV dealer and ask them to check the vehicles tow rating before you buy it.

I once had a customer that found the camper they wanted and went to purchase a new truck. The salesperson told him the truck could tow 10,000 pounds. He went on to show my customer where 10,000 pounds was stamped into the hitch receiver on the back of the truck. The 10,000 pounds stamped in the receiver is what the receiver itself is rated for. It has absolutely nothing to do with the tow rating for the truck. My customer bought the truck and brought it to us to have the brake control and wiring done. I looked the truck up in my book and it was rated to tow 5,400 pounds. The camper weighed 6,000 pounds. I could write another book about stories like this, but our goal is to prevent this from happening to you.

There are many things to consider before you buy a tow vehicle. How often do you plan to tow? Where do you plan to tow? Is this vehicle going to be used strictly for towing, or will you be using it for everyday driving too? Are you interested in a pop-up, travel trailer or fifth wheel? How much does the camper you want weigh? Once you have answered these questions you can start looking for that perfect tow vehicle.

The manufacturer determines a vehicles tow rating. It is the maximum amount of weight that the vehicle can safely tow. The manufacturer takes many factors into consideration when determining a tow rating. They look at the vehicles engine size, transmission, axle ratio, chassis, suspension, brakes, tires, cooling capacity and many other things. Now this may all sound complicated, **but the bottom line is how much can the vehicle safely tow**. Do not assume that just because you're buying a truck it can tow a lot of weight. Most manufacturers offer vehicles with tow packages. A tow package upgrades the vehicles suspension, brakes, tires, and cooling system. They also add items like engine and transmission oil coolers to protect the vehicles major components when you are towing.

Vehicle Classifications

You need to have a basic understanding of vehicle classifications as it pertains to towing. **Light duty** vehicles include many SUV's, mini vans and light duty trucks. These vehicles have tow ratings up to 3,500 pounds. **Medium duty** vehicles will vary depending on how the vehicle is equipped. One important factor is the rear axle ratio. You can take identical vehicles, with the only difference being the axle ratio, and there can be several thousand pounds difference in the tow ratings. Very briefly, the axle ratio is a comparison of how many times the drive shaft rotates in relationship to the rear wheels. For example a ratio of 3.73:1 means the drive shaft turns 3.73 times while the wheels turn once. The higher the numeric value the better the vehicle will tow, and the higher the numeric value the more gas the vehicle will use. We will categorize medium duty vehicles with tow ratings up to 5,000 pounds. **Heavy duty** vehicles like ¾ ton and 1-ton trucks have tow ratings up to 10,000 pounds and **super heavy duty** have ratings over 10,000 pounds. Super heavy-duty vehicles are designed to tow these amounts of weight.

> **Note:** Trailer Life magazine publishes an annual tow vehicle rating guide, www.trailerlife.com

Properly matching the tow vehicle to the trailer is critical to safe towing. You don't want to find out, when you're descending a steep mountain, that your tow vehicle cannot handle the load. You also don't want expensive repair bills, due to premature failure of major components, because the load is too heavy for the vehicle.

Trailer Weights

There has always been confusion when it comes to trailer weights. I can't begin to tell you how many times I have seen people read the manufacturers weight label on the outside of the trailer or fifth wheel and assume that they can't tow it. The data plate on the outside gives you the Gross Vehicle Weight Rating (GVWR). This is not the actual weight of the trailer; it is the maximum amount of weight that the trailers axles, brakes, tires and other components can support. The trailer might weigh 5,000 pounds, but the GVWR may be 7,000 pounds. This means that you could add 2,000 pounds of weight to the trailer before you reach the GVWR. You need to consider how much weight you will add to the trailer when you are calculating this number. You never want to tow a trailer that exceeds the GVWR. The components on the trailer are not designed to exceed the GVWR and it can be extremely dangerous, **or fatal.**

Any manufacturer that is a member of the Recreation Vehicle Industry Association (RVIA) is required to have a weight rating label inside the trailer that will give you more weight information. Look for it on the back of a cabinet or closet door. It will provide information on the Gross Vehicle Weight Rating (GVWR), the Unloaded Vehicle Weight (UVW) or Dry Weight (DW), which it is commonly referred to, the weight of the fresh water tank and LP gas when full, and the Cargo Carrying Capacity (CCC) for the trailer.

The UVW is the actual weight of the trailer as manufactured at the factory. You also want to find out if this weight includes options on the trailer. When a dealer orders a trailer they list the options they want on it. These options include, but are not limited to, the roof air conditioner, awnings, stabilizer jacks, and a spare tire. You can see how quickly weight can add up on the trailer.

Be careful when you look at the weights in the manufacturers brochures. In most cases these weights are for the base model trailer without options, and depending on what they consider to be options the weight can change drastically. It is not uncommon to see a brochure weight of 5,000 pounds, but the actual weight of the trailer is 5,700 pounds or more. 700 pounds can make a big difference when your tow vehicle is on the border of its maximum tow rating.

Before we go any further you will need to have a basic understanding of tow vehicle and trailer weights.

Understanding Weights

Gross Vehicle Weight Rating (GVWR) is the maximum permissible weight of the vehicle when fully loaded for travel. The tow vehicle and the trailer each have GVWR.

Unloaded Vehicle Weight or Dry Weight (UVW) is the actual weight of the trailer or truck as built at the factory. The UVW does not include passengers, cargo, fresh water, LP gas, or after market accessories.

Cargo Carrying Capacity (CCC) is the maximum permissible weight of personal belongings that can be added. CCC is equal or less than GVWR minus UVW, full fresh water weight, and full LP gas weight.

Gross Axle Weight Rating (GAWR) is the maximum allowable weight that an axle is designed to support. The tow vehicle and trailer each have GAWR.

Gross Combined Weight Rating (GCWR) is the maximum permissible weight of the tow vehicle and trailer **combined** when both are fully loaded for travel.

Gross Vehicle Weight or Gross Trailer Weight (GVW), (GTW) This is not a rating; this is the actual weight of the tow vehicle or trailer when they are fully loaded for travel.

Tongue Weight (TW) is the amount of weight pressing down on the vehicle's hitch from the coupler of the trailer when the trailer is fully loaded for travel.

Mark J. Polk

Matching the Tow Vehicle with the Trailer

Armed with this information, let's look at a typical buying scenario. Let's say that we know that our tow vehicle is rated to tow 8,800 pounds and it has a GCWR of 15,000 pounds. When I account for the cargo in the truck, three additional passengers, and after market accessories my actual tow rating is 8,040 pounds. Keep in mind that any weight you load in or on the truck reduces the tow rating by that amount.

Tow rating for the vehicle	8,800 lbs.
Cargo in the tow vehicle	- 150 lbs.
Three passengers	- 450 lbs.
Dealer installed options	- 160 lbs
Actual tow rating	**8,040 lbs.**

The Towing Formula

Now let's look at our towing formula: **Tow Vehicle GCWR − Tow Vehicle GVW = the Maximum GVWR for a trailer we can purchase.**

The GCWR for our truck is 15,000 pounds. Now I subtract the GVW of the truck when it's fully loaded for travel and this equals the maximum GVWR of a trailer I can consider purchasing. The only way to determine the actual GVW of the tow vehicle is to take the fully loaded vehicle to a set of scales and have it weighed. The GVWR can be found on the Safety Compliance Certification label, located on the exterior left front corner of the trailer.

Tow vehicle GCWR	15,000 lbs.
Tow Vehicle GVW	- 6,832 lbs.
Maximum GVWR of Trailer = 8,168 lbs.	

So let's say we found a trailer with a floor plan we like that has a GVWR of 8,000 lbs. The UVW or Dry Weight of the trailer is 6,350 pounds. Keep in mind we have to add any dealer installed options, cargo loaded in the trailer, any water we add to the fresh water holding tank and LP gas. This gives us a gross trailer weight of 7,075 pounds. Ask the RV salesperson to show you the weight label on the inside of the trailer for accurate trailer weights. Unloaded Vehicle Weights found in a manufacturer's brochure are normally for the base model of the trailer and do not include options the dealer may have ordered on the unit. In the majority of cases there is a significant difference between the GVWR and the UVW of the trailer.

UVW or DW of trailer	6,350 lbs.
Dealer installed options	+ 100 lbs.
Cargo in the trailer	+ 300 lbs.
Water 8.3 X 32 gallons	+ 266 lbs.
LP gas 4.23 X 14 gallons	+ 59 lbs.
Gross Trailer Weight	7,075 lbs.

Let's see if this will work: Remember our GCWR is 15,000 pounds. When we subtract the weight of our **fully loaded tow vehicle** and our **fully loaded trailer** we still have 1,093 pounds to spare before we exceed our GCWR.

Tow Vehicle GCWR	15,000 lbs.
Combined Weight of (fully loaded) Tow Vehicle & Trailer	- 13,907 lbs
	= 1,093 lbs. to spare

This method will almost always work, unless you have the tow vehicle and the trailer loaded to their maximum GVWR, which when added together can exceed the GCWR. **This is more likely to happen when the tow vehicle is a light duty vehicle like a mini van, small SUV or light duty truck.** In this situation you simply add the GVWR of the tow vehicle to the GVWR of the trailer then select a tow vehicle that is rated to handle the combined weight.

Mark J. Polk

If your original calculations are based on estimates, you need to verify all weights by going to a set of scales and properly weighing the vehicle and trailer. Keep in mind there are many other weight factors and considerations we did not even touch on. The Gross Axle Weight Ratings (GAWR), tires, tire inflation, proper hitch work, trailer brakes and much more need to be addressed. I cover a lot of this information in my "Trailer Towing, Weights, Hitch Work & Backing" DVD.

Remember to include all of these factors in your weight calculations.

➢ Add the UVW of the trailer; make sure that it includes all options.
➢ Add the weight of any aftermarket accessories like a battery or satellite dish.
➢ Add the weight of any cargo you put in the trailer.
➢ Add the weight of water and LP gas that will be on the trailer.
➢ Water weighs 8.3 pounds per gallon. LP gas weighs 4.2 pounds per gallon.
➢ Add the weight of all passenger's in the tow vehicle.
➢ Add the weight of any cargo in the tow vehicle.
➢ Add the weight of any after market equipment added to the vehicle.

The 75% Rule for Towing

We can take this one step further to build in an even better safety margin. A gasoline engine will lose three to four percent of its available power for every 1,000 feet above sea level. Ford Motor Company recommends a reduction in GVW and GCW of two percent for every 1,000 feet above sea level to maintain engine performance. That's where the 75% rule of thumb comes in to play. **The 75% rule ensures a built in margin of safety and is a good rule to follow if you plan to tow in higher elevations.** At 10,000 feet above sea level you would need to reduce vehicle ratings by 20% to maintain performance. Before we apply the 75% rule, let's reduce our ratings to see how much we can safely tow at

10,000 feet above sea level. In our example we will use a tow vehicle with a GCWR of 15,000 pounds.

Tow vehicle GCWR X 80% to get a 20% reduction
15,000 lbs. X 80% = **12,000 lbs.**

Tow vehicle GVWR X 80% to get a 20% reduction
8,800 lbs. X 80% = **7,040 lbs**

12,000 lbs. minus **7,040** lbs. = **a maximum tow rating of 4,960 lbs.** at 10,000 feet above sea level.

This is where we apply the 75% rule. The 75% rule will calculate the most weight we should tow to still maintain maximum performance. It works like this.

Tow vehicle GCWR X 75%   15,000 lbs.
                            X   75%
                           11,250 lbs.

Tow vehicle GVWR X 75%   8,800 lbs.
                            X 75%
                           6,600 lbs.

11,250 lbs. minus **6,600** lbs. = **maximum tow rating of 4,650 lbs.** at 10,000 feet above sea level. By applying the 75% rule and keeping our trailer weight at or below 4,650 lbs. we can keep the tow rating below the maximum 4,960 lbs. required to maintain maximum vehicle performance.

By applying whichever of these methods works best for your particular needs, combined with the proper hitch work and brakes, you can be assured of a safe and proper match between your tow vehicle and trailer. However, the only way to get true and accurate weights is to weigh both the tow vehicle and trailer when they are fully loaded for travel.

Proper Hitch Work (Safety versus Disaster)

Now that we have selected our tow vehicle and matched it with the right trailer, we need to discuss proper hitch work. This is not a popular subject, because after you buy the trailer the RV dealership hits you with this added expense. **But, we have only solved half of the equation to safe towing when we matched the tow vehicle with the trailer.** You guessed it; the other half is proper hitch work.

I would like to clarify something before we get started. Most people refer to the part that is bolted to the frame of the tow vehicle as the hitch. This is actually the hitch receiver. It receives the hitch head or ball mount. The hitch receiver is rated to handle a specific amount of weight, and has nothing to do with the tow vehicle tow rating. The rating for the hitch receiver must be greater than the amount of weight being towed. There are a few terms you will need to be familiar with in this section.

Weight Carrying Hitch (WC)

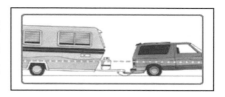

A weight carrying hitch means that all of the weight of the trailer is supported by the hitch itself. WC hitches are used for lighter trailer applications. Too much weight directly on the hitch can affect the steering and handling of the tow vehicle. If you're towing a lighter trailer with a WC hitch and experience problems with the steering and, or sway you may need a **Weight Distributing Hitch (WD)**. With the loaded trailer hooked up to the tow vehicle, stand back and look at it. If the lowest point is where the trailer couples to the hitch, talk to your RV dealer about a WD hitch.

Weight Distributing Hitch (WD)

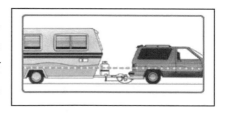

This is when additional hardware is used to distribute a percentage of the trailers tongue weight to the axles of the tow vehicle and the axles of the trailer. WD hitches are used to tow heavier trailers and allow the tow vehicle to handle better. They are extremely helpful with short wheel base tow vehicles.

Tongue Weight (TW)

TW is the amount of the trailers weight that is pressing down on the hitch ball. TW is a critical factor in how well the trailer will tow. Ideally for trailers that weigh over 2,000 pounds, TW should be 10 to 15 percent of the trailer weight. Take the **Gross Trailer Weight (GTW),** which is the actual weight of the loaded trailer, and multiply it by .10 and .15. This will give you the tongue load range you want to be in. Too much TW can cause poor steering, handling and braking. Too little TW can cause the tow vehicles rear wheels to lose traction and contribute to trailer sway.

Sway Control

Sway is a side-to-side fishtailing motion. There are many factors that can cause sway such as a poorly designed trailer, improper loading, improper hitch work, crosswinds, and transfer trucks passing you. Sway controls are designed to dampen the swaying motion. There are two basic types of sway control, friction and cam action. Both are quite effective if used with the right hitch application.

Hitch Receiver Classifications

GVWR and TW will determine the hitch receiver that is needed. Never exceed the lowest rated component in your towing system.

Class I Hitch Receiver: This is a light duty WC hitch receiver that is rated for up to 2,000 pounds, with a maximum TW of 200 pounds.

Class II Hitch Receiver: This is a medium duty WC hitch receiver that is rated for up to 3,500 pounds, with a maximum TW of 350 pounds.

Class III Hitch Receiver: This is a heavy duty WC hitch receiver that is rated for up to 5,000 pounds, with a maximum TW of 500 pounds.

Class IV Hitch Receiver: This is a heavy-duty hitch receiver. If used as a WC hitch it is rated for up to 7,500 pounds with a maximum TW of

Mark J. Polk

750. If used with WD hitch it is rated for up to 12,000 pounds with a maximum TW of 1,200 pounds.

Class V Hitch Receiver: This is an extra heavy-duty hitch receiver. If used as a WC hitch it is rated for 12,000 pounds with a maximum TW of 1,200 pounds. If used with a WD hitch it is rated for 14,000 pounds with a maximum TW of 1,400 pounds.

Note: These weight limits refer to the GVWR of the trailer being towed.

Some Class III and all Class IV and V hitch receivers can be used as either a WC or WD hitch, but they are only capable of towing WD hitch weights if you are using the required WD hitch components. Check the rating label on the hitch receiver. It will give you the WC and WD ratings.

Fifth Wheel Weight Considerations

Out of all of the types of trailers manufactured 5th wheels present the biggest problem when dealing with weight issues. The leading problem is the amount of weight being placed directly on the rear axle of the tow vehicle. The Recreation Vehicle Safety Education Foundation (RVSEF) stated that more than 50% of the trucks pulling 5th wheel trailers we have weighed exceed their maximum towing rating. They go on to say that there are tow vehicles, designed specifically for RV trailers, which are capable of handling units in excess of 40,000 pounds. Be sure that you match your trailer to your truck.

You need to pay special attention to weight ratings when you are considering a 5th wheel. We discussed earlier that tow ratings for vehicles do not include passengers, cargo and after market accessories. They also do not include the hitch weight, that for a 5th wheel is usually 18% to 25% of the overall trailer weight. When you add all of this weight together, it is easy to not only exceed the vehicle tow rating, but to exceed the vehicles Gross Vehicle Weight Rating (GVWR), Gross Axle Weight Rating (GAWR) and the Gross Combined Weight Rating

(GCWR). You never want to exceed any weight ratings. Not only will it prematurely wear major components out on the tow vehicle, but you are jeopardizing yourself and your loved ones safety. The only way to get accurate weights, and be sure that you are not exceeding weight ratings, is to weigh the tow vehicle and 5th wheel when they are fully loaded for travel.

Fifth Wheel Hitch Ratings

Fifth wheel hitch ratings range from 14,000 pounds to 30,000 pounds. A professional should always do hitch selection and installation. Fifth wheel hitches allow you a more stable and safe way to tow larger, heavier trailers as long as the tow vehicle is capable of handling the additional weight. The hitch can easily

Courtesy of Reese Products
www.reeseproducts.com

be removed from the bed of the truck by removing some pins when you're not using the hitch. When towing a fifth wheel with a short bed truck ask your dealer about a slide hitch to prevent the front of the trailer from contacting the cab of the truck when you are making sharp turns.

Hitch Ball & Ball Mount

Towing your trailer safely involves more than just selecting the right class of hitch receiver to use. The hitch ball and ball mount also have maximum weight ratings they are capable of handling. Hitch balls have three basic measurements, the ball diameter, the shank diameter and the shank length. Ball diameter sizes come in 1 7/8", 2" and 2 5/16". The ball size must be the right size for the coupler on the trailer you are towing, and be rated to tow the trailers GVWR. The hitch ball base and shank play a major role in the hitch balls weight rating. The ball mount is the removable portion of the hitch that slides into the hitch receiver.

For Weight Carrying (WC) hitches it may be necessary to find a ball mount with a drop or rise to help level the trailer when its hooked up to the tow vehicle. Ball mounts are also rated by the amount of weight they

Mark J. Polk

can safely tow. An adjustable ball mount is used for heavier trailer applications. Adjustable ball mounts allow the ball to be raised, lowered or tilted to compensate for trailer tongue weight and to attain proper height adjustments. Adjustable ball mounts are normally used with Weight Distributing (WD) hitches.

> **Note:** Always check the receiver, the hitch ball and the ball mount to make sure that the weight you are towing does not exceed the hitch components capacities.

Weight Distributing (WD) Hitch & Adjustments

A WD hitch system, or load equalizing hitch system as it is commonly referred to, is designed to **distribute** the trailer tongue weight to the axles on the tow vehicle and the axles on the trailer. When you distribute this weight, the results are a better handling and safer tow vehicle and trailer. There are different types of very effective WD hitches available on the market.

A weight distributing hitch system is made up of spring bars, (#3 in photo) or equalizing bars, a ball mount (#2 in photo) that is designed to accept the spring bars and snap up brackets that are mounted to the

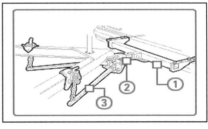

trailers frame. The spring bars have chains that hook to the snap up brackets. You adjust the tongue weight distribution by changing the length of the chains. Spring bars come in different sizes. When choosing the WD hitch make sure the spring bars are rated to handle the amount of TW the trailer has. For example if the TW is 600 pounds you could not use spring bars rated for 550 pounds. You would have to move up to 750-pound bars.

For a WD hitch to work properly it must be adjusted properly. I strongly recommend that you have a qualified RV dealer make these adjustments. The ball mount has to be adjusted to the proper height for the trailer and the spring bars have to be adjusted to distribute the weight evenly to all of the axles on the tow vehicle and trailer. If you do decide to make these adjustments yourself, follow the hitch manufacturer's directions. Too much tension on the bars can cause the tow vehicle to loose traction especially on slippery roads. Too little tension on the bars can affect the tow vehicles steering and handling characteristics.

Safety Chains and Breakaway Switch

Safety chains are used on trailers in case of a hitch failure. One end of the chain is attached to the trailers A-frame, and the other end to a permanent fixture on the tow vehicle, normally the receiver. The chains are crossed, "X" to form a saddle that would prevent the coupler from contacting the road surface in the event of a separation. The breakaway switch is designed to activate the trailers brakes if the trailer accidentally separates from the hitch when you are traveling. The breakaway switch lanyard needs to be connected to a permanent fixture on the tow vehicle. Remember to disconnect the lanyard when you unhook the trailer from the tow vehicle. If the breakaway switch pin is pulled out accidentally, the trailer brakes will engage.

Electric Brake Controller

Electric brake controllers are an essential component to safe trailer towing. The brake controller is installed inside the tow vehicle and supplies the power from the tow vehicle to the trailer's electric brakes. There are two types of electric brake controllers, time delay activated and inertia activated. Time delay or solid-state controllers apply gradual voltage to the trailer brakes using a time delay circuit. A pendulum circuit that applies gradual voltage to the trailer's brakes activates inertia or pendulum type controllers. Both types of brake controllers allow you to adjust the amount of braking power and they both have manual overrides that can be used to activate the trailer brakes without using the vehicle brakes. The override feature can be used when descending an incline, to assist in slowing down and to prevent premature brake wear on the tow vehicle. It is also helpful in regaining control if the trailer begins to sway or fishtail.

> **Note**: A professional should install the brake controller and tow vehicle wiring.

Sway Controls

I'm sure that you have heard horror stories about trailer sway. As mentioned earlier, sway is a side-to-side fishtailing movement. There are many factors that contribute to trailer sway, and many ways to control sway. Our emphasis here is the type of hitch work that can be installed on the trailer to dampen the effects of trailer sway. There are several different types of sway controls available.

Friction Sway Control

Friction sway controls use friction to dampen the pivotal movement where the trailer coupler connects to the ball mount. It does not prevent trailer sway, but once the forces of sway begin the friction helps to control the sway. The amount of friction can be adjusted for different

Courtesy of Reese Products
www.reeseproducts.com

trailer weights and towing conditions. Before backing the trailer up you need to disconnect the friction sway control.

Other types of sway controls are designed to control sway before it even starts. The Equalizer Sway Control hitch offers a four point sway control and a weight distributing hitch in one package. Sway controls should be installed by a qualified RV service center.

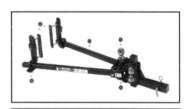

Courtesy of Equalizer Hitch
www.equalizerhitch.com

Transmission Oil Coolers

Vehicle transmissions are perhaps the most overworked component in the drive train when subjected to towing. Transmission oil coolers are like radiators for your transmission. The transmission oil circulates through the cooler and is cooled by airflow. If your tow vehicle does not have one, it is the best investment you can make. They are inexpensive and can save you costly repair bills for a damaged transmission.

Travel Trailers versus 5th Wheels

This is probably a good time to broach this age-old question. Do I buy a travel trailer or 5th wheel? There are many factors that need to be considered when making this decision. A lot of fulltimers buy 5th wheels because they have what I refer to as better road manners. What I mean is they tow and handle better than a travel trailer and it is virtually impossible to get any trailer sway because the hitch weight is directly over the tow vehicles rear axle. On the other hand, a 5th wheel usually costs more, is heavier, and in most cases requires a more expensive tow vehicle. You need to consider how you will use the trailer and how much traveling you expect to do. If you want to tour the country, a 5th wheel is probably the way to go. If you only plan on going to the beach twice a year it would be more cost effective to purchase a travel trailer.

Loading the RV

An entire book could be written on this topic. It is probably the least understood, and most grossly overlooked subject when it comes to RV's. We discussed earlier that every component in the towing system has weight limitations. The tow vehicle, hitch receiver, ball mount, hitch ball, spring bars, trailer tongue weight, axles, tires and brakes. The entire system is only as strong as the weakest component in the system.

The Recreation Vehicle Safety Education Foundation (RVSEF) explains it like this: Each axle on your RV has a Gross Axle Weight Rating (GAWR), established by the axle manufacturer. This number establishes the maximum weight that should ever be on the axle! The number is found on the same data plate with the GVWR. Here, however, is an example of where truck ratings do not apply very well to RVs. The GAWR is based on all of the components of the axle, including the suspension, wheels, bearings, spindles, and tires. When all of the components are considered, the GAWR is based on the weakest link in the system. For example; a typical ¾ ton pick-up truck rear axle, with single 16" load range E tires has a GAWR of 6,084 pounds. If you check the sidewall of the tires, you will note that each tire has a rating, or limitation of 3,042 pounds. Since there are two tires, then 3,042 X 2 equal 6,084, thus the GAWR. But, consider carefully what we just did. We added the two tires together to get the GAWR, so we know that we can't arbitrarily load the axle so that one side has a greater load than 3,042 pounds. This now brings us to a very important conclusion: **GAWR assumes that the axle is loaded equally on both sides!** And herein lays the source of many an RV tire failure. RVs are seldom loaded evenly from side to side, and in fact, it is not unusual to weigh a unit that is more than 2,000 pounds heavier on one side than on the other.

They go on to say, our database reveals that 10% of the units that exceed a tire rating, do so without exceeding GAWR. This means, that because the unit is heavier on one side, these owners, had they taken their RV to a truck scale which weighs each individual axle, would not have detected the tire overload. Now they depart the scale, with a false sense of security that all is well, and down the road, when that tire fails, they reason that it must have been a defective tire, since they were not over the GAWR. This is why RVSEF weighs RVs by each individual tire, so that not only do we determine the weight of the unit, but its weight distribution as well.

Proper loading and weight distribution in your RV is critical. If you load too much weight in front of the trailers axles you increase the trailers tongue weight and in some cases can affect the steering and handling of the tow vehicle. The opposite is true if you load too much weight behind the axles, taking weight off of the tongue can result in trailer sway. Loading too much weight on one side of the trailers axles can result in premature tire failure.

Many RVs today offer large storage compartments on one side or in the back and caution must be used when loading your supplies. It is easy to take advantage of these large spaces, and can lead to poor weight distribution and overloading one area of the trailer. You also need to keep in mind the trailers GVWR and the GCWR. If you load too much in the trailer it can exceed the GVWR and many people take advantage of the cargo space available in the tow vehicle and exceed the GCWR. Both of these conditions are extremely dangerous. You should load the trailer and the tow vehicle the way you would for a trip, including water, LP gas and people, and go to the scales and have it weighed.

Note: You can find more information on how to weigh your RV in Chapter 10

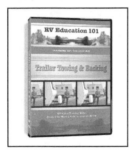

Our Trailer Towing, Weights, Hitchwork & Backing DVD covers all of this information in depth. See the RV Education 101 order form at back of book.

Chapter 4

Selecting and Buying Your RV

Which RV Type is Right for You?

Now that you have a better understanding of the types of RV's, you need to decide which type is right for you. I pointed out a few pros and cons to help guide your decision, but there are many other things you must consider too. How do you plan to use your RV? How much money are you willing to invest for the RV? Will storing the RV present a problem?

Let's start with how you plan to use the RV. If you really like to get away from it all and go camping in the backwoods you will be limited to what size RV will work for you. In this situation a pop-up or truck camper might be your best choice. On the other hand, if you are planning to travel cross country and not spend much time in any particular spot, a motorized RV might make more sense. If you have a favorite destination you go to all of the time a travel trailer or park model would probably work best. If you are going to be spending a great deal of time in the RV like fulltiming, or taking extended trips, a fifth wheel or motorhome would work better for you.

Another factor is how much you can afford to pay for an RV. If you are going to finance the RV, what monthly payment will you be comfortable with? Keep in mind that this is something you might only be using a few weeks out of the year. It's common for first time RV buyers, on a budget, to start out with a pop-up or a less expensive RV that fits their budget. If you know for a fact that a motorhome is the right choice for you but you can't afford the higher monthly payment you might want to consider a used motorhome that fits your budget. You can always upgrade to a larger RV or more expensive RV when you are in a better position to afford it.

Where will you be storing the RV when you're not using it? Do you have room to store it at your residence and if so are RVs allowed where you live? These considerations often times affect the decision on what type of RV you buy. A pop-up might fit in your garage but a 36 foot Type A motorhome might not even fit in your driveway. If there are codes that won't allow RV's where you live, or the RV you want is too big to store at your residence, check into where you can pay to store it. Is the cost and distance to the storage facility reasonable?

Should You Rent Before You Buy?

Some people are cut out for the RV lifestyle and other people aren't. You might get caught up in the excitement at an RV show, or in the thoughts of traveling the country in an RV and purchase one on impulse, only to find out it's not right for you. The golden rule is if you purchase an RV you have to use it! So how do you know if RVing is in your blood? It's easy! Rent one before you buy one. Find a local RV dealer, RV rental company, or a campground that offers rental units and try it out. The cost of renting an RV is significantly less than buying, especially when you discover you don't really like it. You can rent RV's for a weekend or for several weeks. Don't confuse not liking RV's with not understanding how to use the RV. A trip can be ruined if the rental company does not spend enough time showing you how everything operates. If you decide to rent an RV before buying one check out our RV training videos at **www.rveducation101.com** before you rent. It will make your rental experience more enjoyable and you will know for sure if RVing is right for you.

New Versus Used

This would probably be a good time to discuss if you should buy a new RV or a used RV. I touched on this subject briefly when we talked about how much you can afford to pay for an RV. Cost is one of the main factors concerning new versus used, but there are several other factors to consider too. If you're only going to use the RV two weeks out of the year, a used RV might be your best decision. On the other hand, if you are planning on going fulltiming or traveling cross country, a new RV with a full warranty would be a better choice.

Speaking of warranty, if you do decide a used RV is your best choice, check to see if there is any type of warranty available. If you buy a used RV from a private owner it is normally AS IS with no warranty. This is true with many RV dealers too. Replacing an RV refrigerator or other major appliance can be very costly. Most RV dealers will offer an extended service plan or contract if the used RV meets the service plan criteria. You can also purchase these plans from RV clubs and reputable websites on the Internet. The age of the unit will factor into the cost of the plan but you should be able to **negotiate** with the dealer concerning a service plan. Make sure you read all of the fine print and understand exactly what is covered and what is not covered in any type of service plan or contract you purchase. Many times service plans offer different levels of coverage based on the cost of the plan. You also want to be sure that other RV dealers and repair facilities will honor the service plan you purchase. It won't do you any good if you need repairs while you're traveling and nobody will honor the plan.

Another factor to consider between buying new or used is how long you plan to keep the RV. What I mean by this is if you buy an RV with the thought in mind that as soon as you get your next pay raise you're going to upgrade to a larger RV, it would be best to consider buying used. RV's depreciate, they do not appreciate. If you buy a new RV and trade or sell it within the first couple of years you will lose a substantial amount of money. In many cases a used RV has already suffered the brunt of the depreciation and you don't stand to lose as much if you get rid of it sooner. This of course will depend on how much you pay for the used RV. Most RV dealers use the NADA guide for Recreation Vehicles to determine used RV pricing, **www.nada.com**. Used RV prices are based on the age of the unit, the condition, options and mileage, if it's a motorized RV's. The NADA guide has wholesale and retail pricing for used RV's, and all NADA pricing assumes the RV is in good condition, and proper working order. Ask to see the NADA price for the unit you are considering purchasing or look it up on the Internet. For accurate figures you will need to know the make, model, year, options and for gasoline motorhomes, the chassis manufacturer and mileage. **You wouldn't pay full Manufacturer Suggested Retail Price (MSRP) for a new RV, so you shouldn't pay full NADA retail price for a used RV either.** Some used RV's are in more of a demand than others, but if the used RV is in good condition and everything operates properly a fair price would be somewhere between NADA wholesale and retail price.

Another consideration when thinking about purchasing a used RV is the finance terms and interest rates. Because the RV is used, banks offer shorter finance terms and higher interest rates compared to new RV financing. See the finance section of this chapter for more information.

If you decide to purchase a used RV make sure that all of the systems and appliances operate properly, and that there is no type of hidden damage that can't easily be seen. Damage caused by water leaks can be hard to detect and extremely costly to repair. If you are not knowledgeable about RV's you should take someone with you who is, to inspect the unit you are considering purchasing. It may be possible to hire somebody to thoroughly inspect the unit before you buy it. Most RV dealers will give you a walk through orientation of the RV and demonstrate that everything is operating properly. I recommend that you purchase an RV training video on the type of RV you are buying and view it prior to the scheduled walk through. You will have a much better understanding of how everything works and you can ask more targeted questions.

Note: See order form at back of book or **www.rveducation101.com**

Be sure to consider the cost, how you plan to use the RV, warranty, and how long you plan to keep the RV when deciding whether to buy new or used.

Mark J. Polk

RV Manufacturers

This is as good a time as any to talk about RV manufacturers. The Recreation Vehicle Industry Association (RVIA) represents the manufacturers of 95% of all RV's made in the United States. One thing you will want to do in your search for your RV is verify that the RV manufacturer is a member of RVIA. If they are, the RV will have an oval shaped RVIA seal displayed on the exterior, usually located by the entrance door. This seal means that the RV manufacturer is in compliance with more than 500 safety requirements regarding electrical, plumbing, heating, and fire and life safety. These safety requirements are established under the American National Standards Institute (ANSI) A119.2 Standard for Recreation Vehicles. If you don't see the seal don't buy the RV.

> **Note:** RVIA offers a good, searchable database of RV manufacturers at **www.rvia.org**

There are a lot of RV manufacturers. Many of these manufacturers offer several different types and brand names of RVs. It can be a bit confusing at first. Some manufacturer's only manufacturer one type of RV, like travel trailers or maybe truck campers or pop-ups. Some only manufacture motorhomes and some manufacture everything from pop-ups to high end diesel pushers. For example, Winnebago Industries, Inc. only builds motorhomes, but at the time this book was written they had 18 brand names between the three types of motorized RV's. Another example is Fleetwood Enterprises, Inc. They manufacture every type of RV and at the time this was written had 29 brand names available among these types of RV's. There are even manufacturers that have acquired other manufacturers and now use the old name as one of their brand names.

I know it sounds confusing but bear with me and I'll try to explain it in easy to understand terms. In a way it compares to RV dealerships. Some dealers only sell one type of RV, like travel trailers, but might stock a couple different brands of travel trailers built by different RV manufacturers. Other RV dealers sell every type of RV made and stock brands from many of the different RV manufacturers.

There are several reasons for all of these different types and brands of RV's. One reason is there are a lot of RV buyers out there with different tastes, different ideas about how to use an RV and different budgets. Most RV manufacturers build RV's in different levels. They offer entry level units for first time buyers in lower price ranges. They offer what I refer to as mid-line units for the more experienced RVer with middle of the road pricing. And they offer high end RV's for RVers with expensive taste and these RV's have expensive price tags.

These levels are usually offered in each type of RV they build too. What I mean is, if a manufacturer builds travel trailers they will usually have an entry level travel trailer, a mid-line model and a high-end model each having their own brand name. The same applies to pop-ups, truck campers, Sport Utility Trailers, fifth wheels, park models and motorhomes. Now it might make a little more sense why there are so many different brands. It is your job to sort through this wide array of choices and figure out what type, brand and manufacturer is right for you.

I used to compare it to the automobile industry. Once my customers knew what type of RV they wanted I would ask them to tell me if they were shopping for a Chevrolet, Buick or a Cadillac. Then I knew where to start. These different levels also mean that different materials are used to build the RV, different levels of features are offered, and different chassis and drive train components are used. You always need to keep in mind that you get what you pay for. There is absolutely nothing wrong with buying a Chevy, and if you buy a Chevy you get a Chevy.

Selecting an RV manufacturer also involves selecting an RV dealer that handles the manufacturer's product. The next section is dedicated to finding the right RV dealer for you.

Mark J. Polk

Finding the Right RV Dealer

There is a lot involved with finding the right RV dealer to do business with. This section is intended to provide you with the information you will need to make sure you are dealing with the right RV dealer.

Reputation

For starters you need to find a reputable RV dealer with a reputable, professional staff. Someone that is willing to take care of you after the sale. If at all possible talk to some other people who have dealt with the dealership in the past. A reputable dealer wants your business and they want you to return to them for future business. I have been in many RV dealerships that I wouldn't hesitate to do business with and I have been in others that I couldn't leave soon enough. Don't be afraid to ask them to give you a tour of the dealership. Look at the service department. Do they have certified technicians? Do they have the capability and facilities to do routine maintenance and warranty work on the units they sell? Look at their Parts and Accessory department. Do they offer a good selection of parts and accessories? Do they have a good selection of RVs to choose from? How long have they been selling certain manufacturer brands? How long have they been in business?

RV Shows

A good place to start your search for a reputable RV dealer is at some local RV shows. RV shows are usually scheduled during the slow period of the year, the winter months, to help jump start the selling season. RV dealers from miles away will attend these shows. If at all possible you want to find a dealer that is within a reasonable distance from where you live. As bad as it sounds, if you buy from an out of state dealer or one far from home, the local RV dealer may not give you the best service after the sale.

When you attend an RV show don't be afraid to ask questions about the RV dealership and the products they offer. There are some great deals offered at some RV shows and with all of the excitement, and a good salesperson, it's easy to make a hasty purchase. Remember, you're at the show to check out the dealers and you need to visit the RV dealer's physical location before you buy. If they can offer a great deal at the show, chances are they can offer a great deal after the show, unless the offer included a manufacturer discount or rebate for show dates only. Let them know you might be interested in a particular unit or deal, but you want to visit the dealership before you buy.

There is a lot of ground to cover at an RV show and a wealth of information available. Not only will you find a good selection of RV dealers to check out, but there will be every make and model of RV imaginable too. RV shows are a great place to do some comparison shopping. Keep in mind that RV's are available in entry, mid-line, and high-end models. When comparing prices, make sure it is apples to apples. One RV may look like another one, but you need to compare the options, construction, equipment and features they both have to offer. See who offers the best deal but remember if the dealer goes out of business next month, or isn't equipped to work on the RV, your best deal may turn out to be a bad deal.

RV shows aren't just for RV dealers to showcase their products. RV shows are a great source for information, from knowledgeable representatives, on every aspect of the RV industry. You will find information on campgrounds and RV resorts, aftermarket RV products, RV accessories and free RV seminars. Some of these seminars might be helpful to you in making some of your buying decisions. Check with the show office on seminar topics and times. RV shows are also a good place to talk to RV manufacturer representatives and other industry experts. Many of the RV manufacturers send knowledgeable representatives to assist RV dealers with their products. Don't be afraid to talk with other RVers at the show. Many of these people have years of RV experience and knowledge of different products. So what are you waiting for? Find out when the next RV show will be in your area and make it a point to attend it. Oh, and don't forget to wear some comfortable walking shoes!

Mark J. Polk

Brand Loyalty

When you are shopping at an RV dealership or RV show, find out what brands of RV's the dealership offers and how long they have carried these product lines. If a dealer has been selling a particular brand or product for a long period of time there is probably a good reason why. You want the most for your money, but you also want a manufacturer that builds a quality product and stands behind their product with a no hassle warranty. Look for manufacturers who have been building quality RV's for a long time and dealers who have been selling these products for a long time. New manufacturers and dealerships come and go, but the reputable ones have been around for many years. This is why it is important to ask questions and to physically visit the RV dealership.

Sales Department

A reputable RV dealer will in most cases have a reputable, professional sales staff to assist you. If you feel comfortable with the dealership and would like to look at some of the RVs on the lot, it's time to find a salesperson. This is not difficult because they will usually find you first. **It is extremely important that you feel comfortable, and trust the sales person.** If you don't feel comfortable ask to speak to some body else.

Don't be afraid to help the sales person help you. By this point in time you have a basic idea of what type of RV you want. Tell them what your needs are, what you want, your price range and how you plan to use the RV. A knowledgeable sales person can be a real asset, especially if you are new to RVing. They know the products, prices and what is in the inventory, and can be very helpful if they have some idea of what you want. If you prefer to look by yourself, ask for their business card and keep notes so you can ask any questions you have when you talk with the salesperson later.

RV salespeople should be knowledgeable about the products they sell. Don't be afraid to ask them questions about the products they offer. How is it constructed? Why should you buy one brand rather than another? What are some of the unique features and benefits of the product? Remember, you are the one taking it home, using it and paying for it, not the salesperson. This is a major investment and you need to know that you are buying the right RV from the right person and the right RV dealership.

If you find an RV you like, get the brochures and other information available on it, look over all of the specifications and take the time to research the product and the manufacturer. The Internet is a good place to do some research. Don't rush into it, you can find a lot of information about the particular product if you just do a little research.

Avoiding High Pressure Sales

Stay away from the high pressure sales tactics or you might be going home with an RV sooner than you want, bigger than you want and more expensive than you want. It's hard for some RV buyers to say no and for some it just seems easier to go with the flow. This is never truer than in a high pressure sales situation. You have probably encountered high pressure sales at some automobile dealerships you have visited in the past. If you visit a RV dealership and see any indications of high pressure sales techniques it is time to leave. There are a lot of RV dealerships out there and a lot of RV sales people. **Find one you trust and feel comfortable dealing with.** If you don't feel comfortable, more than likely there is something wrong.

Parts & Accessories Department

When you visit the RV dealership you should check out the Parts & Accessories department too. Parts are the things the RV needs to work properly and accessories are the nice to have things that make your camping trips go smoother and more fun. The dealer should stock a reasonable amount of repair parts for the product lines they sell. In today's marketplace it is possible to get parts delivered overnight in most cases, but that doesn't mean the dealership doesn't need to stock some common repair parts too. If a dealership offers a good selection of parts & accessories it is a good indication of being a reputable dealership. Parts and accessory suppliers will not work with RV dealers who are not established with a proven track record.

Service Department

I mentioned earlier that it is important to make sure the dealership you buy from has the capability and facilities to do routine maintenance and warranty work on the units they sell. You wouldn't buy a new automobile from a dealership without a service department and RV's should be no different. You will need to have routine maintenance and warranty work done on your RV.

Ask the salesperson to show you the maintenance facilities and to introduce you to the service writer if they haven't already done so. Ask them if they have certified RV technicians and how long their service department personnel have been employed by the dealership. Long term employment and certified technicians are other indications of a reputable RV dealership.

From **www.rvia.org** ~ The RVDA-RVIA RV Service Technician Certification Program is a collaborative industry program developed by dealer, manufacturer, and supplier representatives. The program is designed to make the nation's nine million RV owners even more satisfied with their motorhome, travel trailer or truck camper by creating a network of qualified, professional RV technicians across the country.

Some Things to Consider Before You Buy

I mentioned earlier that it is important to know what your needs are, what type of RV you want, how you plan to use the RV, and how much you can spend. So far we have talked about the different types of RV's, which type is right for you based on your needs and how to select the right RV dealer to do business with. Now comes the fun part. Hopefully you have decided on what type of RV you want and where you will buy it, now you get to go shopping for it. But remember this is a major investment, take it slow and don't rush into making a buying decision.

A good example of this is a couple I once had shopping for a travel trailer. The one thing they were sure of was that they wanted bunk beds for their three young children. I had several floor plans available on the lot, with bunk beds, to choose from. I showed them the first model and a few moments later they were convinced that this was the trailer for them. The husband liked the pass through storage compartment that could accommodate his fishing gear and the wife fell in love with the interior colors and décor. They purchased the trailer and I saw them at the dealership after they used it for the first time. They told me all about their first trip and how fun it was, but said they wish they would have given more thought to the floor plan before they bought it. The living room was on one end of the travel trailer, the kitchen was in the middle, and the bunk beds and bathroom were on the other end. She told me the kids were constantly going from one end to the other and she could never get anything done in the kitchen. This is just one example of how you can make a hasty buying decision.

A Valuable RV Buyers Checklist
Regardless of the type of RV you decide on, here is a valuable checklist pointing out some things you need to consider before you buy.

> **What type of floor plan will work best for you and your family?**

You will quickly discover that there are many different floor plans available to choose from. Some floor plans were designed with two people in mind and others with six or eight people in mind. There are floor plans with front bedrooms and others with rear bedrooms. There are split bathrooms, with the shower on one side and the sink and toilet on the other side, and bathrooms where everything is located together. There are walk-through bathrooms where you must walk through the bathroom to get to another room. There are floor plans with no slide outs and others with multiple slide outs. There are center kitchens, front kitchens and rear kitchens.

Mark J. Polk

I think by now you get the point. Find the floor plan that works best for you and how you plan to use the RV. If you find a floor plan you like ask to see it with the slide outs in the stored position. Can you still walk through the RV and access everything when the slide outs are in? Will this be a concern when you are traveling?

If you find a particular RV that you like but the floor plan is not exactly what you wanted, look in the manufacturer brochure for optional floor plan arrangements available in that model. In many cases there will be a different bedroom, kitchen, or other configuration available. The dealer will be happy to order the RV configured the way you like it. This will involve a waiting period until the unit can be built and shipped, but it can be well worth the wait to get it the way you want it. In some cases it may be possible for the dealership to call their manufacturer sales representative and try to locate one already built the way you want it.

Keep in mind that it is nearly impossible to find a perfect floor plan with everything exactly the way you want it and where you want it. RV's are designed with stringent weight requirements and other space and size considerations. Find a floor plan that will work for you and your family. I guarantee there is one out there for you.

> **Do you plan to travel cross-country with the RV or is it going to be set up at one location and left there?**

I mentioned earlier that one consideration for the type of RV you purchase was to determine if you will be traveling in your RV, or if it will be set up at one location and left there. If you plan to leave the RV at your favorite vacation destination, it would be wiser to purchase a travel trailer or recreational park trailer rather than a motorhome. You pay more for a motorhome because of the chassis, engine and drive train and you wouldn't have any use for it. Before you purchase a travel trailer or RPT select the lot where it will be set up. Check with management on the exact dimensions allowed for that particular lot, then pick out the RV that will fit there. Keep in mind the additional space required for any slide outs. If you buy the RV first, it may not fit on your favorite lot.

If you plan to travel a great deal, a motorhome or fifth wheel might be the way to go. Some RVers choose a motorhome because they take longer trips and don't really stay in one place for long periods of time. You also have the benefit of access to all of the amenities while you're traveling. If you stay in one place for a few days or weeks at a time a fifth wheel or larger travel trailer works well and you have the tow vehicle for transportation.

> **If you're going to be towing the RV, is the tow vehicle capable of handling the weight of the RV and do you have the proper hitch work to safely tow it? (See Chapter 3)**

This is a subject that is often times overlooked. If you already own the tow vehicle you need to select a trailer that is properly matched for the tow vehicle. A better scenario is to find the travel trailer or fifth wheel you want before you purchase the tow vehicle. This way, you can get a tow vehicle that can safely handle the weight of the trailer you want. I have met many people who were disappointed to find out that their vehicle couldn't tow the RV they wanted. Most vehicle salespeople do not understand tow ratings. Before you purchase a tow vehicle do your research on tow ratings. A reputable RV dealer can usually assist you in determining the correct tow rating for a particular vehicle.

> **Note:** Another good source to check on tow ratings is **www.trailerlife.com.** Each year Trailer Life magazine publishes an annual towing guide. It lists all of the makes and models of vehicles and their tow rating. Pay particular attention to any footnotes.

> **How many people will be in the RV and what are the sleeping requirements?**

You may have already addressed this question during the "which RV is right for you section." But when you are actually in the shopping mode it needs to be addressed again. When a brochure states that a certain RV model sleeps six it is usually referring to one bed that sleeps two people,

Mark J. Polk

a fold out or jack knife sofa that sleeps two people and a dinette that converts into a bed and sleeps two people. The two people on the sofa and the two people on the dinette better be small people. Most dinettes and sofas are not big enough to accommodate two grown adults.

Some RV's will have sofa sleepers which are much larger than a jack knife sofa. A jack knife sofa is a sofa that folds out to make a bed. Check out the real sleeping arrangements before you buy. Don't be afraid to lie down on the bed and try it out. Even the fixed beds in RV's are not the same as regular beds you would find in your home. If a brochure states the RV has a queen size bed it will usually only meet the width or length requirement of a real queen size bed, but not both. This is because RV's are limited in space and must compromise to make things fit. Bunk beds are another option available for additional sleeping arrangements, but make sure you the check weight restrictions. Many RV bunk beds are rated for 150 pounds.

> **Can you walk around the entire bed or is it built into the corner of the walls?**

Some RV's have beds that are called corner beds. They are designed to save on space, or to make use of what space is available. They are usually used on smaller, shorter RV floor plans. These beds are built into a corner of the RV. There are a few things to consider with this type of bed. You cannot walk around the bed. If you are on the inside and you need to go to the bathroom in the middle of the night, you either crawl over the other person or they have to get up to let you out. The bed is more difficult to make because there is no room to move around and it is built against the wall. On the other hand if you are limited to what size RV you can tow, or you want a smaller motorhome that is easier to drive and maneuver, and you want a fixed bed this can be the way to go. Not all RV's have fixed beds. In many models the only beds are the converted dinette and the jack knife sofa.

> ## Is there enough seating space?

This is something else you will need to check out. If you have a family of six, and you are buying a pop-up, can everybody sit comfortably when it is raining outside and everyone is inside the RV? Or, if you are buying a motorhome are there enough seat belts to accommodate the number of people traveling in the RV? The number of seatbelts will usually be the same as the number of people the RV can sleep. When everybody is relaxing in the evening and you're going to watch a movie can everybody get a decent seat and still see the television?

> ## Do you need a slide out or multiple slide outs for additional living space? If you get slide outs, how is the RV interior affected when they are in the stored, travel position?

I would guess that more than 2/3's of the RV's built today have one or more slide outs. They really open up a floor plan and once you see one it is difficult to go back to an RV with no slide outs. Before you buy your RV, make sure you and everyone else involved can live in the space it has to offer. There is absolutely nothing wrong with an RV that doesn't have slide outs, just make sure it is right for you.

I briefly touched on this earlier. If you get a unit with slide outs, check the floor plan when they are in the travel position. I have seen many floor plans that are not user friendly when the slide outs are in the travel position. The day will come when you need to use something in the RV and you can't extend the slide out. Make sure you can get to the bathroom and other items like the microwave or thermostat and other controls. See what is blocked by the slide outs. Some older and smaller campgrounds or state park facilities cannot accommodate RV's with slide outs on both sides of the RV. It may be necessary to leave one in the travel position while you are camping.

➢ **Is their enough outside storage, and are the storage compartments large enough to accommodate what you plan to take?**

Look inside all of the exterior storage compartments. Is there enough room for what you need to take along? Where will you put the lawn chairs, the fishing gear and what about the golf clubs? It can be frustrating to buy an RV and never have enough outside storage. Your wife might not like seeing the fishing poles in the shower all of the time. On the other hand, some of today's RV's offer abundant storage space. The natural tendency is to take advantage of all the space you have, but in some cases it is easy to overload the RV and exceed some of the weight ratings, especially tire weight ratings. Take what you need, but don't just try to fill space. Don't forget to weigh your RV when it is fully loaded for travel. If you exceed weight ratings it may be possible to redistribute the weight. If that doesn't work, you will need to remove some of the cargo. See Chapter 10 for information on weighing your RV.

➢ **Is there enough closet, cabinet and drawer space for all of your personal belongings?**

This is another area that needs to be checked out thoroughly. Close your eyes for a minute and think about what you will need to take with you on a camping trip. Extra clothes and shoes for everybody, beach towels and regular towels, extra bedding, games and toys, canned goods, food and snacks, plates and glasses, oh, and what about pots and pans. This is just a short list. Now, where are you going to put it all?

How much drawer space is available for clothing and how many drawers are there in the kitchen? How much closet space is there? Is it enough? What about cabinets? Check it out now, so you don't regret it later.

> **How much counter space does the RV have in the kitchen? Is it enough?**

It is quite common for RV's to have limited counter space in the kitchen or galley area. Look at the counter space and take a moment to think about how you plan to use it. Make sure it will work for you. Is there room for preparing meals? Is there room for a coffee pot, toaster and to use an electric skillet? If you take something out of the refrigerator or the oven is there room to put it on the counter top?

> **Where is the dinette table in relation to the range, oven and the refrigerator? Does it make sense?**

Basically, is the kitchen or galley configured in a way that will work for you? Is there room to move and to work in the area? Remember the story about the children constantly going through the kitchen to get to other rooms on opposite ends of the RV. Where is the dinette located? Keep in mind it might be used as a bed too.

> **Are there windows where you want windows?**

Windows in an RV are important for several reasons. Windows help with ventilation, they offer us a view and some are even emergency escapes. If you're parked next to a beautiful lake you will want a good view from where you are sitting in the living room. Windows on both sides of a room promote good cross ventilation. Take a moment to sit down and look around. Are there windows where you want them? Are there windows where you don't want them?

> **Can you reach the overhead cabinets, how about the microwave?**

Make sure you can not only reach the overhead cabinets, but that you can reach into them if you are trying to take something out or put some thing in. It is frustrating to use a step stool every time you need something from the cabinets. I once sold a unit to a couple and the microwave was mounted up so high that the wife could not reach it, let alone take something that is extremely hot, out of it. We didn't realize it until after they bought the unit and it was too late. Check the height of everything before you buy. Conversely, many microwaves are also mounted too low and that can present a different set of challenges with young children.

> **Is the A/C ducted throughout the unit? If not, will it cool the entire unit?**

RV air conditioners are mounted on the roof of the RV. Some RV's are cooled from one central location where the A/C comes through the roof. Other RV's have A/C ducting between the ceiling and roof of the RV, with vents in all or most of the rooms in the RV. Some larger RV's have two roof mounted air conditioners. If the RV is cooled from one central location will it cool the entire RV? This is not a problem with pop-ups or a smaller RV, but it can be with larger RV's. Keep in mind that doors may be closed at times making it even more difficult to cool the RV without ducting.

Note: Some RVs are now manufactured with air conditioners below the floor, in a storage unit. RV consumers should be aware of, and test RV's that may have this type of A/C unit. These are appearing more as manufacturers raise the interior height of motorhomes, and a roof top AC could put the total height of the RV over 14 feet.

> **Do you prefer a split bathroom where the shower is separate from the toilet and sink, a walk through bathroom or a bathroom where everything is located together?**

We talked about this briefly when we discussed RV floor plans. Now we really need to think about it. A split bathroom is one where the shower is located separately on one side of the RV, and the toilet and sink are located on the other side, each having their own doors. The advantage is that somebody can take a shower while somebody else can use the bathroom facilities. Sometimes these are arranged so if you open both doors, it will close off the hallway area, giving you access to all of the facilities and more space to move around.

There is also what is referred to as a walk through bathroom. This is where you literally have to walk through the bathroom to get to another room, usually a bedroom. These are nice large bathrooms, but you need to decide if it will work for you. They work well for two people, but not always for several people. There are doors that close off the bathroom from the other rooms, but if you are in the bedroom and somebody else is in the bathroom you are stuck, somebody is going to be inconvenienced.

The third type of bathroom is where everything is located together on one side of the RV with a bathroom door. Size becomes an issue here. You need a bathroom that is large enough to move around in. Regardless of the type of bathroom you decide on, don't be afraid to stand in the shower and sit on the toilet. See if you can move around and see if you have enough head room. Can you bend over and use the sink? Is there enough counter space in the bathroom for a box of tissue paper and other bathroom articles? Check it out before you buy.

> **How much fresh water can you take with you? Is it enough?**

RV's come equipped with a fresh water holding tank. This tank is used to store potable water to use while you are traveling to your destination and if you are dry camping, where no water source is available. Fresh water holding tanks can be as small as 10 gallons in a pop-up and up to 100 gallons in some larger RV's. Find out what size water tank the RV has and determine if it is enough for the type of camping you plan to do. This information is usually available in the manufacturer brochures. If you plan to stay in one place, that has a water source available, this may not be an issue but if you plan to travel a lot and do any type of dry camping it can be a major issue.

Mark J. Polk

> How large are the gray water and black water holding tanks? Are they large enough for the way you plan to use the RV?

While we're on the subject of holding tanks, there are two others that you need to be concerned with. The RV will have what is referred to as a gray and black water holding tank. The gray water tank collects the dirty water from the sinks and shower and the black water tank is for the toilet. These holding tanks are used to store the contents of the tanks until they can be emptied at a dump station or campground sewer hook up. The sizes of these holding tanks are extremely important if you travel long distances without access to a dump station, or dry camp without hook ups. Some tanks store as little as 20 gallons (a few quick showers) and some store up to 60 or more gallons. This information is usually available in manufacturer brochures.

> How much LP gas does the RV hold? Is it enough for how you plan to use the RV?

Another concern is how much LP gas you can take with you. LP gas is used for the range and oven, the refrigerator in the gas mode, the water heater and the furnace. The furnace will consume more propane than the other appliances. On pop-ups and travel trailers, LP gas is stored in bottles or cylinders on the front of the trailer. There are two typical sizes. Twenty pound bottles (like on an outdoor grill) are used on pop-ups, and the taller 30 pound bottles are used on travel trailers and fifth wheels. A pop-up usually comes with one 20 pound bottle. An option that is available on some pop-ups is to add an additional 20 pound bottle. This works well if you do some long term camping in a pop-up. Travel trailers and fifth wheels usually come with two 30 pound bottles which is adequate for most types of camping.

Motorhomes have LP tanks permanently attached to the vehicle chassis frame. These tanks come in all different sizes and this is what you need to check if you plan to do some extended camping away from where you can get more LP gas. Some tanks are small, about the size of one 30 pound bottle and others are much larger about the size of four or more 30 pound bottles.

LP gas can be measured in pounds or gallons. One gallon of LP gas weighs 4.26 pounds. To give you some idea of how much LP gas you have a 20 pound cylinder holds 4.7 gallons and a 30 pound cylinder holds about 7 gallons. Make sure the RV has enough LP gas for how you plan to use it.

> ## Is the RV you are considering too big or too small for your needs?

I've seen it happen time and time again. People buy an RV and within a couple of months decide they need a bigger or a smaller one. In most cases it is buying too small and then trading for a larger RV. This is something you need to give a great deal of thought to. Try to look into the future and imagine how you will like the size of the RV you are considering purchasing.

What I've noticed is people are sometimes intimidated by the thought of towing or driving a 30 foot plus RV, so they buy a small one and once they discover that it is no problem they want something bigger with more room. Another scenario is you have a tow vehicle that is limited in the amount of weight you can tow, so you purchase a small RV and six months later upgrade the tow vehicle and want a larger RV. Both of these situations can be extremely costly. Remember, RV's don't appreciate they depreciate. If you trade too soon you will pay for the depreciation just like an automobile.

> ## If you want a motorhome, drive it before you buy it.

I can't tell you how many times I've seen people buy a new or used motorhome without driving it first. One of the main reasons you are buying a motorhome is so you can drive it. What if you discover that you don't like something about the way it drives after you have already bought it? It may be that you would have preferred something with more power or you don't like the view from the driver's seat or many other things. If you are somewhat intimidated to drive it ask the salesperson to take you to an area where there is very little traffic, but if you're going to buy a motorhome drive it first.

> ## What type of electrical system does the RV have, 30 Amp or 50 Amp?

You should be aware of whether the RV you are considering has a 30 amp electrical system or a 50 amp electrical system. We'll discuss the RV's electrical system more in depth later, but basically what it boils down to is if you have a 30 amp system (the most common found on RV's) and you are plugged into a 30 amp service, you can use up to 30 amps of appliances or electronic equipment before you experience any problems. To give you some idea, the roof air conditioner uses about 12 to 14 amps, a coffee maker uses 6 to 8 amps and a microwave 8 to 12 amps. So with a 30 amp system you would not want to use all three of these items at the same time. It's really just a matter of being aware of what you can and cannot use at the same time. A 50 amp system allows you to use more **if you are plugged into a 50 amp service**.

Thirty amp hook ups are common at campgrounds and many campgrounds offer both 30 and 50 amp sites. There are electrical adapters available to go from 30 to 50 amps, 50 to 30 amps and down to a standard 20 amp household outlet. We offer a 10 minute DVD titled **"Recommended RV Essential Items"** that shows you what items you will need for your camping trips to go smoother. Most of these items are available through Camping World or your local RV dealer.

Note: See order form at back of book or **www.rveducation101.com**

> ## Do you need a generator?

Generators make an RV fully self-contained. You have instant electricity at the push of a button. It's a nice feature to have electricity while you are traveling. If you enjoy dry-camping a generator can be extremely useful.

Almost all motorhomes come equipped with an onboard generator, and there are some fifth wheels, Sport Utility Trailers and truck campers that come equipped with generators, or in many cases you have the option to add a generator. As long as you have a fuel supply you have electricity.

Note: There are RV generators that can run on gasoline, diesel or propane.

Pop-ups, travel trailers, and many fifth wheels do not have generators. This doesn't mean that you can't purchase a portable generator to take with you. It really depends on the type of camping you plan to do. If you do use a portable generator keep in mind the carbon monoxide. Place the generator away from the campsite so the exhaust is not going inside the RV. Make sure the carbon monoxide detector is operating properly on RV's that come equipped with generators.

> **Do you like the interior fabrics, colors, upholstery, and wood treatment?**

I mentioned earlier that interior colors and fabrics are not a good enough reason to base purchasing an RV on, but you do need to like the interior treatments. I have actually walked into RV's before and turned around and walked back out just because of the type of wood used. Some things appeal to some people and not to other people, like colors, fabrics and wood treatments.

Fortunately, RV manufacturers realize this. Most RV's are available in different interior colors and other treatments. If you find a model that you really like but don't like the interior treatments look in a brochure or ask the salesperson what other colors are available. They will have samples available and may even have some other floor plans in stock with other color combinations that you can look at.

Mark J. Polk

> **Where is the TV or TV stand located in relation to the seating arrangements?**

This may or may not be an issue but I've heard several complaints about it in the past. First, look at where the TV is located or where the TV hook-up is located. Can it be seen from all of the seats in the RV? Some RV's have the TV located at ceiling level and others are low to the ground. Is it to high or too low for everybody to comfortably see and watch? How many TV outlets do you prefer? Many RV's have TV hook-ups in the bedroom and the living area, and some also have outside TV connections.

> **What about a phone jack and a cable jack?**

Something else to consider is if you will need a phone jack or a cable jack. Lots of campgrounds offer phone and cable service for an additional fee. Keep in mind what we discussed about RV's being available in different price levels. If you are going to purchase an entry level unit some of these features may not be available.

> **Does the RV have an awning? If so, where is it situated; does it interfere with any storage compartments or windows etc?**

Did the RV come equipped with an awning? Sometimes the awning hardware will interfere with a storage compartment door or other item on the RV. There is nothing that can be done about it, you just need to be aware of it and make sure it is something you can live with.

> **How long is the warranty on the RV? Do you need extended coverage to protect your investment?**

Check to see how long the warranty period is and what it covers. If it's a motorhome you will have separate coverage for the coach and for the chassis. On other types of RV's make sure the warranty covers the entire

RV. The warranty on the RV is very important and it is your job to understand exactly what is covered and for what time period. During the warranty period you need to perform routine inspections on the RV to make sure there are no problems that need to be taken care of. You will want any problems documented by the RV dealership just in case there are future problems with the same area. Most reputable manufacturers and dealerships will strive to take care of warranty related problems.

We discussed extended coverage when we talked about new versus used. If you plan to keep the RV for a long period of time you may want to check into some type of an extended service agreement. It is less expensive to purchase extended coverage on a brand new RV than it is on a used RV. Most plans will allow you to add extended coverage as long as it is still covered by the original warranty, but it will be based on used rates at that time. You also want a plan that will be honored anywhere and anytime you need to use it. Read the fine print so you know exactly what is covered and what's not covered. Many of these plans base the pricing on the extent of coverage. Ask the dealership to explain the service plan in detail and compare prices with other plans available to you through other avenues. We'll talk more about extended service plans later.

> **Note:** It's a good idea to keep an accurate log of all maintenance that you perform on your RV, and all maintenance that is done at the RV dealership. This information can be very beneficial in warranty or extended claims disputes.

➤ How is the RV constructed?

RV manufacturing techniques have been refined over the years and RV's built today just keep getting better. You should have some idea of how the RV is constructed. If a manufacturer is proud of their construction process they will talk about it in their brochures, on their website and they will train the people selling their products to inform you about it.

Mark J. Polk

Many manufacturers offer plant tours or videos on the construction process too.

Your salesperson should be aware of how the RV was constructed and should be able to point out some features and benefits concerning the RV's construction. Is it wood frame or aluminum frame construction? What type of roofing material is used and how long is the roofing material warranty good for? Can you walk on the roof? If it's a travel trailer or 5th wheel do you prefer a corrugated aluminum or fiberglass exterior? Aluminum exteriors are more difficult to keep clean than fiberglass. If it's a pop-up, how is the roof and the box constructed, and is it a good lift system. What type of fabric is used on the pop-up sides and how long is the warranty good for. These are just a few questions you should be asking or finding answers to, pertaining to how the RV is constructed.

> **If you're buying a motorhome, do you want gas or diesel? Which type is more practical for how you plan to use it?**

In many cases, but not all, a diesel motorhome will cost more money and depending on how you plan to use the RV will often times determine if you will benefit from this higher investment. If you plan to fulltime or RV across the country a diesel might be the way to go. If you only plan to take a couple of two week trips a year it probably isn't worth the added expense. Gasoline RV chassis' have come a long way in recent years. They have better power trains and greater Gross Vehicle Weight Ratings (GVWR) than the gasoline chassis of a few years ago. The gasoline chassis price has increased too, but in most cases is still less than a diesel. Regardless of the type of chassis' you decide on, do your homework. It goes back to the different levels of RV's built. There are entry level diesel pushers and high end diesel pushers and there are entry level and high end gasoline motorhomes. This means there are different chassis', transmissions and engines used in different models. Talk to your RV dealer about these different chassis' and drive trains used and decide which one is best for you. Remember, you get what you pay for.

This checklist is not all-inclusive but it should help you make a more informed decision before you purchase an RV. Another important consideration is what options on the RV. Let's take a look at what that's all about.

Understanding RV Options

When an RV is manufactured it starts out as a base or standard model. Then there is a list of options that can be added to it. Many of the manufacturer brochures and websites will list these available options. Depending on the type of RV it is, options include but are not limited to, items like the roof air conditioner, awning, stabilizer jacks, hydraulic leveling jacks, roof rack and ladder, back up camera, generator and much more. On a pop-up, depending on the model, options could include a water heater, refrigerator, furnace, outside shower, dual LP gas bottles and more.

When a dealer orders an RV they order the options that they feel will help sell the RV, based on their experience. On the other hand, they can limit the options to make the price more appealing. You must decide what options you want or need. Sit down with your sales person and review what options are on the RV and what options are available. Most RV's are available in different interior colors and treatments too. If you find a model you really like, but don't like the interior treatments, look in a brochure or ask the salesperson what other colors are available. They will probably have some other floor plans in stock with the other colors that you can look at. If you find a floor plan you really like, but it's not equipped the way you want, have the dealer order one for you. I know that waiting is difficult, but remember slowww down, it will be worth the wait to get the RV you really want.

Buying Your RV

The actual RV buying process consists of several steps. You have already determined which type of RV is right for you and you have researched the RV dealership and the RV manufacturer. You used the RV buyer's checklist to narrow your choice down to a particular RV that suits your needs. The remaining steps involve negotiating the price of the RV and what your financing options are. I can't tell you exactly how much to pay for an RV or whether you will get a great deal, ultimately that is up to you. What I can do, is offer you some insight, ideas and suggestions on some of the aspects involved with negotiating and financing your new or used RV. These final steps of the buying process are where you will either make a good, sound purchase, or make a poor, uninformed purchase. The goal here is to meet somewhere in the middle, where you the buyer and the RV dealer both get a fair shake. Keep in mind the RV dealer must make a reasonable profit to stay in business and to be there to take care of you after the sale.

Negotiating the Selling Price

When you find the perfect RV for you, be prepared to sit down and talk price. This part of the sales process is referred to as the closing. RV dealers do business in different ways so it would be impossible for me to explain exactly how the buying process will work for you. Chances are the salesperson will want to get you back inside and write up some type of basic sales agreement that he or she can present to the sales manager. Some RV dealers give the salesperson full authority to close the deal, but more than likely they will want you to speak with the Finance and Insurance (F&I) manager.

Either way, be prepared. Have a plan. **Never commit to anything until you have discussed and agreed on the price.** The first step is to negotiate the price. Let them know if they offer the RV for the right price that you are willing to do business **today.** This will motivate them to try and get your business. Don't worry about finance terms right now; you're not going to buy it if the price isn't right. At this point in time you have probably only seen or been told the Manufacturer Suggested Retail Price (MSRP) if it's a new RV, or the asking price if it's a used RV. RV dealers use different methods to determine how much profit they **must** make on a unit to be profitable and stay in business. It will be your job to negotiate the price down to the lowest acceptable margin the dealer will accept. Some people are uncomfortable when it comes to negotiating. You can bet the finance manager isn't uncomfortable and you shouldn't be either. If you are, I recommend you take somebody who isn't, along with you. Remember, RV dealerships do this every day. They know what works and what doesn't work when it comes to closing a deal.

There are several factors that will determine how you will negotiate the selling price of the RV. The Manufacturer Suggested Retail Price (MSRP) if it's a new RV, the asking price if it's a used RV, if there is a trade-in involved or if it's a cash deal (no trade), just to name a few. There are different ways to negotiate the price too, but the bottom line is to know in your mind that you negotiated down to the lowest acceptable price the dealer is willing to take for the unit.

Let's start with the Manufactured Suggested Retail Price or MSRP. The MSRP is exactly what it says, a suggested retail price. This is nothing more than a starting point for the negotiation. When an RV manufacturer determines the MSRP there is a built in margin that allows the RV dealer the flexibility to negotiate a deal when there is a trade-in involved. Let me try to explain this in terms that are easy to understand. Because RV's can be financed over a long period of time, and the fact that an RV depreciates, owners are often times upside down with their current RV. Upside down is a term used when you owe more money on the RV than the RV is actually worth. When you finance an RV for 10, 15 or even 20 years you are paying the interest on the loan, back to the bank, before you pay on the principal. What this means is, for the first several years you have the loan the RV is depreciating, but you still owe most of what you initially paid for it. If you decide to trade the RV during these first few years you are basically upside down.

The MSRP is inflated to help the RV dealer help you when you are in this type of situation. On the other hand, if you don't have a trade-in there is a substantial amount that can be negotiated off of the MSRP. How much the MSRP is inflated is the big question on everybody's mind. It's really difficult to say because different manufacturers use different methods to set the MSRP. They want to be competitive with other manufacturer pricing on like products, but at the same time offer their

Mark J. Polk

RV dealer network the best pricing possible for negotiating all types of buying scenarios.

Several times throughout the book I discussed the different types of RV's, and that within these types there are different price levels. RV's are built to meet different needs and different price levels. This means that the margin built into the MSRP will vary depending on the type of RV, and if it's an entry level, mid-line or high end model. If you're not trading something in you could expect to save 10 to 15% off of MSRP for less expensive RV's like pop-ups and entry level units. On more expensive RV's and high end units you could expect to save 15 to 20% off of MSRP. This is by no means set in stone, but in most cases it will result in a fair deal for both you and the RV dealer.

When negotiating the price, the F&I manager will act as though they are at the lowest possible selling price. It is your job to make sure. When you reach their lowest price you will usually know it. They will absolutely refuse to go any lower. If it's a cash deal (no trade-in involved), and you are within the percentage off MSRP for the type of RV it is, one way to find out if you're at the lowest selling price is to ask them to throw something in on the deal. Ask for something fairly expensive, like hitch work, if you're buying a trailer or a tow bar, to tow a vehicle, if it's a motorhome. If they refuse to do it there is a good chance they are at their lowest acceptable price. If they agree to do it there is usually more room left to negotiate.

If you're negotiating on a used RV there are other factors involved. Did the dealership bring the unit in at a good price so they can offer it at a fair price? If they put too much money in it they will want to get more out of it. How long has it been on the lot? A dealer wants to move used inventory because this is where some of their money is tied up. To get a percentage of the profit out of a deal where a trade-in is involved they need to sell the used unit. If it's been on the lot for a while they may be more motivated to sell. The longer it sits on the lot the less it's worth. Don't be afraid to ask what the book value is. Ask to see it or look it up on the Internet at **www.nada.com** and compare it to the asking price.

Negotiating for a used RV is like a new one as far as getting to the lowest price the dealer will accept.

If the used RV is on consignment by an owner for the dealer to sell, make sure the price is within range of the NADA book value. Some RV owners are upside down with their financing on the unit. They owe more than the RV is worth and they want to pay the loan off. The dealer has to make some money selling the unit on consignment too. Do some research on the RV and make a reasonable offer for the owner to consider.

Let's get back to the negotiating. **If you still doubt that you have reached the best price, the best thing to do is leave.** Tell the Finance & Insurance manager you need to go home and think about it, **or that you want to check with another RV dealer.** They want your business right now. They don't want you to leave and if there is any room left to negotiate they will probably offer it to you at this point. They want one of two things to happen right now. Close the deal and get your signature on all of the legal paperwork, or if they think you are going to leave they will ask for a deposit to hold the unit. Do not be in rush to sign on the dotted line. **When you have reached their lowest price you are in control.**

Negotiating the price of the unit is only the first step. We will talk about interest rates and finance terms in a little while. Right now ask them to show you all of the other costs involved with the deal and to explain each of them to you. Different states have different taxes involved with purchasing an RV. There are registration and licensing fees, and there may be additional parts required like hitch work and the labor rates for installing these parts. Make sure anything that was agreed on by the sales person or the F&I manager is written in the sales agreement. Some fees are not necessary and can be waived. If you don't understand a fee or if you don't think a fee makes sense, question it. You should not have to pay for a walk through orientation of the unit you are buying. Make sure there are no hidden fees or costs. Rather than the RV dealership being in control, you need to take control. Ask for their best price in writing with all costs shown on the paperwork. If they won't give it to you in writing, **LEAVE**.

This is when you will need to make a decision. At this point you can leave and do some comparison shopping with another dealer or if you feel that you negotiated the deal to the lowest price possible you can stay and continue working on the deal.

Ask yourself:
- ➢ Do you like this dealership?
- ➢ Do you feel like you have been treated fairly?
- ➢ Can they take care of you after the sale?

Keep in mind the importance of a reputable dealership. If you do leave, you risk somebody else buying your perfect RV before you come back, which I have seen happen more than once. If you stay, it's time to talk about some finance rates and terms.

Using Your Bank or Theirs
If you decided to move forward with the deal it's time to talk about financing unless you're going to pay cash. You really need to understand what your finance options are, because any money saved during the negotiating process can be lost during the finance process.

One of the first considerations is whether to use your bank or one of the dealer's banks to finance the RV. Most conventional lenders are not set up to finance long term RV loans. Your bank might be willing to finance it but on a shorter term, which results in a much higher monthly payment for you. One of the nice things about an RV is that the RV specialty lending banks will give extended terms so you have a lower monthly payment and they offer competitive rates. The term of the loan is based on the dollar amount financed, and some high dollar loans can be financed for up to 240 months. It's not uncommon for an average priced travel trailer to be financed for 120 months. This not only helps to get the payment within your budget but it will free up money allowing you to use your new RV more often. If you're looking for a payment that will fit your budget a longer term loan can help; but keep in mind what I said about paying back the interest to the bank before you pay on the principal. Check with your bank and the RV dealer's banks to see who can offer the best term to fit your needs.

Finance Terms & Interest Rates

Let's talk a little more about finance terms. One advantage to a longer term loan is a lower monthly payment. The average RV buyer will trade RV's every few years. If this is the case wouldn't it make more sense to save a couple hundred dollars every month on your payment when you're not going to pay the full amount of interest anyway? This goes back to how good of a job you did negotiating the price of the RV. If you saved a significant amount of money when you bought the RV you will be in better shape when it's time to trade. It's also common for RVers to pay off an existing loan or to refinance the loan before it reaches the full term. **Most RV loans are simple interest, fixed rate loans, and there is no penalty for paying the loan off early.**

If you do plan to keep your RV for a long period of time and you are in a position to make higher monthly payments you can finance it on a shorter term to avoid the long term interest payments. One other advantage to a long term RV loan, at the time of this writing, is that the interest paid is tax deductible (in the USA) as a second home on many types of RV's. Talk to your RV dealer, and accountant, about which RV's qualify for this deduction. You need to determine what term will work best for you, based on your individual needs, when you are financing your RV.

Now let's talk about interest rates. Interest rates affect what your monthly payment will be and the total amount of money you will pay for the RV if you keep it for the life of the loan. Keep in mind that buying an RV is considered a luxury item and you must have good credit to secure a loan, especially from the RV specialty lending banks. A bank will consider an applicant with an average credit history, but if you are approved it will be at a higher interest rate because the bank is taking a higher risk. The good news is that a good credit rating equates to good interest rates. I said a moment ago that any money you saved during the negotiating process could be lost during the financing process. It is quite possible for the finance manager to make more money on the financing than the dealership made on the sale of the RV. RV lending banks offer RV dealerships competitive interest rates in an attempt to get the RV dealers loan business. The finance office will then offer you an interest rate in an attempt to get your business. If they get a higher interest rate from you than the bank offered them, they get paid what is called participation. **Interest rates are something you must compare before you sign a bank contract.** Get a quote from one of the RV dealer's banks, one from your bank and one from an Internet lending source that finances RV's. **Find out what the current interest rates are and if you have above average credit don't settle for higher rates.** It will really pay you to do your home work on interest rates before making the deal.

> **Note**: You can be pre-approved for a certain dollar amount before you even go shopping for your RV and then compare the rates you were given, with what the RV dealership can offer. You can check with some reputable RV Internet lending sources too.

Trade-in or Sell Outright

If you already have an RV and you're planning to get another one you need to decide if you're better off trading your current RV in, or if you should try to sell it outright. There is no easy answer in what will be best for you, but there are a couple of things to consider. If your RV is worth what you still owe on it or if it's already paid off you would be better off trying to sell it outright. An RV dealer cannot afford to put more than wholesale into a used RV, and in most cases it will be less than wholesale.

Try to remember when we talked about the MSRP being inflated, in case a customer has a trade-in. Let's say your current RV is paid for. Now just for an example let's say that you want to buy an RV that has an MSRP of $20,000, but the dealer could actually sell it for $17,000 and make a reasonable profit. Now say your trade-in has a NADA retail value of $10,000 and a wholesale value of $7,000. Are you with me so far? The most a dealer would ever give you is the wholesale value. So they take the difference between the MSRP of the new RV and what they can actually sell it for, which is $3,000 and add it to the $7,000 wholesale price they will actually put into your trade. You're under the impression that they are giving you 10,000 for your trade and you're paying $20,000 for the RV. They take the $20,000 minus the $10,000 for your trade and you will finance $10,000 for your new RV.

Now let's say you were able to sell your RV outright for $9,000. You go back to the dealership and **negotiate** the best deal on the same $20,000 RV, and they are willing to sell it for $17,000. You pay $9,000 down and you only have to finance $8,000 for the same RV. You save $2,000.

The problem goes back to most people owing more money on their RV than it is actually worth. If you still owe more on your RV than it is worth it would probably be difficult to sell outright. In this situation ask for some figures on a trade-in. The dealer might be able to roll what you owe into the new RV loan. Let's take a look using the same figures, but instead of your trade being paid for, now let's say you owe $12,000, the retail value is $10, 000 and the wholesale value is $7,000. The new RV has a retail price of $20,000 but the dealer could actually sell it for $17,000 and make a reasonable profit. They take the difference between the retail price of the new RV and what they can actually sell it for, which is $3,000 and add it to the $7,000 wholesale price they give you for your trade. Now they take the $20,000 for the new RV minus the $10,000 for the trade leaving a balance of $10,000.

Next they take the $12,000 you still owe on your current RV and add it back in for a balance of $22,000 for the new RV. You put 15% down ($3,300) and finance $18,700 for the new RV. These are very basic figures just to give you an idea of what might be best for you based on your current situation.

If you decide selling your RV is the best route for you, but you don't know how or where to begin, talk to an RV dealer about putting it on consignment. Selling on consignment simply means that the RV dealer will show and sell your unit for a pre-determined charge or fee. You will be responsible for keeping insurance on the unit while it is on the dealer's lot, and you are responsible for paying the balance still owed to any financial institution when it is sold. Read the consignment contract carefully before you agree to the terms. Determine how much you will need to get out of the RV and work all of the details out with the RV dealer. Another option you have is to sell the RV outright. You can advertise through different types of media and handle the sales transaction yourself.

Extended Service Plans

We talked earlier about how the finance department can also make money on the deal. One way was through the interest rate. Other ways are through selling you extended service plans, various insurance policies, tire guard plans, paint protection and more. It will be up to you to decide if these extras are worth the price. I do think extended service plans are great as long as you understand a little about them and how they work. When you are doing the finance paperwork on your RV most RV dealers will offer some type of extended service plan that you can purchase. Before you agree to purchase a plan make sure you understand all of your options. **Do not be pressured into buying an extended service contract.**

If you buy a new RV and purchase an extended service plan that covers both the coach and the chassis the plan would take over the day after all of the original factory warranties expire. For example, if you purchase a seven year extended service plan and the motorhome has a one year warranty on the coach and a three year warranty on the chassis the service plan would be in affect for six years after the coach warranty expires and for four additional years after the chassis warranty expires. The advantage of purchasing the plan when the RV is new is that it will be less expensive for a new unit as opposed to a used unit. Most plans can be purchased anytime up until the factory warranties expire if you don't purchase the plan when you initially buy the RV. Some extended service plans will offer coverage on used units that meet the plans criteria if you purchase the plan when you buy the used unit. Coverage on a used unit will cost more. It is usually based on the age of the unit and the mileage if it's a motorized RV.

I mentioned if you buy coverage for the **coach and the chassis**. That's because most of these service plans offer different levels of coverage. You may only want additional coverage on the coach portion or on the chassis portion. In addition to different levels of coverage, plans are available for different terms.

Make sure you read and understand the extent and time period of coverage before signing any agreements. If you don't understand something, ask to have it explained to you. You will also want to make sure that the company offering the plan is reputable and will be acknowledged by other RV dealers and RV repair centers. It should offer coverage in all of the USA and/or Canada. If you plan to travel outside your country of origin make sure the coverage is still available. You will also want to check on how a claim is paid. I have seen cases where you pay for the repairs up front and then get reimbursed when you send in a copy of the service order or repair bill. If the repair facility agrees to file the claim most plans only require that you call for approval before any repairs are made. **A good plan should be transferable if you sell your RV, it should be renewable so you can extend the coverage and it should offer a pro rated refund if coverage is terminated during the term of the contract.**

Pricing for these plans will be based on several factors. I have already mentioned some, the length of the plan, the extent of coverage, if the RV is new or used, the age and mileage, and the deductible. The deductible can range from 0 to over $200. This is not bad considering a $500 or $1,000 average repair bill if an appliance fails. Some items on the RV, like slide outs and entertainment systems may not be covered unless you pay an additional surcharge. Make sure you understand what these items are and if you want them to be covered by the plan.

Do not be pressured into purchasing a plan. Ask your RV dealer to give you a price on the plan they have to offer and then you can shop around and compare pricing for extended service plans. Just make sure

Mark J. Polk

the plans you are comparing offer similar coverage. There are reputable extended service plans available through RV clubs and on the Internet.

> **Note:** Research and know in advance what you plan to do about an extended service plan before you go in to sign the finance paperwork.

Emergency Roadside Assistance

Don't get an extended service plan confused with an emergency roadside assistance plan. Some service plans do offer additional coverage and protection like a towing service or tire repair service, but most don't. Many RV manufacturers include an emergency roadside plan for a certain time period when you purchase a new RV. If the RV you buy does not come with one, I recommend you look into and purchase a good roadside assistance plan. It can be the difference between a good vacation and a ruined vacation. This is something else you will want to shop around and compare prices on before you buy. RV clubs offer discounted rates to members and there are many plans to choose from.

Picking Your Unit Up

The day you have been waiting for has finally arrived. Today you go to the dealership and pick up your new RV. You are very excited and can't wait to get it home and show all your friends and family. When you go to pick the unit up you will be overwhelmed by the vast amount of information given in a short period of time. The dealer gives you a walk through of your new RV, but by the time you get home you forgot half of what they told you, and you're not really sure if they covered everything. I recommend that you purchase an RV training video or DVD for the type of RV you are purchasing prior to your delivery date. This way you can view it first and familiarize yourself with the RV and how everything operates, and you will be able to ask more targeted questions during the walk through. You can also review it as many times as you need or like after you get it home.

> **Note:** See order form at back of book or **www.rveducation101.com**

RV Financing FAQ

Will one RV lender offer better interest rates than another RV lender?

Interest rates change frequently. If the prime rate goes up RV finance rates will go up too. RV lenders send updated rate sheets to RV dealers whenever their rates change. RV specialty lenders watch each other closely and if one lender lowers rates the other lenders will generally follow suit. They will usually stay within a quarter to a half point of each other.

Are there other factors that will determine what interest rate I get?

Yes, there are several factors that will determine the rate you get.
1) It depends if the RV is new or used. A used RV (normally over 3 or 4 years old) will get a higher interest rate than a new RV will.
2) Your down payment will affect your interest rate. If you finance the RV on a zero down program the interest rate will be higher.
3) The term on the loan will affect the interest rate. The shorter the term the higher the rate, the longer the term the lower the rate.
4) The amount financed will affect the interest rate. The lower the dollar amount the higher the rate, the higher the dollar amount the lower the rate.
5) Your credit history (credit rating or score) will affect the rate. The better your credit score the lower the interest rate.
6) Carefully read the section on finance terms and interest rates in this chapter.

Should I shop around for a better rate, or will the rate they offer be the best rate I can get?

You should be aware of what the current rates are for RV loans and based on the criteria listed determine if you are getting the best possible rate you can get. If you think you qualify for a lower rate, by all means try securing a better rate elsewhere. There are several RV specialty lenders on the internet that would like your business and will offer competitive rates.

Mark J. Polk

Do not however let too many lenders run a credit check on you in an attempt to get a lower rate. This can backfire so be selective about who is running credit checks. If lenders make several inquires on your credit history your credit score will be lowered causing you to get a higher interest rate. The reason for this is when banks see numerous inquires they are under the impression that you are having trouble securing a loan and could be a credit risk to the bank. While we're on this subject, when the RV dealer is going to run a credit check make sure you tell them to only submit your application to one lender. Some unscrupulous finance personnel think it's easier to submit your credit application to all of the banks at one time, leaving you with numerous credit inquires.

Can you explain more about financing an RV with no money down?

There are usually a couple of lenders that will offer no money down finance programs. These programs will have certain guidelines to qualify. The type of RV, dollar amount, term of the loan and your credit rating can all factor into these types of programs. The finance rate will usually be higher too.

What length of term can I expect to get on an RV loan?

The term of the loan will be based on the dollar amount financed and the age of the RV. Some RV lenders are offering 20 year loans on financed amounts over $100,000 and loans ranging from $25,000 to $99,000 can qualify for 15 year loans. Loan amounts between $10,000 and $25,000 may qualify for 10 to 12 years repayment terms.

Why would anybody want to pay the interest on a 15 or 20 year loan?

The biggest advantage of a long term loan is you get a lower monthly payment. Financing $100,000 for 240 months at 7% interest would be $775 a month. The same loan for 120 months would be $1,161 a month. You save almost $400.00 a month. But keep in mind you will have little or no equity if you try to trade within the first several years.

There are several things you need to consider when you determine what the best term would be for you.

1) How much can you afford to pay every month? The term of the loan directly affects the monthly payment.

2) How long do you plan to keep the RV? If you only plan to keep it for 3 or 4 years you won't be paying all of the interest anyway. The downside to this is you won't have any equity built up in it either.

3) If you plan to refinance the loan, or pay the loan off before the full term, a longer term loan would probably make more sense.

4) If you plan to keep the RV for the life of the loan a shorter term loan might be better for you. Make sure you can handle the higher monthly payments and the more you can put down initially the better.

Can I finance an RV with below average credit?

RV's are basically considered a luxury item, so the criteria to finance an RV are more stringent than it is to finance an automobile. There are lenders that will finance below average credit but interest rates will be higher.

How is the interest on an RV loan calculated?

The majority of RV loans from RV specialty lenders are simple interest fixed rate loans. What this means is you will only pay interest on the principle owed, and in most cases there is no penalty for paying the loan off early. If you choose to pay more than your required monthly payment you can shorten the term of the loan and save on interest.

Can I write the interest off on my income taxes?

Yes, a fully self contained RV is considered a 2nd home and all of the interest paid is deductible, if you are not already deducting the interest on a 2nd home. At the time of this writing an RV is considered a qualified residence if it is one of the two residences chosen by the taxpayer for purposes of deductibility in the tax year as long as it provides basic living accommodations, meaning it has cooking, sleeping and bathroom facilities with fresh water and waste water holding tanks. Talk to your tax advisor about what is required to write the interest off on your RV.

Will I need a down payment and if so how much?

Down payments will vary slightly between RV lenders but 10 to 20% down, in the form of cash or a trade-in, is usually the range. There are programs that offer low down, or no down payment but this will usually increase the interest rate. Most banks want to see your good faith commitment to the loan.

Do I have to have insurance on the RV to get a loan?

Yes, insurance is required when you close on the loan. The bank will not loan the money until they have proof of insurance. See Chapter 5 on RV insurance.

Should I finance the RV or pay cash?

It is my personal opinion that it makes more sense to finance your RV purchase. If you finance the RV you can maintain your personal financial status without liquidating any assets. You can also take advantage of writing off the interest on your income taxes if the RV qualifies.

Chapter 5

RV Insurance 101- Protecting Your Recreation Vehicle

Content for this chapter was provided by National Interstate Insurance Company and Explorer RV Insurance Agency, Inc.

I have mentioned several times that your new or used RV is a major investment. To protect your investment you need the proper type of insurance coverage. There are several major insurance companies that specialize in RV insurance and I strongly recommend that you use one that does specialize in RV's. You might have a great insurance company for your home and automobiles, but an auto policy can't begin to cover the complexities of an RV. You need specialty coverage like vacation liability, total loss replacement, personal effects and much more.

When you insure your new motor home or travel trailer, the choices you have in insurance companies and coverage can be very confusing. The intent of this chapter is to explain the benefits and options you have with a specialty RV policy. To help make it easier to understand RV insurance I divided this chapter into four primary sections. The first section discusses the basics of RV and auto insurance. This section will apply to you regardless of what insurance company you choose to go with. The second section explains additional specialty RV coverage that can be used to create a customized RV insurance policy to fit your needs exactly. The third section explains different valuation and loss settlement techniques that most RV specialty insurance carriers can offer you. The fourth section explains some effective ways to reduce your RV insurance premium and it provides some different ways you can buy RV insurance.

Section 1- RV and Auto Insurance Basics

I know I just said that an auto policy will not suffice for an RV, but there is a great deal of overlap between RV and auto policies. If you have a motorized RV, you will need some of the same coverage's provided by

85

an auto policy plus specialized RV coverages. Bear with me and I will attempt to explain this without confusing you.

Regardless of the insurance company you decide to use, there are a handful of basic coverage's you will need to have in your policy. Again, this coverage is very similar, if not identical, to the coverage you have on your personal auto insurance policy. This coverage can be broken down into two different categories; liability and physical damage. All motorized RV's will have some form of liability coverage. Towable RV's like travel trailers and 5th wheel trailers do not have any liability coverage. However, if you own a travel trailer or 5th wheel the section on liability may contain information helpful to you regarding the vehicle you use to tow your trailer.

Liability Coverage

There are a number of coverage's that fall under the category of liability coverage including Bodily Injury, Property Damage, Uninsured Motorist Bodily Injury, Underinsured Motorist, Uninsured Motorist Property Damage, Personal Injury Protection and Medical Payments. Some of these coverage's vary by state. I know this sounds confusing, but you'll have a much better understanding of liability coverage's after you read a brief generic description of each type.

Note: The Department of Insurance in the state you live in can be an excellent resource for additional information regarding state specific coverage's. Most states offer a Consumer Buyer's Guide on their website that will explain state specific nuances to each of these coverage's.

Bodily Injury is third party coverage. This means it provides protection for claims due to injuries to a passenger in your vehicle (other than you or a family member) or passengers in another vehicle, or pedestrians. It provides you, the owner/operator of a motor vehicle, with protection for your legal liability due to the ownership, maintenance or use of your RV. It is very important to select a limit that is high enough to protect your assets. You may be responsible for any amounts, related to injuries received to the third party, over and above the limit on your insurance policy. You can also purchase a separate umbrella policy that sits over all of your liability limits on your cars, your house and your motorized RV. This type of policy is not discussed in detail here, but provides protection above your Bodily Injury limit and up to the limit of the umbrella.

Property Damage is also a third party coverage, and provides protection for claims due to damage to other people's property. For example, Property Damage would pay to repair damage to the bumper of a car that you rear-end in an accident. **Bodily Injury and Property Damage** limits typically work together and can be either a split limit or a combined single limit. A typical split limit has a different limit for damages to each person, each accident and property damage. For example, a common split limit would be $100,000/$300,000/$50,000. This means that for Bodily Injury coverage you have a maximum limit of $100,000 per person for each person injured not to exceed $300,000 per accident and a $50,000 limit for Property Damage. A common single limit for Bodily Injury and Property Damage is $300,000 meaning you have $300,000 to pay for all injuries and property damage arising from any one accident. It can be split any which way between injured parties and damaged property. Bodily Injury and Property Damage are required for all motorized RV's. For travel trailers and 5th wheel trailers liability follows the unit towing the trailer, so Bodily Injury and Property Damage coverage's are not necessary.

Uninsured Motorists (UM) and Underinsured Motorists (UIM) coverage's can be first or third party coverage's. UM provides protection for injuries you or someone else sustains in an accident due to the fault of another party when the at-fault party does not have any insurance. UIM provides protection for injuries you or someone else sustain in an accident due to the fault of another party when the at-fault party does have insurance, but not enough insurance to cover your damages. UM

Mark J. Polk

and UIM are sold on a split limit and combined single limit basis, just like Bodily Injury and Property Damage.

Uninsured Motorists Property Damage (UMPD) provides protection for damage to your vehicle caused when your vehicle is struck by another party that does not have insurance. This would also be covered by Collision coverage, but UMPD typically has a lower deductible ($100 or $250) than the deductible on Collision coverage.

Personal Injury Protection (PIP) is also known as "No-Fault Coverage" and can be a first or third party coverage. This is a statutory coverage **that is only available in some states** and provides protection for injuries sustained in an accident regardless of fault. In a true no-fault state your insurer pays for your injuries, and the other party's insurer pays for their injuries regardless of who is at-fault. PIP benefits are state mandated and can include medical expenses, lost wages, funeral expenses and substitute services. If you live in a PIP state, you should consult your insurance agent or the department of insurance for more information on the PIP options and rules that pertain to your state.

Medical Payments can also be a first or third party coverage. This coverage provides protection for injuries of someone in your vehicle, including yourself, up to a specified limit. Medical Expense coverage is available in most states.

Liability Limits- When getting quotes on insurance, you will have to make several decisions about limits. You should pay close consideration to the liability limits you select. Liability coverage protects the insured in the event that the insured's negligence causes bodily injury or damage to property of others, and the insured is legally required to pay for damages.

Bob Isbell, the RV Team Leader at Explorer RV Insurance Agency, recommends to his clients that they have higher liability limits, and never only carry the state minimum requirements for liability coverage. In the event of a lawsuit, the claimant will pursue damages in correlation with the financial position of the individual causing the damages. Therefore, Bob Isbell personally recommends his clients get liability limits at least as high as "the value of their home plus one year of income." Bob's recommendation to clients seeking to reduce their premium is that they raise their deductibles if necessary, rather than decreasing their limits of liability. "After all," he said, "liability insurance is not very expensive."

Physical Damage Coverage

This would be a good time to talk about two of the common coverage's that fall under the physical damage section of the policy; Comprehensive and Collision. Comprehensive coverage is also commonly referred to as Other Than Collision. Comprehensive provides coverage for damage to your vehicle resulting from "other than a collision." Common examples are fire, theft, windstorm, hail, or flood damage. Collision provides coverage for damage to your vehicle that results when your vehicle strikes another object. Both of these coverage's are subject to a deductible, and for both coverage's raising the deductible lowers your premium.

Section 2 –Specialty RV Coverage's

I mentioned earlier that there are a number of specialty coverage's available, designed to protect you and your property. Specialty RV coverage's are what differentiates RV policies from auto policies. Adding your RV to your auto policy is inadequate because it fails to cover many of the things included in a specialty RV policy. For example, most RV insurance provides coverage for awnings, furniture, permanently installed items and fixtures, and plumbing and electrical systems unique to RVs.

Typical RV policies also provide unlimited towing and roadside labor coverage. Auto policy towing coverage is often inadequate for RV expenses. With most auto policies, the towing reimbursement is usually on a per occurrence basis. Because the fees to tow an RV or to change an RV tire are much higher than the same for an auto, these fees often exceed the per occurrence limits on an auto policy.

Mark J. Polk

Another consideration for RV owners is that they get the benefit of specialized claims service when they choose to insure their RVs with specialty RV insurance as opposed to having RVs put on auto policies. The adjusters assigned to claims by insurance companies with specialty RV products usually have expertise with RVs, losses to RVs, and settling the value of the loss. Let's take a look at some more of these specialty RV coverage's available to you.

- **Diminishing Deductible** – Under this coverage your physical damage deductibles could be reduced 25% for each claim free year you have with the company. After four claims free years, your deductibles would be $0. Any comprehensive or collision losses would reset the deductible.

- **Emergency Vacation Expense coverage-** is also unique for specialty RV policies. This provides coverage to pay for temporary living expenses if your RV is inoperable due to a covered loss and you are more than 50 miles from your home.

- **Vacation Liability** – Provides campsite liability for you while you are using your recreation vehicle as a vacation residence. For example Vacation Liability could cover damage caused by your campfire if it gets out of control or if you accidentally hit someone with a horseshoe.

- **Fulltimer's Coverage's-** This is very important coverage to insured's who use their RVs year round as their residence. There are three Fulltimer Coverage's available:
  - o **Fulltimer's Personal Liability-** This provides personal liability type coverage to fulltime users of RVs, which usually equates to five or more months of use per year. This coverage is even available to individuals who do not own their own home, and is similar to the personal liability coverage on a homeowner's policy.
  - o **Fulltimer's Secured Storage Personal Effects-** Many fulltime RVers keep some of their personal property in

storage. With this option, the insured can get coverage for these items in storage. Typically, the insured will have to create a schedule of these items, and the insurance company will have specified limits for the value of this personal property.

o **Fulltimer's Medical Payments**- This option provides coverage of medical expenses resulting from an accident that occurs while the vehicle is used as a permanent or primary residence. Insurance companies will likely require that the insured also has Fulltimer's Personal Liability coverage in order to qualify for medical payments coverage.

> **Note**: Many insurance policies contain exclusions for using your RV as a permanent or primary residence. Often the Fulltimer's Liability endorsement removes these exclusions from the policy. In other words if you are a fulltimer and do not carry Fulltimer's Liability you may be subject to policy exclusions.

- **Personal Effects** – provides coverage for loss to personal belongings used in conjunction with the RV.

- **Mexico Physical Damage Coverage**– Provides comprehensive and collision coverage for the insured vehicle while traveling in Mexico. The insured is required to purchase Mexican liability coverage too.

- **Mexican Liability Coverage-** While most RV insurance provides physical damage coverage while traveling in Mexico, it does not provide Mexican Liability Coverage. When traveling in Mexico by auto or RV, you must have Mexican Liability Coverage from a Mexican Insurance Company, which you can buy from US-based brokers or at the border. Type this link into your Internet web browser to read a very informative article by Jim Labelle, about properly insuring yourself to travel south of the border.

http://es1.mexicaninsuranceonline.com/press/mre_tm2003.html

- **Schedule Personal Effects Coverage**- Provides coverage for the loss of expensive personal belongings used in conjunction with the RV. The insured must have appraisals for these items.
- **Adjacent Structure coverage** may be available for storage sheds, screened rooms, or carports on owned or rented lots.
- In addition, you may be able to get coverage for roadside assistance, a utility trailer, a golf cart, or scooter.

Section 3 - Valuation and Loss Settlement Options

There are several different physical damage valuation options that may be available to you when you insure your Recreation Vehicle. If you do not add any special coverage's that change the "default" valuation provisions in your policy you will have coverage on an Actual Cash Value (ACV) basis. ACV represents the value of the unit at the moment just prior to the loss. **In other words, ACV includes consideration for depreciation.**

- **Loss Settlement**- When you have a total loss to an automobile, the insurance company pays out the book value of the automobile, which is usually the N.A.D.A. (National Automobile Dealers Association) book value. However, because of the higher values of RVs and the effects of depreciation, a total loss can leave an RV owner with a payout far less than what is owed on the loan – leaving the individual to pay the remainder of the loan not covered by the insurance payout.

> **Note**: Specialty RV insurance offers other loss settlement valuation methods that can protect you, the RV owner from the effects of depreciation.

- **Total Loss Replacement**- If your vehicle qualifies you may be able to purchase Total Loss Replacement (TLR) coverage for your policy. **This valuable coverage protects you against**

depreciation. Typically if you have TLR coverage and your vehicle is a total loss during the first five years, the insurance company will replace your vehicle with a brand new vehicle. After the first five years, the valuation provision switches to a purchase price provision and you would receive the original purchase price of your recreation vehicle, so you are still protected against depreciation. In the event of a total loss of an RV, TLR coverage requires the insurance company to pay you the equivalent of a new unit of the same model, body type, class, size and equipment if you decide to replace your RV. You would have to replace your unit in order to receive this payout. If you choose not to replace your unit, you would only receive the actual cash value of your unit, which is basically the market value of the unit. Typically, this coverage is only eligible for the original owners of the RV. As you can see, Total Loss Replacement protects against the high costs of depreciation.

- **Purchase Price Guarantee-** This is another specialty coverage type that protects the insured against the effects of depreciation in the event of a total loss. Purchase Price Guarantee typically applies to the RV in its first 10 model years. In the event of a total loss, the insurance company will pay the insured the purchase price they paid for the vehicle. The Purchase Price Guarantee option is available instead of Total Loss Replacement when the vehicle is more than 5 years old but less than 10 years old, or if the vehicle is less than 5 years old, but the individual is not the original owner of the vehicle. A common stipulation with this option, however, is that the owner must have purchased the unit within the prior 12 months to be eligible for this coverage.

- **Agreed Value Coverage-** In order for Total Loss Replacement to work, the insurance company needs to be able to obtain a comparable replacement unit at the time of loss. Many RVs are difficult to value. For example, with custom bus conversions the market value of the unit cannot always be determined by the Kelly Blue Book, NADA or the bill of sale. There isn't such a market available for most custom bus conversions. Under Agreed

Mark J. Polk

Value coverage the insurance company and the insured agree on the value of the unit prior to the loss. The rating basis under Agreed Value coverage is based on the indicated market value of a qualified appraisal. These appraisals must then be updated every 3 years to substantiate the "Agreed Value". In the event of a total loss, the Agreed Value is paid to you. This option, however, does not fully protect against the effects of depreciation like Purchase Price Guarantee for Total Loss Replacement coverage's.

> **Note:** To discuss Specialty RV Insurance Coverage, or to get an RV insurance quote from Explorer RV Insurance Agency, Inc call:
> 1-888-774-6778
> **www.explorerrv.com**

Now that you have a better understanding of how basic insurance coverage's work and how important it is to get specialty RV coverage, let's take a look at various ways you can reduce your insurance premium.

Section 4- Ways to reduce your RV insurance premium

There are several ways you can reduce your insurance premium, including:

- Memberships in RV Associations
- Memberships in RV Manufacturing Associations
- Successful completion of driving safety courses
- Clean driving record
- Multi-Policy Discount (treated differently by each insurance co.)
- Improve your credit score
- Homeowners discounts
- Paid-in-Full discounts
- Adding a security device to your RV such as an audible alarm will often qualify for a discount.

Many insurance companies provide discounts to customers who are members of some type of RV association or club. Discounts vary by insurance company. Here is a list of some of the associations that National Interstate Insurance Company provides a 5% discount for, if you are a member.

AAA-Plus Camping World Pres Club Coast-to-Coast Escapees Family Campers	FMCA Good Sam Club Happy Campers Club Thousand Trails

Association discounts are often given for participants in RV manufacturing associations and clubs too. Here is a partial list of manufacturing associations that qualify a candidate for a 5% National Interstate Insurance Company insurance discount.

Coachmen Caravan Club Georgie Boy Owner's Club Gulf Streamers Int'l RV Holiday Rambler RV Club Int Allegro Fam MH Club Jayco Jafari Club Marathon Coach Club Int'l Monaco International Club	Newell Owner's Club Newmar Owner's Club Prevost Prouds Prevost Owner's Group Spartan Chassis Club Wings RV Club (Shasta) Winnebago Motorsport Club Winnebago-Itasca Club

Driver safety courses often qualify an RV owner for discounts with some insurance companies. An insurance agent can inform you of what programs qualify for discounts. Here are some examples of driver safety courses:

- 55 Alive through AARP (not tailored to RV driving)
- Lazy Days offers an RV Driver Confidence Course (is tailored to RV driving)
- Qualified driver safety courses are often offered at large RV rallies such as at FMCA (Family Motor Coach Association) rallies

Most insurance companies, including National Interstate Insurance Company will not stack discounts. As an example, even if you are a member of multiple qualified associations and you have taken a qualified driver safety course, the insurance company will most likely give you one 5% discount.

A clean driving record will reduce your insurance premium. It usually takes 3 years (36 months) for accidents and moving violations/citations to stop impacting your insurance rates.

Another way to reduce your premium is to buy multiple policies from the same insurance company. This is called a multi-policy discount. As an example, companies like National Interstate Insurance Company offer discounts when an individual buys an RV policy and a companion auto policy.

Homeowner's discounts are also common and some companies offer discounts if you pay in full up front.

Use of Credit

Most insurance companies now use credit scores in their insurance pricing. Insurance companies have data that supports the use of credit, and actually believe one's credit score is the best predictor of their future losses. Credit usage is not allowed in all states, so it varies from state-to-state and carrier-by-carrier. Your credit score can heavily impact your insurance rates, so improving your credit score may improve the premium you pay. There is much debate about using a person's credit rating to help determine insurance pricing. You can type this link into your internet browser to read an article in Reactions Magazine, listing both sides of the debate on the use of credit in insurance pricing. http://info.insure.com/auto/creditscorecontroversy0103.html

Drew West, the RV Product Manager for National Interstate Insurance Company, stresses the importance of using and distinguishing insurance scoring from credit scoring.

"Insurance credit scores are different from financial credit scores, even though both scores use only information from credit bureau data. While financial credit scores are used to predict the likelihood of future delinquency on credit accounts, insurance scores were developed to predict the likelihood of future insurance losses. Insurance scores consider trends in the consumer's credit management practices and have been found to be very predictive of the frequency and severity of future losses. An independent test studying our policyholders revealed a definite correlation between an individual's insurance score and the likelihood that they would experience an insurance loss. Past research ("The Relationship of Credit-Based Insurance Scores to Private Passenger Automobile Insurance Loss Propensity") An Actuarial Study by EPIC Actuaries, LLC ~Principal Authors – Michael J. Miller, FCAS, MAAA and Richard A. Smith, FCAS, MAAA *has shown that people with certain patterns of behavior in their credit history display a higher likelihood of filing claims with their insurance company. Insurance scores enable us, the insurer, to offer discounted premiums for those who have a record of responsible credit management."*

How to Buy RV Insurance
There are 3 primary channels for buying RV insurance:

- Through an Agent
- Buying Direct
- Online Quote Services

Through an Agent

Agents represent insurance companies and act as an intermediary between insurance companies and the consumer. There are two different types of agents:

Captive or Exclusive Agents

These are agents like State Farm agents who represent a full range of products from one carrier. These agents will usually only sell insurance products from one carrier. As an example, a State Farm agent will only sell State Farm products.

Independent agents

These agents typically represent a variety of insurance companies. Therefore, they have the ability to generate competitive quotes from several insurance companies. Independent agents can provide more insurance options for a consumer and help match the consumer's unique needs and preferences with an appropriate insurance option. For example, Explorer RV Insurance is an independent agency that sells products of National Interstate Insurance Company, Great American Insurance Company, Drive Insurance from Progressive, RLI, PersonalUmbrella.com, and several others.

Buying Direct

More and more insurance companies are selling directly to the consumer rather than through agents. Examples of companies doing this are Progressive Direct, and GMAC. Many consumers prefer the independence of shopping for insurance themselves and have a greater comfort level purchasing insurance this way. Many first-time RV insurance buyers, however, prefer the counsel of an agent.

Online Quote Services

There are an increasing number of online quote services that help match consumers and insurance providers. As an example, U.S. Insurance Zone

www.usinsurancezone.com enables consumers to get quotes. These online quote services don't sell insurance directly, but facilitate a relationship between interested consumers and insurance providers. In other words, they help match buyers and sellers of insurance.

RV owners can find RV insurance through many RV dealerships and some RV associations too. Some of these organizations have their own internal insurance agencies and licensed agents which enables them to sell insurance policies. Other dealerships and associations have formal referral relationships with insurance agencies or insurance companies that sell direct.

Commercial Usage of RVs

If you want to lease/rent your RV, you will first want to explore your insurance options. The cost of insurance for having rental coverage can be very high and few insurance companies offer it. If you rent your RV without such coverage's, however, there are usually exclusions in your RV policy that prohibit such use. Therefore, if a renter has an accident or causes damage, your insurance company will most likely deny the claim.

If you intend to use your RV for other business uses, such as a mobile hotel, an onsite business location, a mobile service business, or other sales-related uses, the RV must be under a commercial policy. Most commercial vehicle policies do not have specialized RV coverage's. A few companies, such as National Interstate Insurance Company, offer a commercial policy for RV's used in business.

Note: To discuss Specialty RV Insurance Coverage, or to get a quote on RV insurance from Explorer RV Insurance Agency, Inc. call:
1-888-774-6778.
www.explorerrv.com

Mark J. Polk

Explorer RV Insurance Agency, Inc.
Proudly Endorses RV Education 101 Products.

Specialized RV Insurance you can't pass up!

Your RV lifestyle is special. Your RV insurance should be just as specialized. Whether you are a part-time RV enthusiast or you call your RV home, Explorer RV Insurance Agency, Inc. can provide you with customized coverage at a great price. We will also consult with you to help you understand the unique nature of RV insurance and determine if you qualify for any discounts offered by the insurance companies we represent.

To get advice on your RV insurance or request an insurance quote, please call us or provide the following information on this form and return it to Explorer Insurance Agency, Inc. by mail or fax (see below for contact information). An Explorer representative will contact you to discuss your insurance needs.

EXPLORER RV
INSURANCE

Featuring National Interstate Insurance Company

Name_____

Home Phone_____ Cell Phone_____

Email_____

Street_____

City_____ State_____ Zip_____

Year/Make/Model of RV_____

P.O. Box 568
Richfield, OH 44286
Phone: (888) 774-6778
Fax: (330) 659-6687
Email: Explorer@ExplorerRV.com
www.ExplorerRV.com

Explorer markets a variety of insurance products including RV, auto, medium duty truck, boat, motorcycle, ATV, horse trailer, umbrella, and mobile home insurance. Explorer markets insurance across the U.S. except Hawaii and the District of Columbia.   Ad #RVEdB07

 *The RV Book*

Chapter 6

Using Your RV

The LP Gas System

LP gas is a camper's best friend. It provides us with warmth on a chilly day, hot water to shower with, cold food in the refrigerator and the capability to cook on the road the same way you do when you're at home. When we need it it's there, instantly providing us with all of the amenities and creature comforts we are accustomed to. We don't really even think about it, it's taken for granted that when you push that button, almost like magic it responds to your demands.

What is LP Gas?

But what is LP gas? Should we be afraid of it, or just continue to take it for granted? Liquid propane, more commonly known as LP gas gets its name because it is stored in a liquid state. When LP gas is manufactured it is compressed and stored under pressure, which causes it to liquefy. When the pressure is released, the liquid turns back into a vapor. LP gas is odorless, colorless and tasteless. To assist you in detecting a leak an odorant is added to the gas when it is manufactured. If you are not familiar with the odor of LP gas, the next time you go to a qualified fill station ask the attendant to let you smell it. Most people describe the smell as being similar to rotten eggs, or as having a garlic odor.

We'll get back to more characteristics of LP gas in a minute, but first let's address the second question. Should you be afraid of it? You should respect LP gas, because all gases have dangerous characteristics. If you check for gas leaks using an open flame you are certain to be in danger. I guess what I am trying to say is that LP gas is one of the safest of petroleum products if it is handled properly. More times than not, when

Mark J. Polk

there is an accident involving LP gas it is due to negligence or improper handling.

LP gas is portable, safe when handled properly and it's very efficient, so it only makes sense that it is used in RVs. I mentioned a moment ago that LP gas is compressed in a liquid state and stored in containers. Because of the amount of pressure involved, the containers are manufactured under very stringent codes.

LP Gas Cylinders & LP Gas Tanks

There are two basic types of containers, Department of Transportation (DOT), and American Society of Mechanical Engineers (ASME). The DOT containers, more commonly called cylinders, are the upright type that you see on pop-ups, travel trailers, fifth wheels or your BBQ grill.

The ASME cylinders are referred to as tanks and are mounted horizontally like the type you would see on a motorhome.

Regardless of the type, all LP gas containers are only filled to 80% of their capacity to allow for expansion when the temperature around the container rises. LP gas cylinders are equipped with Overfill Protection Devices or OPD valves to prevent them from being overfilled. LP gas can be

measured in weight or in gallons. You may have heard somebody say that the gas cylinders on their travel trailer are 30 lb. cylinders, or they may say their cylinders hold 7 gallons apiece. One gallon of LP gas weighs 4.26 pounds.

LP Gas Regulator

When you open the valve to the LP gas cylinder the liquid gas turns back into a vapor and goes into a two stage regulator. In the first stage, the pressure coming out of the cylinder is reduced significantly. The second stage reduces it to the required 11 inches of water column to run

the appliances properly. On a travel trailer the two-stage regulator is located between the LP gas bottles. It is also an automatic changeover regulator. Let me explain. First, you open the gas valves on both bottles. The LP gas bottle that the lever is pointing towards is your supply bottle. The other bottle is your reserve bottle. When the supply bottle is empty the regulator will automatically change over to the reserve bottle without disrupting your camping. When a bottle is empty the green indicator on the top of the regulator turns red letting you know the bottle is empty. When it's empty you can switch the lever over making the reserve bottle your new supply bottle. Now you can turn the empty bottle off, disconnect it and take it to be filled, while you still have LP gas. On a motorhome the LP gas regulator is located by the LP gas tank. This is still a two-stage regulator, but there is no automatic changeover because there is only one tank.

LP Gas Leak Detector

There is also an LP gas leak detector inside the RV that will set off an alarm to alert you if there is a gas leak. LP gas leak detectors are normally located close to floor level because LP gas is heavier than

air and it will settle towards floor level if there is a leak. If you ever smell LP gas when you're camping, or if the LP gas leak detector alarm goes off, you could have a leak somewhere in the system.

If the LP gas detector alarm goes off:

➢ Extinguish any open flames, pilot lights and do not smoke, or touch electrical switches.

➢ Evacuate the RV and turn off the main gas supply valve.

➢ Leave the door open and do not return to the area until the odor clears.

➢ Have the system checked out by a qualified technician before using it again.

> **Note:** False alarms can be caused by hair spray, perfume, cleaning solvents and low battery voltage.

LP Gas Do's and Don'ts

➢ Do remember to turn the main gas supply on when you're ready to use a gas appliance.

➢ Do have the system checked if you suspect a leak, disturb the gas system, or at least once annually.

➢ Do take the proper steps to safely transport, store and use LP gas cylinders.

➢ Do review all cautions and warnings on the LP gas system and appliances in your owner's manual.

⊘ Do not use an open flame to check for leaks.

⊘ Do not use the range burners or oven as a source of heat; it is not vented outside and **depleted oxygen can cause asphyxiation**.

⊘ Do not go to a gas station to refuel unless you extinguish any open flames and, or pilot lights and turn LP gas appliances off.

⊘ Do not transport LP gas cylinders inside a vehicle.

⊘ Do not be afraid of LP gas, but **do** respect it and handle it properly.

LP Gas Appliances

When the LP gas leaves the regulator it goes through a low-pressure manifold to the furnace, the refrigerator when it's in the gas mode, the range top and oven, and the water heater.

The Water Heater

Most RVs manufactured have a water heater with the exception of some pop-ups and some other smaller RV's. The majority of RV water heaters have six gallon water tanks, and some have ten gallon tanks. If you have a water heater it will operate on LP gas, and some operate on electricity too.

There are two basic types of water heaters, manual and Direct Spark Ignition (DSI). A manual water heater requires you to light it using a hand-held striker. A DSI water heater can be lit by simply turning on a switch. Before you light any water heater you need to make sure the water tank is full of water. To see if the tank is full, with the RV either hooked up to a water source or if you're using the 12-volt water pump, turn a hot water faucet on and see if you get a steady flow of water. If it is spitting air, the tank is not completely full. Allow the water heater tank to finish filling and make sure the LP gas supply is turned on.

If you have a manual type water heater look at the control dial and you will see an **Off, On** and **Pilot** position. To light the water heater move the selector to the Pilot position. You will notice it is spring loaded. Hold it down in the pilot position and using a striker light the pilot light.

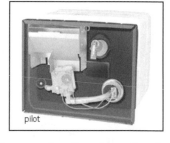

Continue holding it in this position for several seconds after the pilot is lit. When you release the knob and the pilot light stays lit, turn the knob to the ON position and the burner will light. You should see and hear a nice strong, blue flame. If you get a weaker yellow flame it's possible that your air inlet isn't adjusted properly or that there is an obstruction around the burner.

Mark J. Polk

You have a heat selector at the back of the manual gas valve to control the water temperature. It's preset by the manufacturer, usually at 140 degrees, about the same as what you would find in your house. You should only have to light the water heater one time unless a strong wind happens to blow the pilot light out.

If you have a DSI water heater all you need to do is locate the water heater switch, inside the RV, and turn it on. Make sure the water tank is full and the LP gas supply is on. The water heater will light automatically. If it doesn't light the first time, turn it off, wait a minute and try it again.

> **Note:** Always follow the manufacturer's instructions to light and operate the type of water heater in your RV.

Once the water heater has ignited it will cycle on and off as required to keep the water hot, as long as you have LP gas. It will take 20 to 30 minutes to heat the water to temperature. Depending on how much hot water you plan to use, you can leave it on for your entire camping trip, or you can just light it 30 minutes before you need hot water.

> **Caution:** Keep children away from the outside water heater vent. It can get extremely hot.

Some water heaters offer an additional feature where it can also operate on electricity. If you are plugged into an electrical source, just turn the water heater switch on in the electric mode. Keep in mind that it will draw from 9 to 13 amps when it's in the electric mode and always make sure there is water in the tank so you don't damage the electric heating element. You should always drain the water heater tank when you are not using the RV.

> **Caution:** Never drain the water heater when the water is hot or when it is under pressure.

This could result in severe burns. To relieve the water pressure, turn off the water supply and open a hot water faucet. Allow sufficient time for the water to cool down before draining. To drain the water heater, locate and open the outside water heater access door. The drain plug, or petcock is located in the bottom left hand corner of the water heater compartment. Remove the plug and open the pressure relief valve on top of the water heater to assist in draining.

The Range and Oven

A typical RV gas range and oven is similar to what you might find in your house, with the exception that most new RV ranges only have three burners. The front burner is a high output burner. Some burners have built in automatic igniters, making it very simple to light the burners. Just turn the knob to the light position and rotate the knob until the burner lights. On a range that doesn't have automatic igniters you can use a striker. Turn the burner to the light position and use the striker to light the burner. To light the oven, turn the selector knob for the oven to the pilot **ON** position and light the pilot inside the oven using a striker.

The pilot and burner assembly is located under the tray in the oven. When the pilot is lit you will see a small pilot flame. Once it's lit, turn the selector knob to a higher heat range setting and the pilot light will burn stronger. When it reaches a certain temperature the gas valve releases gas and the burner lights. This can take several seconds. After the burner lights you just set the temperature control to the desired heat setting for what you are cooking.

Some pop-ups have an LP gas range that can be used inside and outside. You simply turn the main gas supply off at the range inside, disconnect the quick disconnect, and hook it up to the external gas supply provided to use it outside. Other pop-ups give you two separate ranges, one for inside and one for outside.

Mark J. Polk

LP Gas Tip: When you change a gas bottle there is a possibility you will get air in the gas lines. A good habit to get into is to light the range burners first. What this does is help evacuate any air out of the system to make it easier to light the other appliances.

Warning: Never use the range burners or oven as a source of heat. It is not vented outside and depleted oxygen can cause **asphyxiation**.

The RV Furnace

If you have a forced air furnace in your RV it will operate off of LP gas. Heat in your RV will either come from vents located throughout the RV or it will be ducted in the floor. To turn the furnace on, all you need to do is locate the thermostat. It's possible that you will have a separate thermostat just for the furnace. If this is the case, slide the small lever on the bottom of the thermostat to the

"**ON**" position and raise the temperature selector to the desired temperature. On most RVs, the same thermostat will control both the heat and the air conditioning. Move the selector to the "**heat**" position and raise the temperature selector to the desired temperature. In a few seconds you'll hear the furnace fan motor come on. In less than a minute the furnace will ignite and you can feel heat coming from the vents. The furnace will cycle on and off just like the one in your house does.

Note: Always follow the manufacturer's instructions to light and operate the type of furnace you have.

Caution: Keep children away from the outside furnace exhaust vent. It gets extremely hot.

The Refrigerator

The next appliance we want to discuss is the refrigerator. The refrigerator in your RV will work off of LP gas or electricity. It's not like the refrigerator in your house. An RV refrigerator doesn't have a compressor, or any moving parts for that matter. It works off of the principle of absorption. Instead of applying cold directly, the heat is drawn out, or absorbed. The theory is, when there is an absence of heat there is cold. Basically your RV refrigerator uses heat, either from an electric heating element or LP gas flame. The heat starts a chemical reaction and then through evaporation and condensation causes it to cool. It also works off of gravity, freezing the freezer compartment first and then dropping down to the refrigerator compartment.

The initial cool down process can take four to six hours. You should turn the refrigerator on the day before you plan to leave on a trip, and before you put any food in it. When you do load the refrigerator the food you put in should already be cold, and the food put in the freezer should already be frozen. Putting cold food in the refrigerator, rather than adding warm food, lets the refrigerator work more efficiently. One common mistake made is to over pack the refrigerator. There has to be space between the foods to allow for air to circulate throughout the compartment. In most situations you will have access to a store where you can buy food. A two to three day supply should be enough.

Turn the refrigerator on and if you are plugged into electricity it will go into the auto mode on electric. If you have a battery on the RV and you unplug the power cord it would automatically switch over to LP gas, as long as the LP gas bottles are open. You also have the option to manually put the refrigerator in the LP gas mode.

Most have an automatic igniter, so as soon as you switch it to the gas mode it will light the burner. If it fails to light, a check light will come on to let you know that it didn't light. You can turn the refrigerator off, wait a minute, turn it back on and it will reset and light. If the check light comes on, whether the refrigerator is on gas or electric there is something wrong. It might be that there is no gas in the bottles, the RV is not

Mark J. Polk

plugged in or the battery is weak. Try to identify the problem and take care of it.

To keep the refrigerator operating efficiently in the LP gas mode there is some routine maintenance you can perform. Remove the outside lower vent cover to access the back of the refrigerator. With the refrigerator turned off ensure all connections are clean and tight. Turn the refrigerator on in the LP gas mode and a look at the flame. If the flame is burning poorly, a yellow colored flame, or if the refrigerator isn't operating properly in the gas mode it's possible that the baffle inside the flue is covered with soot. Soot, rust and other debris can fall down and obstruct the burner assembly. When this happens it will be necessary to clean the flue and the burner assembly. Turn the refrigerator off again and locate the burner. Directly above the burner is the flue. The baffle is inside the flue. Wear a pair of safety glasses and use an air compressor to blow air up into the flue. After the flue is clean use the compressed air to remove any debris from the outside refrigerator compartment. Now, turn the refrigerator on in the LP gas mode to make sure it is working properly. Look for the bright blue flame.

> **Note:** For a thorough cleaning of the flue and baffle it will be necessary to have an authorized RV service center do it for you. While it's there have them to do an LP gas pressure test and leak test too. This should be done annually.

Some RV refrigerators have a manual temperature control and some have a built in temperature control. Normally a temperature setting of three or four will work fine. If it is extremely hot or cold outside it may be necessary to raise or lower the setting. The outside temperature directly affects the operation of the refrigerator. Extremely hot weather will directly affect the refrigerators efficiency. When it's really hot outside try parking your RV with the side the refrigerator is on in the shade. Periodically inspect and clean the refrigerator door gaskets. Check them for a good seal. Place a dollar bill behind the seal and close the door. It should stay there and not drop. When you try to pull it out there should be some resistance felt. Do this in several different places and have any damaged seals replaced.

Try to limit the amount of times you open the refrigerator or freezer doors and the length of time you leave the doors open. Every time the door is opened it loses a few degrees. On a hot summer day it won't take long to lose all of its  cooling capacity. Last but not least you should always have a thermostat in the food compartment. Food will begin to spoil at temperatures above 40 degrees.

Pop-up Tip: Most refrigerators on pop-ups operate off of three different power sources, LP gas, 120-volt AC, and 12-volt DC. In the gas mode you will need to follow the instructions and light the burner. Once it is lit it will do the rest.

Note: All RV's need to be fairly level for the RV refrigerator to operate properly.

Mark J. Polk

The RV Water & Waste Management System

RV Water Systems

The water system of an RV has many similarities to the one in your house. They both need a source of potable water supplied to them. This water source in turn supplies water to the water heater, the kitchen sink, bathroom sink, shower, and toilet. In your house the waste water that goes down the sink and shower drains, and the waste flushed down the toilet goes into a septic tank or a city sewer system.

Your RV has two waste water holding tanks similar to a septic tank. The gray water tank collects waste water from the sinks and shower. The black water tank collects waste from the toilet. There is a monitor panel in the RV that will allow you to check the tank levels so you will know when they need to be emptied.

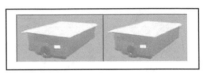

Surface Mount Display:
Surface Mount Display monitors
up to four holding tanks.

I mentioned a moment ago that you need a source of potable water for your RV. Most campgrounds will provide a potable water source to hook up to. You just connect a potable drinking hose from the water source at the campground, to the city water inlet of the RV and you have water supplied throughout the RV.

Now let's say that you want to get away from it all, you want to do some remote type camping where there is no water supply, better known as dry camping. What do we do for water? Sure, you want to get away from it all but no one said anything about not being able to take a shower. This is where your RV is unique; it has a fresh water holding tank that allows you to carry potable water with you when a water source is not available. The capacity will vary, and can range from 10 to 20 gallons in a pop-up, and up to as much as 100 gallons in some motorhomes.

If you're going to be traveling, or camping where a potable water source is not available, fill your fresh water holding tank, through the fresh water fill, before you leave on your trip. The monitor panel lets you know how much water is in the fresh water holding tank.

> **Note**: Water weighs 8.3 pounds per gallon. If you're going to take 40 gallons of fresh water, you just added over 300 pounds of additional weight to the RV. Take just enough water to get to your destination.

Water from the fresh water holding tank is supplied throughout the RV by a 12-volt DC, demand type water pump. The pump will require a 12-volt deep cycle battery if you don't have access to an external electrical source. You simply

turn the switch on, usually located by the monitor panel, the pump pressurizes the system and you have water.

At the end of your camping season you drain the water system, winterize the RV and put it in storage for the winter. One problem with this is that on most RV's when you drain the fresh water holding tank there is still some water left in the tank. Let's say you do manage to drain all of the water out of the tank. There is still moisture in the water system. Just imagine what can grow in that moist tank and in the water lines while it sits for three or four months. I'd rather not think about it.

This is the water tank that you drink from and the water you use to wash dishes and take showers with. We cannot assume that it will stay safe and fresh like the water system in our home. Contaminated water is extremely dangerous. We not only have to deal with a water system that hasn't been used for sometime, but when we travel in the RV we hook our water system up to a different water source every time we stop to spend the night some where. We hook up to city water, well water, and eventually contaminated water. You've probably heard people say don't drink the water if you go to Mexico. Well that can be true anywhere. We

Mark J. Polk

stopped at a campground one night just to get a few hours of sleep and I didn't bother to use the water filter. The water coming out of the faucet was cloudy and had small particles suspended in it. There are no guarantees that any water is completely safe for us to drink, but if we take certain precautions we can keep our RV water system safe to use. So where do we start?

First of all, you should always use a white non-toxic drinking hose. Hoses not labeled safe for drinking can contribute to lead and other dangerous chemicals getting in the water. Use the white non-toxic hose for hooking up to the water source and  take along a green or black garden hose for all other uses like flushing out holding tanks or washing the RV. When you're not using the drinking hose, roll it up and connect the two ends together. This will keep dirt and other debris from getting in the hose. The next time you use the hose, run some water through it before hooking it up to the RV.

Water Filtration

Next you need to filter the water going into the RV with a high quality filtration system. Water filters do not purify the water but they can control and remove bacteria, lead and other dangerous contaminants found in drinking water.

You basically have two choices on how to filter your RV water system. You can install an inline water filter directly to the water line that you drink from, or you can filter all of the water going into the RV. I prefer to filter all of the water going into the RV. This helps to protect the entire water system and even filters the shower water to help prevent any skin irritation.

Sanitizing the Fresh Water System

Possibly the most important step you can take is to keep the fresh water system sanitized. At a minimum, you should sanitize the system every spring when you take the RV out of storage, and any time you notice stale water or an odor. It's really quite simple to do. You can start by draining the water heater. Go to the outside compartment where the water heater is located. The drain plug, or petcock is located in the bottom left hand corner. Remove the plug and open the pressure relief valve on top of the water heater to assist in draining.

> **Caution:** Never drain the water heater tank when it's hot or under pressure. To relieve the water pressure, turn off the water supply and open a hot water faucet. Allow sufficient time for the water to cool down before draining.

Next you need to locate the low point water line drains. It may take a while to find them, but I assure you they are there. There will be one for the hot and one for the cold water lines. This is the lowest point in the water system. Open these and let the water drain out. Now, find the drain for the fresh water holding tank and drain all of the water from it. At this point you can turn the water pump on for a moment to force any remaining water out. Do not let the pump continue to run once the water stops draining. Close all of the drains.

What we have accomplished so far was to evacuate the majority of water from the system. Now take a quarter cup of house hold bleach for every fifteen gallons of water that your fresh water tank holds. Mix the bleach, with water, into a one-gallon container and pour it into the fresh water holding tank. Fill the fresh water tank almost completely full of water. Turn the water pump on, open all hot and cold faucets and run the water until you smell the bleach at each faucet. Close the faucets.

If it's possible, drive the RV or pull the trailer so the water can move around to assist in cleaning the entire tank. Let it sit for at least 12 hours. Drain the entire system again and re-fill the fresh water tank with potable water. Open all of the faucets and run the water until you no longer smell

Mark J. Polk

any bleach. It may be necessary to repeat this process again to eliminate all signs of bleach from the water system. Once this is done it is safe to use your water system.

The RV Waste Management System

All about RV Holding Tanks

This would be a good time to talk about RV holding tanks. To start with, I would like to mention something about RV holding tanks that I don't think a lot of RVers are aware of. Many of the free dump stations available to RVers are closing because of chemicals that are harmful to septic systems and because RVers are abusing these dump stations. If we want to have access to these dump stations it is absolutely essential that we use septic safe chemicals (no formaldehyde), and that we clean up after ourselves and do not abuse dump stations.

I mentioned earlier that your RV has what is referred to as a gray water holding tank and a black water holding tank. The gray water holding tank collects dirty water from the kitchen sink, bathroom sink and shower. Some larger RVs have an 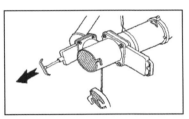 additional gray water holding tank. The black water holding tank is for the toilet. These tanks terminate into one main outlet used to empty the holding tanks. This is where we connect our sewer hose.

Make sure you have the required couplings and connectors. It may be necessary to attach two hoses together to reach the sewer connection. I recommend you only use heavy duty sewer hoses.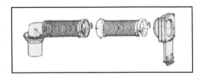

They are not that expensive and they hold up much better. Keep a 10 foot hose and a 20 foot hose available so you can always reach the campground sewer connection. Do not pull or drag the sewer hose on the ground. This will cause it to tear or get pin holes in it. To hook up the sewer hose make sure both valves are closed and remove the sewer cap. Make the connection by putting the hose adapter over the outlet and turn it clockwise until it locks securely in place. Take the other end of the hose over to the campground sewer connection. Use the necessary adapters to make the connection and get a good seal.

It's a good idea to place some weight over the hose so it doesn't jump back out when you drain the tanks. It may be necessary to use some type of sewer hose support to get a good angle from the RV to the campground sewer connection so the tanks drain properly when you empty them. The small valve is for the gray water tank and the large valve is for the black water tank.

One golden rule for RV holding tanks is to never dump the black water tank until it is at least two thirds full. You can check the tank levels at the monitor panel. You want the tank nearly full so the weight and the gravity will force the contents of the tank to drain properly. Another golden rule is to never leave the black tank valve open at the campground and expect the toilet to drain or flush like the toilet in your home. It won't work. When the tanks are full, or nearly full always dump the black tank first, the large valve, followed by the gray tank, the small valve. The gray water tank should also be at least two thirds full. Dumping the gray water tank last will help flush out the sewer hose.

When you're at the campground for an extended period of time you can leave the gray tank valve partially open so it drains as you use it, but remember to NEVER do this with the black tank. If it's time to leave the campground and your holding tanks aren't full you can finish filling them with water and then dump them. Just put the hose down the toilet to finish filling the black tank, or in the shower or bathtub drain to finish filling the gray tank.

Never use your drinking water hose for holding tank maintenance or cleaning purposes. RV drinking hoses are normally white. Take a different color hose for others uses so you can distinguish the difference.

After you dump the tanks you need to thoroughly flush the tanks out. Some RVs have a built in system for flushing the holding tanks. If not there are other ways to do it. You can use a tank wand designed for cleaning and flushing the black tank. The only problem is, you don't know when or if the black tank is really clean and you can't rinse or clean the gray tank with a wand.

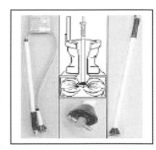

There are other products like the Flush King. It's a reverse flush valve that connects directly to your sewer outlet and rinses and cleans both holding tanks in one simple operation. It's easy to use and it has a see through barrel so you know when the tanks are really clean.

www.flushking.com

Every time you dump the black tank you need to treat it with holding tank chemicals to assist in controlling odors and to break down solids. You should always use environmentally safe chemicals. Enzyme based chemicals use the good bacteria to digest waste and control odors. Formaldehyde based chemicals destroy the bacteria that's needed to break down waste and they can be dangerous to humans and pets. The first step is to add enough water to completely cover the bottom of the tank. Four or five toilet bowls full should be enough, depending on the size of your black tank.

Water will assist a great deal with controlling holding tank odors. You always want the contents of the tank to be covered by water. Next, fill the toilet bowl with water and add the proper amount of holding tank chemicals, usually four ounces for every forty gallons the tank holds. Flush the toilet. Repeat this procedure every time you empty the black water holding tank. Some holding tank chemicals also contain valve lubricants to keep the valves operating properly and extend the valve seals life.

You should always use toilet paper designed for use in RVs. This toilet paper breaks down and dissolves in the holding tank chemicals preventing potential problems with the holding tank, the RV sewer system and the dump station septic system. False holding tank readings on your monitor panel are caused by the holding tank probes being covered by toilet tissue or other debris. If flushing the tank doesn't solve the problem add some water and a couple bags of ice cubes to the empty holding tank. Drive or pull the RV so the ice cubes can scrub the sides of the tank. Proper holding tank chemicals will also keep the holding tank probes clean.

Over time grease and residue build up in the gray tank and it causes a foul odor, not to mention how it is affecting the tank and valve assembly. Periodically treat the gray tank with environmentally safe holding tank chemicals to avoid odors from the tank. When the tank is empty you can also add some dishwashing liquid down the drains to help break down grease and residue build up.

Some pop-up campers come equipped with cassette toilets. These toilets have small holding tanks that can be removed and emptied at the dump station when they are full. If the pop-up doesn't come with a toilet you can purchase a portable porta-potti.

There are also portable holding tanks available to collect the waste water from a pop-up that is not equipped with holding tanks, or for other RV's when dump facilities are not available. When the tank is full it can be transported and emptied at a dump station.

Note: Never let the gray or black water drain on the ground.

Following these simple holding tank tips can prevent problems and provide you with long lasting trouble free holding tanks. This is one problem we can all do without!

> **Note**: Whenever you are working with waste evacuation and holding tanks it is a good idea to wear gloves. There are disposable gloves designed just for this. Check with your local RV camping supply store.

> Our RV training videos cover information on RV holding tanks, the water system, LP gas system, electrical system and much more.

Note: See order form at back of book or **www.rveducation101.com**

The RV Electrical System

The electrical system in your RV can seem complex and confusing until you have a basic understanding of how it works. Your RV actually has three separate electrical systems. It has a 12-volt DC chassis system, a 12-volt DC coach system, and a 120-volt AC coach system.

12-Volt DC Chassis System

If it's a pop-up, travel trailer or fifth wheel, the 12-volt DC chassis system gets its power from the tow vehicle battery when the trailer wiring harness is plugged into the tow vehicle trailer receptacle. This operates the trailers tail-lights, brake lights and turn signals. The tow vehicle alternator will also charge the trailer battery if a charge line is wired into the trailer receptacle. The trailer brakes are activated through use of the electronic brake controller mounted in the tow vehicle. If it's a motorhome the 12-volt DC chassis system gets its power from the RV starting battery. We'll talk more about RV batteries in a minute.

12-Volt DC & 120-Volt AC Coach System

We are primarily concerned with the 12-volt DC and 120-volt AC coach systems. 12-volt DC or direct current is electricity supplied by a deep cycle auxiliary battery or batteries. DC electricity flows in one direction, from negative to positive.

12-volt DC electricity is stored in the RV batteries and supplies power for components, devices and appliances that operate off of 12-volts.

120-volt AC or alternating current is the same electricity used in your household. AC electricity reverses or alternates direction 60 times per second, or 60 hertz. 120-volt AC electricity supplies power to all of the 120-volt appliances and electronic equipment in your RV. The majority of campgrounds you go to will provide you with an external 120-volt electric source to plug into. Your RV has a heavy-duty power cord that is normally about 20 to 25 feet long.

Depending on the type of RV you have, or purchase, it will either have a 30 amp or 50 amp electrical system. When you plug into the proper campground electrical source it will supply power throughout your RV. You must have a 120-volt AC power source if you are going to use the microwave, roof air conditioner, the refrigerator in the electric mode, electronic equipment and the 120-volt electrical outlets.

For the most part everything else in the RV works off of 12-volt DC power. When you're plugged in at the campground the 120-volt AC current is converted to 12-volt DC current, by the RV's converter, for the items in the RV that work off of 12-volts. Some of these items are the overhead lights, the furnace fan, the fan over the range, the vent fan in the bathroom, the water pump, LP gas leak detector, stereo, and the refrigerator when it's in the LP gas mode. Your RV may or may not be equipped with a battery disconnect switch. If you do have a coach battery disconnect switch it will have to be turned on to use the 12-volt appliances and accessories.

Power Distribution Panel

If you look at the RV's power distribution panel you will see circuit breakers like you have in your house for the 120-volt AC side, and automotive style blade fuses for the 12-volt DC side. If you trip a breaker, turn the appliance off and check the power distribution box. The breakers and fuses are labeled. Try to determine why the breaker tripped and correct the problem. Turn the appliance off, reset the breaker and turn the appliance back on. If an overhead light quits working, check the bulb first, if the

bulb is good check the fuse. You should keep some spare fuses and bulbs in a drawer.

If you're not plugged into an external power source you can still use the 12-volt DC system if you have a 12-volt deep cycle battery or batteries on your unit. As long as the battery or batteries are charged you can use everything in the RV except the microwave, roof air conditioner, the refrigerator in the electric mode and the electrical outlets. You can check the condition of the battery at the monitor panel. To get an accurate reading of the battery check it when the RV is not plugged into electricity, and turn a couple overhead lights on to put a small load on the battery.

If you have a motorhome, or if you're going to purchase a motorhome, it will have a battery for the 12-volt automotive system and an auxiliary battery or batteries for the 12-volt coach system. The coach battery is charged whenever the motorhome is running; the generator is running, or when it's plugged into an external electrical source.

RV Generators

Motorhomes also provide an additional source of 120-volt AC power with an onboard power generator. This unique feature offers you the convenience of 120-volt AC power whenever you need it, making the unit fully self-contained.

AC power generators are rated in kilowatts. One Kilowatt (KW) equals 1000 watts so a 4KW generator would be capable of producing 4000 watts. The fuel supply for the generator comes directly from the motorhome fuel tank. The system is designed so that when the fuel tank gets to a 1/4 tank the generator will stop running, so it doesn't use all of the fuel in the motorhome. Some motorhomes have an automatic switch over from an external power supply to the generator. Other motorhomes require you to plug the motorhome power cord into a generator receptacle on the motorhome when you use the generator.

I have always been an advocate of monitoring the AC line voltage coming into your RV. Campground electricity can fluctuate a great deal.

Mark J. Polk

If you don't know what the voltage is coming into your RV, you risk damaging thousands of dollars worth of electrical appliances and electronic equipment.

Digital Voltmeter

Every RVer should invest in some type of digital voltmeter that plugs directly into a 120-volt outlet in your RV. There are several types available and they are inexpensive compared to the repair costs for damaged electrical equipment and appliances. I recommend one that can test campground polarity,
measure AC line voltage and, if you have a generator, measure AC frequency.

You should always test the campground wiring for improperly wired circuits before you plug your RV in. Before you plug your RV power cord into the electrical supply make sure any breakers are turned off. Plug the RV in and turn the breaker on. Now you can plug the digital meter into a 120-volt outlet where
it will be easy to monitor throughout your camping trip. By monitoring the AC voltage throughout your trip you can protect thousands of dollars worth of electrical equipment and appliances in your RV. If AC voltage drops below 105-volts or goes above 130-volts you should turn electronic equipment and appliances off until the power is restored.

When you use your generator set the digital meter so it will measure or count the AC frequency output of the generator. Frequency is the number of times that electricity alternates per second. Appliances are designed to operate at 60 cycles per second, or 60 hertz. When you use your generator the governor in the generator must hold the speed constant at, or close to 60 hertz from no load on the generator to a full load. Depending on the load placed on the generator, AC voltage can range from 105 to 130 volts and the frequency can range from 58 to 63 hertz. The meter will let you know when the generator is not operating within the proper ranges and you can have it checked out and repaired before any damage occurs.

Extension Cords & Electrical Adapters

If it's possible you should try to avoid using an extension cord when making electrical connections at the campground. The gauges of the wire used in standard household extension cords are not suitable for RV electrical hook-ups. Eventually you will be put in a situation where you will need to use an extension cord. It's a good idea to purchase an RV extension cord that is compatible to the electrical system of your RV. If you do purchase an extension cord somewhere else it should be 10-guage wire and always use as short of an extension cord as possible.

There are RV electrical adapters that will go from your RV type plug and size down to household type outlets; and adapters that go from household type outlets to all types of campground RV connections. It's nice to have these adapters on hand when you need them, but you must exercise caution and use common sense when you use them.

If you have a 30-amp electrical system and you are hooked up to a 50-amp service, use your RV electrical system exactly the same way you do when you're plugged into a 30-amp service. In other words, don't try to run anymore than you normally would. On the other hand if your RV is a 30-amp or 50-amp system, and you use an adapter to plug the RV into a 15 or 20-amp outlet, you severely limit what you can operate in the RV. In this situation you should only use the appliances or electronic equipment that is absolutely necessary. The air conditioner alone can draw 14 to 16 amps when the compressor engages. If you try to use the air conditioner with other appliances or electronic equipment turned on you risk damaging those items. If you place too much of a demand on these electrical adapters, or use them for extended periods of time they

Mark J. Polk

can overheat and melt resulting in damage to the RV power cord or the electrical system.

Even when you're plugged in to the proper electrical service for your RV you still need to be selective about what you are using. If you try to use too much, the RV will let you know by tripping a breaker in the distribution box and hopefully no harm will be done.

Ground Fault Circuit Interrupter (GFCI)

The RV also has what is called a Ground Fault Circuit Interrupter or GFCI. This is designed to protect you in the event that you plug something into a receptacle and there is moisture or water present. The GFCI will trip automatically. Several outlets can be wired on the GFCI circuit so if you plug something into an outlet and it doesn't work check the GFCI to see if it needs to be reset.

120-Volt RV Appliances

Air Conditioner

The air conditioner in your RV will be one of two types. It will either cool from one central location or it will be ducted throughout the ceiling of the RV. Some larger RVs will have two roof air conditioners. In most cases, the thermostat that controls the air conditioner also controls the heat. It's very simple to operate, just move the selector to the cool position and the temperature selector to the desired temperature. You also have a fan mode if you just want to circulate some air. If the A/C unit comes through the roof of the RV and cools from one central location the controls are on the A/C unit itself.

Periodically remove and clean or replace the AC filters. You can wash, rinse and thoroughly dry the filters or vacuum them with a small vacuum cleaner. The air conditioner will work more efficiently with clean filters. If it is an older RV with two roof mounted air conditioners it may not be possible to run them both at the same time. Running both of them can exceed the maximum amperage of the RV's electrical system. On many newer RV's you can run both air conditioners at the same time, but you will be limited as to what other electrical items you can use.

Refrigerator

We briefly discussed the RV refrigerator in the chapter on LP gas. Whenever you are plugged into electricity the refrigerator will switch to AC unless you manually set it to operate in the LP gas mode. If you have an auxiliary battery on the RV and you unplug the RV power cord it will automatically switch over to the LP gas mode, as long as the LP gas is turned on and you have gas in the bottles or tanks.

Getting the most from your RV Refrigerator

I receive a lot of questions about how to make your RV refrigerator work more efficiently. RV refrigerators, for the most part, are efficient. In many cases it is something the owner does that makes the refrigerator less efficient.

There are several things you can do to help the refrigerator do its job more efficiently. First and foremost the RV must be fairly level for the refrigerator to operate properly. Older RV refrigerators required more precise leveling, but even the newer models need to be close to level for optimum performance. Over time a cooling unit operated out of level will be permanently damaged. Traveling with the refrigerator on will not cause problems because the liquids and gases in the cooling unit are constantly moving around. They don't collect and stay in areas of the cooling unit like they can in a stationary, out of level refrigerator.

There has to be space between the foods to allow for air to circulate throughout the compartment. To assist with air circulation you can purchase an inexpensive, battery operated refrigerator fan. Put the batteries in and place the fan in the front of the refrigerator compartment, blowing up. Cold air drops and warm air rises. The fan will improve the efficiency by circulating the air and it will reduce the initial cool down time by up to 50%.

The heat created by the cooling process is vented behind the refrigerator. Air enters through the outside lower refrigerator vent and helps to draft the hot air out through the roof vent. Periodically inspect the back of the refrigerator and the roof vent for any obstructions like bird nests, leaves or other debris that might prevent the heat from escaping.

Another good idea is to install a 12-volt, thermostatically controlled refrigerator vent fan at the back of the refrigerator, or at the top of the roof vent, to assist with drafting the hot air away from the refrigerator. If you are mechanically inclined these fans are fairly easy to install, or you can have your RV dealer install one for you. Either way it's worth it. The fan removes the heat built up behind the refrigerator improving the refrigerators performance by up to 40%.

RV absorption refrigerators do a great job for RVers. They will do an even better job, and last longer, if we apply these simple tips to make their job easier and less demanding.

Microwave

Most RV's will come equipped with a microwave or in some cases it might be a convection oven. You must have electricity to operate the microwave. You operate the microwave the same as you would in your house. Keep in mind if the RV has a 30 amp electrical system you should not use the microwave and the air conditioner at the same time. You risk damaging electronic equipment and appliances.

RV Converters

I briefly discussed what your RV converter does a moment ago. When you plug your RV into an electrical source, or when you use the onboard generator, the converters job is to reduce 120-volts AC down to 12-volt DC. The converter supplies power to all of the 12-

volt appliances and accessories in the RV. If you weren't plugged into an electrical source, your RV battery(s) would supply the power to all of the 12-volt appliances and accessories in the RV. The converter basically prevents your RV battery(s) from draining when you're plugged in.

There are two types of amperage draw concerning your RV. The AC amps we are using and the DC amps we are using. I'll try to explain. When you plug your RV into an electrical source and use 120-volt appliances like the roof air conditioner, the microwave and a TV you are drawing amps from the available supply at the campground, usually 30 or 50 amps depending on your RV electrical system and the electrical supply you are plugged into. When you're plugged into an electrical source and you use DC appliances and accessories like fans, lights, pumps or the TV antenna booster you are drawing amps from the RV converter. Are you more confused now than when we started? Let's try wording this a little different.

Let's say you plug your RV into a 30 amp electrical supply and you only use 120-volt appliances. You're using available amps from the 30 amp electrical supply for whatever 120-volt appliances are running, but the converter is drawing almost 0 amps because you're not using any DC accessories. It will use a small amount for items like the LP gas leak detector, clocks or maybe an aisle light, but not enough to really affect the amperage you are plugged into.

Your RV converter is rated for a certain amperage i.e. 30 amps, 45 amps, 55 amps. In other words a 45 amp converter is capable of running 45 amps worth of 12-volt appliances in the RV. When your RV converter is working at its maximum capacity, which in this case is producing 45 amps for 12-volt appliances and accessories, it is drawing around 5 amps out of the 30 amps available from the campground electrical supply.

Let's say you're plugged in and you're using a couple of 12-volt overhead lights (2 amps) and a ceiling fan (4 amps). In this case your converter is drawing very little from the campgrounds 30 amp electrical supply. In another scenario let's say you're using a lot of 12-volt overhead lights (8 amps), you're running the furnace fan (11 amps), water pump (4 amps), 12-volt television (5 amps), range hood fan (2.5 amps), and the battery is being charged by the converter charger (3 amps). Now, when the converter is running close to its full capacity it draws the full 5 amps from the campgrounds 30 amps, leaving you with 25 amps for other 120-volt appliances and accessories. As you can see it's unlikely that all of this

Mark J. Polk

would be happening at one time. The bottom line is the converter amperage draw will fluctuate depending on the 12-volt demand placed on it.

Your RV converter is also a battery charger. RV converters provide a charge to your RV house batteries whenever you are plugged in to electricity, but only a small portion of the converters amperage rating is used for charging the batteries, normally 3 to 5 amps. This will provide a trickle charge but it is not enough to charge batteries that are completely discharged.

The converter battery charger is designed to keep the house batteries topped off with this trickle charge. Another problem with older RV converters is they charge at a fixed voltage in the range of 13.5 volts. If your batteries are fully charged this can be too much for a float charge and over time it will deplete the water level in the battery's cells. This is why it's important to check the water level in your batteries on a regular basis, especially when you leave the RV plugged in for extended periods of time. You need a three stage charger that can provide a bulk charge then an absorption charge and finally a float charge. Newer RV converters on the market are capable of charging the batteries this way.

Now, to help you out I am including some typical amperage draws for appliances and accessories commonly used in RV's. **Keep in mind I'm not an expert on electricity by any stretch of the imagination.** This is just a basic guide to assist you in how many amps you are using at any given time, so you don't exceed the RV's electrical system. If you need to know exact amperage ratings you can check the data plate on any motors, appliances or electronic equipment you are using. If you can't locate a data plate with this information check the appliance or electronic equipment owner's manual. This information might provide wattage requirements rather than amps.

Here are a couple of simple formulas to help you convert some common electrical terms.

Wattage divided by Volts = Amps

Amps times Volts = Wattage

For Example: 30 Amps X 120-volts = 3600 watts.

> **Note**: One other thing to keep in mind is many RV appliances require more amps to start the appliance than they do to run the appliance. A roof air conditioner can draw 16 amps to start, but may only use 13 amps once it is running.

120-Volt AC Amp Ratings

Appliance or Electronic Equipment	Estimated Amps
Air Conditioner (X number of A/C)	12-16 Amps
Blender	5-6 Amps
Coffee Maker	5-8 Amps
Compact Disc Player	1 Amp
Computer (Laptop)	2-3 Amps
Converter	1-5 Amps
Crock Pot	1-2 Amps
Curling Iron	<1 Amp
Drill	2-6 Amps
Electric Blanket	0.5-1.5 Amps
Electric Fan	1 Amp
Electric Water Heater	9-13 Amps
Electric Skillet	6-12 Amps
Hair Dryer	5-12 Amps
Iron	5-10 Amps
Light (60 watt % 120V)	<1 Amp
Microwave	8-13 Amps
Microwave (Convection Oven)	13 Amps
Refrigerator in AC mode	5-8 Amps
Space Heater	8-13 Amps
Television	1-4 Amps
Toaster	7-10 Amps
Vacuum (handheld)	2-6 Amps
VCR	1-2 Amps
Washer/Dryer	14-16Amps

12-Volt DC Amp Ratings

Appliance or Accessory	Estimated Amps
Aisle Light	1 Amp
CO Detector	1 Amp
Fluorescent Light	1-2 Amps
Furnace	10-12 Amps
LP Gas Leak Detector	1 Amp
Overhead lights (Per Bulb)	1 Amp
Porch Light	1 Amp
Power Roof Vent	1.5 Amps
Radio/Stereo	4 Amps
Range Hood (Fan & Light)	2-3 Amps
Refrigerator (LP Gas Mode)	1.5- 2 Amps
Security System	1 Amp
Television (12-volt)	4-5 Amps
TV Antenna Booster	<1 Amp
TV Antenna Booster 12-volt outlet	Up to 8 Amps
Variable Speed Ceiling / Vent Fan	4 Amps
VCR Recorder / Player	2 Amps
Water Pump	4 Amp

Mark J. Polk

RV Inverters

We just discussed what a converter does, but what is an inverter used for? Your RV batteries produce power in Direct Current (DC) that run at low voltages. Power companies and AC generators produce sine wave Alternating Current (AC), which is used to operate 120-volt

appliances and electronic equipment. An inverter takes 12-volt DC power from your RV batteries and electronically changes it to 120-volt AC.

If you've been RVing for awhile you have probably been in a situation where you needed an inverter at one time or another. Maybe it was when you were dry camping and didn't have access to electricity, or even when you have a generator but it's after quiet hours and you still want to watch a TV program or use the microwave. You don't want to buy a bigger inverter than you need, but you also don't want one that's too small for how you plan to use it.

Inverters are available in small portable units that plug directly into a cigarette lighter or 12-volt outlet; to larger high power, hardwired units that can provide electricity for the entire RV electrical system and are permanently installed in the RV. Many of the inverters found in RVs today are inverter/chargers. What this means basically is that they are inverters, battery chargers and a transfer switch all in one. They act as a battery charger when you're plugged into an electrical source or using the generator

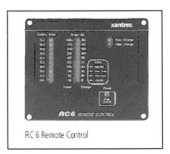

RC 6 Remote Control

and they invert stored DC battery power when no electrical source or generator power is available. Many are capable of transferring from inverter to battery charger automatically.

Inverters are rated in watts and come in a variety of sizes and power ranges from 75 watts to 3000 watts. The size of the inverter you will need depends on several factors. If the majority of your camping is done at campgrounds where electricity is plentiful you may not even need an inverter. On the other hand you might enjoy boon docking where all of your 120-volt requirements depend on batteries and an inverter.

When you purchase an inverter the output capacity must be capable of operating the loads that will be placed on it. Inverters have two different capacity ratings, the continuous output rating and surge capacity rating. Continuous output is the maximum wattage the inverter can output for a long time period. Surge capacity is the maximum wattage the inverter can output during initial start up. All appliances require more power when they initially start, compared to what they use when they are running. They can use as much as two or three times the amount to start that they use to run, so the starting power required for any appliance that you plan to use with the inverter must be within the surge capacity rating.

Let's say you only plan to use an inverter to run one or two small appliances. You might want to use a 19-inch TV, a VCR, and an overhead light all at one time. You total all the wattages, about 96 watts for the TV, 25 watts for the VCR, and 20 watts for a fluorescent light. This is a total of 141 watts. In this case you can probably get by with about a 300 watt inverter. Other RVers use inverters to operate microwaves, coffee pots and other larger appliances which will require a larger more sophisticated inverter.

Another consideration is the type of AC power being produced. There are modified sine wave inverters and true or pure sine wave inverters. Modified sine wave inverters are less expensive and will power most types of appliances. The down side to modified sine wave inverters is that some electronic equipment will not run on this waveform and because it's not true or pure sine wave you may get some electrical noise or a snowy picture on your TV screen. True or pure sine wave inverters

Mark J. Polk

are more expensive, but they are capable of producing power as good as a power company and all appliances and electronic equipment will run the way they are intended to. Microwaves, motors and other inductive loads will run quieter and will not overheat and electrical noise will be reduced. If you plan to use a computer or other sensitive electronic equipment you may want to consider a true sine wave inverter.

Another very important consideration when using an inverter is your RV battery(s). The more electricity you plan to use not only requires a larger inverter, but a larger battery bank too. Batteries are rated in amp hours. The amp hour rating is basically how many amps the battery can deliver for how many hours before the battery is discharged and needs to be recharged. Amps times hours. In other words a battery that can deliver 5 amps for 20 hours before it is discharged would have a 100 amp hour rating. 5 Amps X 20 Hours = 100 Amp Hours. This same battery can deliver 20 amps for 5 hours. 20 Amps X 5 Hours = 100 Amp Hours.

You need to compute the amperages you plan to use and the amount of time you plan to use it to determine if your battery(s) are capable of providing enough stored power. Keep in mind when you make your calculations, when a battery is discharged to 50% of its capacity it is basically dead. What this means is a 100 amp hour battery can really only provide 50% of its capacity before it needs to be recharged. The power, in watts, drawn from the batteries by your inverter is the same as the power, in watts, drawn by the 120-volt AC items, plus about 15% for losses in the inverter.

Since Watts = Volts X Amps, and the 120-volts is 10 times the 12-volts of the batteries, then about 10 times the amperage is required from the batteries than the amperage drawn by the 120-volt loads (ignoring for the moment the inverter losses). For instance, a TV might draw 480 watts from the 120-volt AC supply, which is 4 amps of current. To supply these 4 amps at 120-volts, the inverter must draw 40 amps at 12-volts from the batteries, plus about another 6 amps for the inefficiency of the inverter.

You can estimate your total battery capacity requirements by starting with the tables I am including. In the first table, you will find estimated requirements for 120-volt items. **Note that you need to use the column "Amps at 12 V".** To compute required amp-hours, multiply each entry by the number of hours you estimate you will use the item during the time between battery recharging sessions. **Similarly find your 12-volt loads from the second table** and multiply each of them by their estimated use time in hours. After adding up all the required amp-hours, add about 15% for inverter losses. This gives you an estimate of the amp-hours actually required from your batteries.

Last but definitely not least, you need to consider that any battery power used has to be put back in through some type of effective charging system. Batteries need to be charged in three stages. The first stage is a bulk charge that replaces 80% of the battery capacity very quickly. The second stage is the absorption stage that replaces the remaining 20% and the last stage is the float stage which is a lower voltage designed to keep the battery(s) topped off, but not over charge them.

Many RV converter/chargers charge battery(s) at a fixed voltage in the range of 13.5 volts. This will not recharge batteries that are discharged to 50% and it can be too much for a float charge for fully charged batteries. Once you determine how much battery power you will be using you can decide on an effective charging system. It may be that you only need to keep the batteries topped off with the converter charger, or you might need a complete set of solar panels to put back into your batteries what you are taking out.

Amp Requirements for 120-Volt Items

Appliance	Est. Amps @ 120 V	Est. Amps @ 12 V
Air Conditioner (X number of A/C)	12-16 Amps	120-160 Amps
Blender	5-6 Amps	50-60 Amps
Coffee Maker	5-8 Amps	50-80 Amps
Compact Disc Player	1 Amp	10 Amps
Computer (Laptop)	2-3 Amps	20-30 Amps
Converter	1-6 Amps	10-60 Amps
Crock Pot	1-2 Amps	10-20 Amps
Curling Iron	<1 Amp	<10 Amps
Drill	2-6 Amps	20-60 Amps
Electric Blanket	0.5-1.5 Amps	5-15 Amps
Electric Fan	1 Amp	10 Amps
Electric Water Heater	9-13 Amps	90-130 Amps
Electric Skillet	6-12 Amps	60-120 Amps
Hair Dryer	5-12 Amps	50-120 Amps
Iron	5-10 Amps	50-100 Amps
Light (60 watt % 120V)	<1 Amp	<10 Amps
Microwave	8-13 Amps	80-130 Amps
Microwave (Convection Oven)	13 Amps	130 Amps
Refrigerator in AC mode	5-8 Amps	50-80 Amps
Space Heater	8-13 Amps	80-130 Amps
Television	1-4 Amps	10-40 Amps
Toaster	7-10 Amps	70-100 Amps
Vacuum (handheld)	2-6 Amps	20-60 Amps
VCR	1-2 Amps	10-20 Amps
Washer/Dryer	14-16Amps	140-160 Amps

12-Volt DC Amp Ratings

Appliance or Accessory	Estimated Amps
Aisle Light	1 Amp
CO Detector	1 Amp
Fluorescent Light	1-2 Amps
Furnace	10-12 Amps
LP Gas Leak Detector	1 Amp
Overhead lights (Per Bulb)	1 Amp
Porch Light	1 Amp
Power Roof Vent	1.5 Amps
Radio/Stereo	4 Amps
Range Hood (Fan & Light)	2-3 Amps
Refrigerator (LP Gas Mode)	1.5- 2 Amps
Security System	1 Amp
Television (12-volt)	4-5 Amps
TV Antenna Booster	<1 Amp
Variable Speed Ceiling / Vent Fan	4 Amps
VCR Recorder / Player	2 Amps
Water Pump	4 Amp

RV Batteries

To properly maintain and extend the life of your RV batteries you need to have a basic understanding of what a battery is and how it works. Batteries used in RVs are lead acid batteries. Lead acid batteries have several cells connected in series.

Each cell produces approximately 2.1 volts, so a 12-volt battery with six cells in series produces an output voltage of 12.6-volts. Lead acid batteries are made of plates, lead and lead oxide submersed in electrolyte that is 36% sulfuric acid and 64% water. Lead acid batteries don't make electricity they store electricity. The size of the lead plates and the amount of electrolyte determines the amount of charge a battery can store.

Now it's very important that you use the right battery for the type of application. The battery used to start and run the engine is usually referred to as a chassis battery or a starting battery. Vehicle starters require large starting currents for short periods of time. Starting batteries have a large number of thin plates to maximize the plate area exposed to the electrolyte. This is what provides the large amount of current in short bursts. Starting batteries are rated in Cold Cranking Amps (CCA). CCA is the number of amps the battery can deliver at 0 degrees F for 30 seconds and not drop below 7.2 volts. Starting batteries should not be used for deep cycle applications.

The battery or batteries used to supply 12-volts to the RV itself are commonly referred to as house batteries. House batteries need to be deep cycle batteries that are designed to provide a steady amount of current over a long period of time. Starting batteries and marine batteries should not be used in this application. True deep cycle batteries have much thicker plates and are designed to be deeply discharged and recharged over and over again. These batteries are rated in Amp Hours (AH) and more recently Reserve Capacity (RC).

The amp hour rating is basically how many amps the battery can deliver for how many hours before the battery is discharged. Amps times hours. In other words a battery that can deliver 5 amps for 20 hours before it is discharged would have a 100 amp hour rating 5 amps X 20 hours = 100 amp hours. This same battery can deliver 20 amps for 5 hours 20 amps X 5 hours = 100 amp hours. Reserve Capacity rating (RC) is the number of minutes at 80 degrees F that the battery can deliver 25 amps until it drops below 10.5 volts. To figure the amp hour rating you can multiply the RC rating by 60%. RC X 60%

The two major construction types of deep cycle batteries are flooded lead acid and Valve Regulated Lead Acid (VRLA). Flooded lead acid batteries are the most common type and come in two styles. Serviceable with removable caps so you can inspect and perform maintenance or the maintenance free type. In VRLA batteries the electrolyte is either suspended in a gel or a fiberglass-mat. Gel cell batteries use battery acid in the form of a gel. They are leak proof and because of this they work well for marine applications. There are several disadvantages to gel cell batteries for RV applications. Most importantly they must be charged at a slower rate and a lower voltage than flooded cell batteries. Any overcharging can cause permanent damage to the cells. Absorbed Glass Mat, or AGM technology, uses a fibrous mat between the plates which is 90% soaked in electrolyte. They're more expensive than a standard deep cycle battery but they have some advantages. They can be charged the same as a standard lead acid battery, they don't loose any water, they can't leak, they are virtually maintenance free and they are almost impossible to freeze.

Battery Life Expectancy
The life expectancy of your RV batteries depends on you. How they're used, how well they're maintained, how they're discharged, how they're re-charged, and how they are stored all contribute to a batteries life span. A battery cycle is one complete discharge from 100% down to about 50% and then re-charged back to 100%. One important factor to battery life is how deep the battery is cycled each time. If the battery is

discharged to 50% everyday it will last twice as long as it would if it's cycled to 80%. Keep this in mind when you consider a battery's amp hour rating. The amp hour rating is really cut in half because you don't want to completely discharge the battery before recharging it. The life expectancy depends on how soon a discharged battery is recharged. The sooner it is recharged the better.

What does all of this mean to you? That depends on how you use your RV. If most of your camping is done where you're plugged into an electrical source then your main concern is just too properly maintain your deep cycle batteries. But if you really like to get away from it all and you do some serious dry-camping you'll want the highest amp hour capacities you can fit on your RV.

Deep cycle batteries come in all different sizes. Some are designated by group size, like Group 24, 27 and 31. Basically the larger the battery the more amp hours you get. Depending on your needs and the amount of space you have available, there are several options when it comes to

batteries. You can use one 12-volt Group 24 deep cycle battery that provides 70 to 85 amp hours or you can use two or more 12-volt batteries wired in parallel. **Parallel wiring increases amp hours but not voltage.**

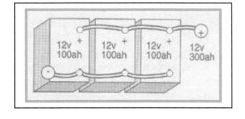

If you have the room you can do what a lot of RVers do and switch from the standard 12-volt batteries to two of the larger 6-volt golf cart batteries. These pairs of 6-volt batteries need to be wired in series to

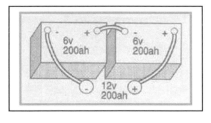

produce the required 12-volts. **Series wiring increases voltage but not amp hours.** If this still doesn't satisfy your requirements you can build larger battery banks using four 6-volt batteries wired in **series/parallel that will give you 12-volts and double your AH capacity.**

Undercharging & Overcharging

The two most common causes for RV battery failure are undercharging and overcharging. Undercharging is a result of batteries being repeatedly discharged and not fully recharged between cycles. If a battery is not recharged the sulfate material that attaches to the discharged portions of the plates begins to harden into crystals. Over time this sulfate cannot be converted back into active plate material and the battery is ruined. This also occurs when a battery remains discharged for an extended period of time. Sulfation is the number one cause of battery failure. The second leading cause of battery failure is overcharging. Overcharging batteries results in severe water loss and plate corrosion. The good news is both of these problems are avoidable.

Battery Maintenance

Before we talk about battery maintenance we need to talk about battery safety. Lead acid batteries contain sulfuric acid which is extremely corrosive and can cause severe burns or even blindness. And the hydrogen gas that batteries produce when they're charging is very explosive. When you work around batteries you need to wear goggles and gloves, remove all jewelry and do not smoke or use any open flames.

> **Caution**: If you accidentally get battery acid on your skin, flush it with lots of water and if it gets in your eyes you need to flush with low pressure water for 15 minutes and call a doctor.

Battery maintenance is actually very simple. By performing theses maintenance procedures every three to six months you can extend the life expectancy of your RV batteries. You should make these checks more often in hot temperatures or during heavy battery usage.

The first thing we want to do is visually inspect the battery for any obvious damage. Any fluid on or around the battery may be an indication that electrolyte is leaking from the battery. A damaged or leaking battery should be replaced immediately. Inspect the battery terminals, cables, and connectors for any damage and for good connections. Look for any signs of corrosion. Corrosion can be neutralized with a 50/50 mixture of baking soda and warm water. Use one pound of baking soda to one gallon of water. Clean any dirty battery terminals and the insides of cable clamps with a post and clamp cleaner. If you remove any battery cables **always disconnect the negative battery cable first. When you reconnect the clamps to the terminals connect the positive cable first.** Never over tighten the battery terminals.

> **Warning:** Do not over tighten terminals. This can result in broken battery posts, post meltdown and/or fire. When you finish, spray the clamps with a battery terminal protector.

Checking the electrolyte level on a regular basis can save your flooded lead acid batteries. Check the water level monthly, and if you leave your RV plugged in with the batteries being charged by the converter battery charger, check it bi-monthly. If your converter doesn't have a three stage charger the battery is getting a constant charge of 13.5 volts. When the batteries are topped off this voltage is too high for a float charge and it can boil off the electrolyte over time. When you add water only use mineral free water. Distilled water is best, and you should only fill the cell to 1/8 inch below the fill well. Overfilling cells will cause battery acid to overflow. When this happens the battery will lose some of its capacity and corrosion will build up on and around the battery. Water should only be added after fully charging the battery unless the water level is below the plates.

Follow these steps for adding water to the battery. Remove the vent caps and look inside the fill wells. Check the electrolyte levels. The minimum level required for charging the battery is at the top of the plates. If it's below the plates, add enough distilled water to cover the plates before you charge the battery. Fully charge the battery before adding more water. When the battery is charged, remove the vent caps and check the electrolyte levels. Add distilled water until the electrolyte level is 1/8 inch below the fill well. Replace and tighten all vent caps.

Warning: Never add battery acid to a battery.

Battery Testing

Visual inspections of our RV batteries are important, but that won't tell us the actual condition of our batteries. We need to test the batteries to determine their state of charge and overall condition.

There are a couple of different ways to check your batteries state of charge. You can measure the voltage with a digital voltmeter or check the specific gravity of the acid with a hydrometer.

Testing the specific gravity is the preferred method but measuring voltage has its advantages. If you have sealed batteries your only choice is to measure voltage and measuring voltage can give you a quick picture of the batteries depth of discharge so you know when they need to be recharged.

If the battery state-of-charge is below 70% the battery needs to be recharged before you test it. The battery should not be tested if it has been charged or discharged in the last 6 hours and preferably 24 hours. This is called an open circuit voltage test. To measure the voltage you need a good digital voltmeter. Using the DC voltmeter check the voltage and compare it to this chart.

% State Of Charge	Specific Gravity Corrected 80 F	Open Circuit 12-Volt	Open Circuit 6-Volt
100	1.277	12.73	6.37
90	1.258	12.62	6.31
80	1.238	12.50	6.25
70	1.217	12.37	6.19
60	1.195	12.24	6.12
50	1.172	12.10	6.05
40	1.148	11.96	5.98
30	1.124	11.81	5.91
Discharged	1.120	11.80	5.90

Whenever possible, you should avoid discharging a battery below 40%. Battery readings that are off of this chart indicate the battery was left discharged too long, or the battery may have a bad cell.

The preferred method for testing the battery's state of charge is to check the specific gravity reading of each cell. You can purchase a hydrometer at an auto parts store for less than ten dollars. The electrolyte is a solution of acid and water so you need to wear goggles and gloves and avoid skin contact. Remove the vent caps and check the electrolyte levels. There has to be enough electrolyte in the cells for the hydrometer to pick it up. If you have to add any water you'll have to charge the battery and then let it sit for at least six hours before testing. Fill and drain the hydrometer at least twice in each cell before taking a sample. Make sure there is enough electrolyte in the hydrometer to support the float. Take the reading and record it, then drain it back into the cell. Test all of the cells and replace the vent caps. If your hydrometer does not compensate for temperature you must correct the readings to 80 degrees F. To do this add .004 for every 10 degrees above 80 degrees F and subtract .004 for every 10 degrees below 80 degrees F. Compare the readings to the chart.

The specific gravity readings should be at 1.277 + or - .007. If any of the readings are low, check and record the voltage levels, put the battery on a complete charge, then take the specific gravity readings again. If any of the readings still remain low, check the voltage levels again and perform an equalization charge on the battery. Equalizing is an overcharge, performed on a flooded lead acid battery, after it has been fully charged. It reverses the buildup of negative chemical effects like stratification, a condition where acid concentration is greater at the bottom of the battery than at the top. Set the battery charger on equalizing voltage and charge the battery. The battery will begin to gas and bubble vigorously. Test the specific gravity every hour. Equalization is complete when the specific gravity readings no longer rise during the gassing stage.

If any readings still register low, one or more of these conditions may exist:

- ➢ The battery is old and approaching the end of its life.
- ➢ The battery was left in a state of discharge too long.
- ➢ Electrolyte was lost due to spillage or overflow.
- ➢ A weak or bad cell is developing.
- ➢ The battery was watered excessively previous to testing.

> **Note:** Batteries with these conditions should be taken to a specialist for further testing or replacement.

Battery Charging

It's important to keep in mind that what you take out of your batteries must be put back in. If it's not done in a timely manner the battery sulfates and can be permanently damaged. You need a three stage charger that can provide a bulk charge then an absorption charge and finally a float charge. There are RV converter chargers on the market that will do this.

If you purchase a multi-stage battery charger you need to know the charging current limitations of the battery being charged. When selecting a charger, the charge rate should be between 10 and 13% of the battery's 20-hour AH capacity. For example, a battery with a 20-hour capacity

Mark J. Polk

rating of 225 AH will use a charger rated between approximately 23 and 30 amps.

> **Note:** For proper charging procedures always follow the battery charger manufacturer instructions.

Batteries should be charged as soon as possible after each period of use or whenever they reach a 70% state of charge or below. The batteries should only be charged in a well ventilated area and keep any sparks and open flames away from a battery being charged. Check the electrolyte levels before and after charging batteries.

If you put your RV in storage it's a good idea to remove the batteries and put them in storage too. This is quite simple to do. When you're removing the battery always remember to remove the negative terminal first. Clean the batteries with a 50/50 mixture of baking soda and water if necessary. Check the electrolyte level and add distilled water if necessary. Test the battery state of charge and charge any batteries that are at or below 80%. A discharged or partially charged battery will freeze much faster than a charged battery. Store the batteries in a cool dry place but not where they could freeze. Batteries in storage will loose their charge. Test the state of charge every month and charge batteries that are at or below 80% state of charge. Completely charge the batteries before re-installing them next spring. For optimum performance equalize the batteries after they are fully charged.

> **Note:** If you are not comfortable performing maintenance on, or working around lead acid batteries, take the RV to an authorized repair center to have battery maintenance done.

RV Generators

When I worked at an RV dealership, every spring our service department was booked with appointments for generators that either wouldn't start, or if they did start they had that all too familiar surging sound. This was a result of letting the generator sit for periods of time without starting and exercising it. Lack of use is one of the biggest problems with generators. In gasoline generators the fuel breaks down and gums up causing hard starting and surging problems. This can happen in as short a period of time as a month or two.

RV generators are what truly make your RV fully self-contained. What a feature, instant electricity at the push of a button. We take electricity for granted in our homes because we don't have to do anything to get it, with the exception of paying our monthly electric bill. This is part of the problem with RV generators, we expect the electricity to be there when we need or want it just like in our house. The problem is this magical source of electricity requires a certain amount of care and maintenance from the owner.

Generator Safety

Safety first! Always keep in mind when you use a generator there is carbon monoxide. You should always inspect the exhaust system on the generator set before using it. Do not operate a generator with a damaged exhaust system. If you're using a portable generator set, make sure the exhaust is directed away from the camping area. Test your carbon monoxide detector for proper operation prior to using the generator. I recommend not running a generator when you or anyone else is sleeping. Observe campground etiquette. Do not run your generator during quiet hours.

Generator Operation & Maintenance

A generator that comes equipped on an RV gets its fuel supply from the same fuel tank the engine uses. When the fuel tank reaches a ¼ tank of fuel, the generator will shut down to prevent you from possibly using all of the fuel without realizing it. The generator will either have an automatic transfer switch, to sense whether you are using shore power or the generator, or you will need to plug the RV power cord into a generator receptacle to use the generator. It is perfectly okay to use the generator while you are traveling. This is one of the reasons you have a generator in the first place. It is actually more fuel efficient to run the generator with the roof mounted air conditioner on, than to use the dash air.

Generators are rated in kilowatts (KW). One kilowatt equals 1,000 watts. So a 4 KW generator would be a 4,000-watt generator. RVs have either 30 amp or 50 amp electrical systems. If you have a 30 amp electrical system and you're plugged into a 30 amp, 120- volt electrical source you can basically use 3,600 watts before you exceed the RVs electrical system. 30 amps X 120-volts = 3,600 watts. This is why a large majority of RV's with a 30 amp electrical system comes equipped with 4,000-watt generators. This of course is also why RVs with 50 amp electrical systems come equipped with larger generators.

RV generators are extremely dependable and in many cases will out last the RV if they are properly maintained and cared for. They do not require your constant attention, just some basic maintenance. The first thing you need to understand about maintaining your generator is that they need to be exercised on a regular basis. This applies to gas and diesel generators. I mentioned earlier that gasoline generators could have fuel related problems in as little as one to two months of sitting idle. This is one of the biggest problems, but it can easily be prevented if you get in a habit of exercising the generator on a monthly basis.

I used to think that I could avoid this by adding a fuel preservative to the fuel tank and then running the generator long enough to get the preservative through the generator set. You definitely should use a fuel preservative whenever the unit will be in storage, but there are many other reasons to start and exercise the generator on a regular basis. Moisture build up can cause damage to your generator. When you exercise your generator it heats up the generator windings and eliminates this moisture build up. This monthly exercise regime also lubricates all of the engine seals and components and helps to prevent carbon build up.

So, what exactly do I mean when I say exercise your generator? For a gasoline generator, you should start and run the generator with at least a fifty percent load for at least two hours every month. It is extremely important that you run it with this minimum rated load. Generators are designed to run with a load placed on them. For a 4,000 watt generator you can turn the roof air conditioner on in the summer time, which is about 2,000 watts, or use a couple of small portable electric heaters if it's cold out. It's always better to let your generator run for longer periods of time than for shorter periods.

Note: Check your generator owner's manual for load ratings specific to your unit.

Other maintenance intervals for generators are based on usage. Your generator set will have an hour meter so you can monitor the usage. Consult your owner's manual for maintenance intervals. Changing the oil and filters on a regular scheduled basis and for seasonal changes is just as important for your generator as it is for your automobile. For extended storage requirements consult your generator owner's manual.

Our walk through DVD titles cover information on LP gas, water & electrical systems. See the RV Education 101 order form at back of book.

Mark J. Polk

Chapter 7

Campground Set-up

Now that you have a better understanding of how the three primary systems of an RV work, LP gas, water & electrical, I am including a checklist to assist you with setting the RV up at the campground. There is a checklist for pop-ups, and one for travel trailers and motorhomes.

Campground Set-Up for Pop-Ups

> ➢ Locate your site and conduct a site survey. Identify where the campground connections are and where to locate the pop-up so you have access to all connections. If you have a slide out make sure there are no obstacles in the way. Allow plenty of room for extending the awning.
> ➢ Remove any friction sway control equipment before backing up.
> ➢ Position and level the pop-up from side to side on the site and double-check all clearances and access to hook-ups.
> ➢ Chock the wheels.
> ➢ Disconnect from the tow vehicle. Level from front to rear.
> ➢ Release all roof latches.
> ➢ Locate crank handle and raise the roof.
> ➢ Some campers prefer to lower the awning when the roof is partially raised and they have easy access to it. If not you'll need a small step stool or ladder to extend the awning later. If you do extend the awning now, finish raising the roof and set the awning up so it is out of the way.

- Install roof supports if applicable.
- Lower the stabilizer jacks. Many manufacturers recommend not lowering stabilizers until the roof is up. Check your owner's manual if you're not sure.
- If you have a slide out extend it now. Lower or install the jacks under the slide out if applicable.
- Lower the entry door and set it in place.
- Pull out the bed ends taking care not to tear canvas, windows or screening.
- Install bed supports.
- Raise the bed bows and install the bed bow supports.
- Attach all canvas as required.
- Complete canvas set up for slide out.
- Put the step out if you haven't already done so.
- Set up the interior of the pop-up.
- Test the campground electricity with a voltmeter for proper polarity and voltage prior to plugging in (if applicable.)
- Pull enough power cord from the compartment to reach the campground electrical connection. Plug into the receptacle that matches the amperage requirements of your pop-up. Use electrical adapters as required. If at all possible try to avoid using an extension cord. Some campgrounds have a circuit breaker in the box that must be turned on to allow electricity to the pop-up.
- Check and make sure the electricity is working in the pop-up. If equipped with a refrigerator turn it on in the electric mode.
- If you have a water pressure regulator, hook it up to the campground water supply.
- If you have an exterior water filter hook it up to the city water inlet on the pop-up. If you don't use a filter attach a 90-degree elbow to the city water inlet to prevent the hose from kinking.
- Attach one end of your potable RV drinking hose (white hose) to the campground water supply and the other end to the city water inlet on the pop-up.

153

➢ Turn the water on and check for any leaks. Make sure you have water coming in to the RV.

➢ When you are hooked up to a city water supply do not use the 12-volt water pump, if equipped. Only use this when you don't have an external water supply and need to draw water from the fresh water tank.

➢ Hook a green or black garden hose up to the gray water drain on the pop-up. Attach the other end to the campground sewer connection. You can purchase an adapter that will provide a good seal at the campground sewer and allow you to make the hose connection. If a campground sewer connection is not available always drain your gray and black water into a portable tote tank and dispose of it properly. Never empty any holding tank contents directly on the ground.

➢ If your pop-up has a cassette toilet treat the tank with chemicals, if you haven't already done so. Treat the holding tank with chemicals every time you empty it. Consult the directions on the cassette toilet.

➢ Turn the main LP gas supply valve on at the bottle.

➢ If you have a water heater and you want hot water at this time be sure that the water heater tank is full of water before you light it. If your water heater has a bypass kit, make sure that it is not in the bypass mode. Open a hot water faucet and when you get a steady flow of water (no air) the water heater tank is full and you can light the water heater. Follow the lighting instructions for the type of water heater you have.

➢ If the campground has a cable TV hook up and your pop-up has a cable connection, hook the TV coax cable from the pop-up to the cable connection.

➢ Set up your awning and screen room if applicable.

➢ Put the outdoor carpet mat down.

➢ Set up the lawn chairs.

➢ Start the BBQ and have fun!!

Another good resource is to purchase a pop-up training DVD. If you forget how something works, just play the DVD as a reminder.

Note: See order form at back of book or **www.rveducation101.com**

Campground Set-Up for Travel Trailer & Motorhome
It would be impossible to cover everything involved with this checklist because of the vast differences between RVs. However most RVs do have many things in common and that is what we will concentrate on. The purpose of this checklist is to provide you with a basic system of what to do when you arrive at your site. Use only the items that apply to your RV.

> ➢ If you are in a motorhome and are towing a vehicle you may want to disconnect the vehicle in the campground registration parking lot before going to your site. Have someone drive the vehicle in front of you to assist in locating your site.
> ➢ Conduct a site survey. Identify where all campground connections are and where you want the RV located to have access to all connections. Take into consideration where slide outs will be and if there is room to put the awning out. Make sure that there are no low hanging branches or other obstacles that will interfere with the RV.
> ➢ Determine if you need to back in or if it is a pull through site. Position the RV on the site and double-check all clearances and access to hook ups.
> ➢ If you have a motorhome, set the parking brake.
> ➢ Level the RV as required.
> ➢ Chock the wheels.
> ➢ Disconnect from the tow vehicle if applicable.
> ➢ Put the stabilizer jacks down if applicable.
> ➢ If you have a motorhome and there is a battery disconnect switch for the chassis battery turn it off to prevent any drain on the starting battery.

Mark J. Polk

- If you have an auxiliary battery disconnect switch for the coach battery(s), turn it on.
- Put the entry steps out. If you have a switch for the steps turn it off so the steps stay out when the door is closed.
- Remove any slide out travel locks. Extend slide out(s) if they won't interfere with making your basic hook ups. Have someone watch for clearance and obstacles in the slide out path. Be sure the driver's seat is not in the way of the slide out.
- Test the campground electricity voltage and polarity with a voltmeter prior to plugging the unit in.
- Pull enough power cord from the compartment to reach the campground electrical connection. Plug into the receptacle that matches the amperage requirements of your RV. Use electrical adapters as required. If at all possible try to avoid using an extension cord. Some campgrounds have a circuit breaker in the box that must be turned on to allow electricity to the RV.
- Check the RV to make sure the electricity is working. If you have a plug in voltmeter, plug it into a wall outlet so you can monitor campground voltage during your stay. Any readings below 105 volts or above 130 volts can be dangerous to your appliances and electronic equipment.
- Turn the refrigerator on in the electric mode.
- If you have a water pressure regulator, hook it up to the campground water supply.
- If you have an exterior water filter hook it up to the city water inlet on the RV. If you don't use a filter attach a 90-degree elbow to the city water inlet to prevent the hose from kinking.
- Attach one end of your potable RV drinking hose (white hose) to the campground water supply and the other end to the city water inlet on the RV.
- Turn the water supply on and check for any leaks. Make sure you have water coming into the RV.

➤ When you are hooked up to a city water supply do not use the 12-volt water pump. Only use this when you don't have an external water supply and need to draw water from the fresh water tank.

➤ Wearing gloves remove the cap from the sewer hose valve and attach the sewer hose to the sewer drain outlet. Be sure to turn it so the locking tabs securely lock in place. Place the sewer hose donut or seal in the campground sewer connection. Attach the other end of the sewer hose in the donut. Be sure and get a good seal and connection.

➤ If you have a sewer hose support set it up now, allowing for a slope from the RV down to the sewer connection to assist in dumping the tanks.

➤ If you're going to be at the campground for a couple of days or more you can slightly open the gray water tank knife valve to allow sink and shower water to drain directly into the sewer. It is the smaller of the two valves. If your only there for the night leave it closed. **NEVER** leave the black tank valve open, the larger valve. You only open the black tank valve when dumping the tank. When the black tank is ¾ full or full, its time to dump it. Dumping the black tank before its near full can cause problems. You will want plenty of water in the gray tank at this time to help flush the sewer hose out. To dump the tanks pull the black tank valve all the way out. Let it drain completely then close the valve. Now open the gray tank valve and allow it to drain completely and flush the sewer hose out at the same time. Close the valve. Treat the black tank with holding tank chemicals every time you dump it.

➤ Turn the main LP gas supply valve on at the tank or bottles.

➤ If you want hot water at this time make sure that the water heater tank is full of water before you light it. If your water heater has a bypass kit, make sure that it is not in the bypass mode. Open a hot water faucet and when you get a steady flow of water (no air) the water heater tank is full and you can light the water heater.

Mark J. Polk

Follow the instructions for the type of water heater you have. There may also be an electric mode on the water heater. It will take a little longer to heat the water but it will conserve your LP gas.

➢ If the campground has a cable TV hook up connect your TV coax cable from the RV to the cable connection. If they don't offer cable raise the TV antenna on the RV. Turn the TV and the power booster on. Pull down on the antenna base plate and rotate the antenna until you get the best reception. If you have cable, do not use the antenna booster.

➢ Open the locking tabs on the outside range hood vent door if you plan to use the range exhaust fan.

➢ Put the outdoor carpet mat down.

➢ Set up the lawn chairs.

➢ Put the awning out.

➢ Start the BBQ and have fun!!

Camping Tip: A 30 amp electrical system on an RV has the capability of using 3,600 watts or 30 amps before you will overload the system. 120-volts X 30 amps = 3,600 watts. Think of it like this, you could use 36 one hundred watt light bulbs and when you turn the 37th one on it will probably trip a breaker. You should never run more than one major appliance at a time i.e. air conditioner or microwave.

Save 50% on your camp site fees

Happy Camper Club!

Nearly 1,200 resorts
USA & Canada
Just $49.95 a year

Toll Free 866.677.6453
www.camphalfprice.com

Chapter 8

RV Safety

Every RVer should know what safety devices are available on their RV and understand how to use them. Most RVs regardless of what type or what size it is will come equipped with several safety devices. RVs come with fire extinguishers, LP gas leak detectors, smoke alarms, emergency escape windows, and in many cases carbon monoxide detectors.

RV Fire Safety

There are approximately 20,000 reported RV fires each year. A large percentage of these fires are transmission related fires on motorhomes. Automatic transmission fluid leaking from the transmission can ignite, and quickly spread if it contacts any portion of the hot exhaust system. Before traveling in your RV inspect the underside for any signs of fluid leaking. Have any potential leaks checked out and repaired immediately.

Fire Extinguisher Inspection

Over 30% of RV fires are caused by shorts in the 12-volt electrical system. Not only do you need a fire extinguisher, you need to inspect it before each trip to make sure it is charged. Look to see if the arrow is pointing in the green area in the sight gauge. If it reads empty or needs charging, replace it or have it recharged immediately. If it's a dry powder type fire extinguisher the arrow pointing in the green doesn't always guarantee that it will work. Every month you should turn dry powder extinguishers upside down, tap on the bottom of the extinguisher and shake it. It should sound hollow, sort of like a drum. If not, continue tapping on it until it sounds hollow and the powder that settled in the bottom is released.

Types of Fire Extinguishers

There are four different types, or classes of fire extinguishers, **A, B, C,** and **D** and each type are used for a specific type of fire.

Class A extinguishers are used for fires caused by ordinary combustibles like paper and wood.
Class B extinguishers are used for fires caused by flammable liquids like grease, gasoline and oil.
Class C extinguishers are used for fires caused by electrical equipment.
Class D extinguishers are used for fires on flammable metals and often they are specific for the type of metal it is.

Some fire extinguishers have multi-class ratings like, **AB, BC** or **ABC** which means one fire extinguisher can be used to put out different types of fires. The National Fire Protection Agency rules that RV's must have a **BC** rated fire extinguisher near each exit. **BC** rated fire extinguishers are used for flammable liquids and gasses like grease, gasoline and oil, and for electrical fires. Many RV fires that happen inside an RV are **Type A** fires caused by common combustibles like paper, and they require a **Type A** fire extinguisher to put them out. This is why, in my opinion you need more than one fire extinguisher for your RV.

It's a good idea to keep a **BC** type fire extinguisher in an outside storage compartment where it is easily accessible. You should also keep a **BC** type fire extinguisher inside the RV and keep an **A** type fire extinguisher inside the RV. If you tow a trailer keep a **BC** type fire extinguisher in the tow vehicle. Having these fire extinguishers available is a great idea but they are worthless if you and the other people traveling in the RV don't know what type of fire they are used for and how to properly use them. Get everybody who will be in the RV together, and make sure they understand the different types of fire extinguishers you have and where they are located in the event of an emergency.

The old style labeling for fire extinguishers, to designate what type of fire they are used for was with the letter **A, B, C or D**

Ordinary   Flammable   Electrical
Combustibles   Liquids   Equipment

Newer style labeling for fire extinguishers include a picture designating the type of fire it is used for.

If it can be used for multiple types of fires it will show the pictures for the types of fires it can be used for and it will have a red diagonal line through the picture of what it cannot be used for.

Using a Fire Extinguisher

The next step is to teach everybody how to properly use a fire extinguisher. There are different types and sizes of fire extinguishers, but for the most part they all work the same way. Teach everybody to remember the word **PASS**. This is an easy way to remember how to use a fire extinguisher, especially during an emergency. **PASS** stands for **Pull, Aim, Squeeze and Sweep.**

> **Pull** the pin located at the top of the fire extinguisher.
> **Aim** the nozzle at the base of the fire.
> **Squeeze** the handle, standing approximately 8 feet away from the fire. Release the handle if you want it to stop.
> **Sweep** the nozzle back and forth at the base of the fire until it is out. Observe the fire to make sure it does not re-ignite.

Fire Escape Plan

Last but not least, you need to have an emergency escape plan. The National Fire Protection agency requires that RV's have emergency escape windows. Make sure everybody knows where the escape window is located and how to use it. It's a good idea to practice using it so you are familiar with how to get out in case of an emergency. You should have an escape plan for the front of the RV and the rear of the RV.

Most important, do not risk your personal safety, or the safety of others, attempting to put a fire out. The first step is to get everybody out of the RV or away from the fire safely. Have somebody call 911 for help and if you can't extinguish the fire within the first minute or so let the professionals put it out. Have a plan for everyone to meet at a pre-determined location once they are outside the RV. Account for everyone.

LP Gas Leak Detector

Your RV also has an LP gas leak detector. This leak detector will set off an alarm to alert you if there is a potential gas leak. It's usually located close to floor level because LP gas is heavier than air and it will settle towards the floor. If you ever smell LP gas when you're camping, or if the LP gas leak detector goes off you could have a leak somewhere in the system. If this happens you should:

➢ Extinguish any open flames, pilot lights and do not smoke, or touch electrical switches.
➢ Evacuate the RV and turn off the main gas supply valve.
➢ Leave the door open and do not return to the area until the odor clears.
➢ Have the system checked out by a qualified technician before using it again.

False alarms can be caused by hair spray, perfume, cleaning solvents and low battery voltage. Whenever you go to have the LP gas refilled or when stopping to refuel the RV the all LP gas appliances should be turned off and the main gas supply valve should be turned off.

Smoke Alarm

A properly working, battery operated smoke detector is critical. Test the alarm mechanism prior to each trip you take to make sure it is working. Change the batteries when you change your clocks twice a year. If you remove the batteries from any safety device while the RV is stored; remove the device from the wall or ceiling and place it where it will easily be seen as a reminder the next time you use the RV.

Carbon Monoxide Detectors

Many RVs come equipped with carbon monoxide detectors. If yours didn't, it's a good idea to purchase a battery operated carbon monoxide detector designed for use in RV's. You never know when you might be parked next to an RV that is running a generator. Carbon monoxide detectors should be located on a wall close to the ceiling since carbon monoxide is lighter than oxygen. Test the detector before each trip to make sure it is operating properly. Read the owners manual so you thoroughly understand how it works. And know what the symptoms of carbon monoxide poisoning are:

- Dizziness
- Vomiting
- Nausea
- Muscular twitching
- Intense headache
- Throbbing in the temples
- Weakness and sleepiness
- Inability to think coherently

> **Caution**: If you or anyone else experiences any of these symptoms get to fresh air immediately. If the symptoms persist seek medical attention. Never run a generator when you are sleeping in the RV.

Mark J. Polk

> **Caution:** Never use the range burners or oven as a source of heat. These LP gas appliances are not vented outside and because of the limited space inside the RV the lack of oxygen can lead to asphyxiation. When you do use the range top burners or the oven for cooking use the range vent fan or open a window.

Emergency Weather Planning

There is nothing like exploring the back roads in your RV. You can go where you want and when you want, in your house on wheels, and because of this, often times you find yourself in a new destination everyday. Something many RVers do not consider, with this freedom to roam, is the weather conditions where you are traveling to, or spending the night. **RV's are great but they are not safe in severe weather like lightning and thunderstorms with high winds, tornadoes and hurricanes**.

When you are at home, you usually know what the weather forecast is from the newspaper, radio or television. When you travel three or four hundred miles a day in your RV the weather conditions can change several times. Many times when you stop for the night somewhere all you want to do is get some rest. The weather is the last thing on your mind. The problem with this is severe weather can occur without much warning, and if you are caught in it, it can be disastrous.

So, what do we do, what's the plan? Plan is the key word here. RVers need to have an emergency plan in case of a severe storm. For starters you need to be familiar with the National Oceanic Atmospheric Administration (NOAA) Weather Radio or NWR. The NOAA Weather Radio is a nationwide network of radio stations that broadcast continuous weather information directly from a nearby National Weather Service Office. They broadcast National Weather Service warnings, watches, forecasts and other hazard information 24 hours a day. Alerts inform people if they need to take some type of action in order to protect themselves, such as "seeking shelter" or "to evacuate an area immediately!" What does this mean to RVers? It means if you owned a battery operated weather radio receiver you could monitor weather conditions no matter where you are!

Portable Weather Radios

Every RVer should own a portable weather radio receiver. Receivers are available at most retail stores that sell electronic equipment. Prices can range anywhere from $25 to $200 depending on the quality of the receiver and its features. I personally own two weather radio receivers. My Midland WR-300 works off of AC power or four AA batteries when the power is out. It has an alert feature that alarms when the National Weather Service issues severe weather announcements or emergency information. I also have a portable handheld Midland 40 channel CB, with a 10-weather channel receiver. It works off six AA rechargeable batteries or any 12-volt receptacle. It is well worth the investment to know what type of weather to expect when traveling or camping in your RV. When we are at home, we use the weather radio receiver in the house. For more information on the NOAA Weather Radio visit their website at **www.nws.noaa.gov**

Emergency Weather Plan

OK, the first step to our emergency weather plan is to get a weather radio receiver if you don't already have one, and to always monitor it when you use your RV. The next step is to develop an emergency evacuation plan, to use in the event of severe weather. When you arrive at a campground, ask at the check-in desk about an emergency plan in case of a severe storm such as a tornado, or a thunderstorm with high winds. If they don't have a plan you need to make your own.

Locate a structure that is safer than your RV, like a bathhouse or the campground office. Always stay on the lowest level possible and away from doors and windows. Brief everybody with you on the emergency plan. Explain to children how to respond to different disasters and the dangers of severe weather, fires, and other emergencies. Instruct children on emergency exits. Instruct them on how and when to call 911. Make sure everybody knows exactly what his or her job is in case of severe weather. Monitor the weather radio for emergency information.

> **Note**: Calling 911 on your cell phone when away from home may not connect you to the local authorities. Understand how your cell phone works with 911 when outside of your home calling area.

> **Note:** Emergency weather watches and warnings are for counties and towns. Always check a map for the county or town where you are staying.

Emergency Supply Kit

Have an emergency supply kit made up and easily accessible. The kit should contain flashlights, batteries, rain ponchos, a portable weather radio, first aid kit, non-perishable packaged or canned food and a manual can opener, blankets, prescription and non-prescription drugs, pet supplies, bottled water and any special items for infants, elderly or disabled family members.

Remember, RV's are not safe in severe weather! This includes severe thunderstorms with high winds, tornadoes and hurricanes. Learn about different types of weather hazards, get a weather radio if you don't have one, create a plan with your family, practice and maintain the plan. Now go RVing and have fun.

Chapter 9

RV Tires

Portions of this chapter are excerpts, courtesy of the Recreation Vehicle & Safety Education Foundation (RVSEF) & Bridgestone/Firestone North American Tire.

Your RV tires are one of the most important components of your RV and probably the most neglected. We all tend to take tires for granted. You know what I mean, when was the last time you checked the inflation pressure in your tires? Especially the inner duals if you have a motorhome. Better yet, when was the last time you had your RV weighed? Overweight RVs and under inflated tires are both unsafe, send operating and repair costs sky high and can cause unexpected downtime. Much of the reason for neglecting our tires is because we don't really understand what is required to properly maintain them.

Weight Ratings

The best place to start is with weight ratings. Weight ratings are established by the manufacturer and are based on the weakest link in the chain. The suspension system, tires, wheels, brakes, axles, and the RV itself all have weight ratings. When you exceed a weight rating, you are overloading one or more components on the RV and risk wearing the component out prematurely or complete failure of the component. In many cases the tires on your RV are the weakest link.

If you've been RVing for a while I'm sure you heard stories about tire failures and blowouts. I can't begin to tell you how many times I've heard people say that the tires on their RV were defective, or my tires only had 12,000 miles on them when I had a blowout. In the majority of cases the truth of the matter is that tire maintenance has been neglected or the RV

Mark J. Polk

was overloaded. The only thing between your RV and the road surface is your tires and the air that is in them. This is the weakest link.

A federal data plate is required by law on all vehicles. It lists the Gross Vehicle Weight Rating and the Gross Axle Weight Rating for the vehicle. The Gross Vehicle Weight Rating or GVWR is one of the most crucial safety factors of your RV. The Gross Vehicle Weight Rating is the maximum allowable weight of the vehicle when fully loaded for travel including, all passengers, all cargo, fluids, and aftermarket accessories. You must not exceed the total GVWR for your vehicle. The Gross Axle Weight Ratings or GAWR is the maximum weight that should ever be placed on a given axle. The GAWR divided by two is the maximum axle rating for each end of the axle. You must not exceed this weight on either end of the axle, even if the total doesn't exceed the GAWR.

In addition to the federal data plate all members of the Recreation Vehicle Industry association RVIA are required to have an additional weight label on the vehicles they manufacture. This label lists additional information not available on the federal data plate and supersedes the federal data plate. There are two versions of the RVIA label depending on whether the vehicle was manufactured from September 1996 through August 2000, or after September 1, 2000. There are also separate versions for motorhomes and for trailers, including 5th wheel trailers.

The only way to know if you are exceeding any weight ratings is to take your RV to the scales and have it weighed. The first step is to find scales where you can weigh your RV. This shouldn't be a problem. You can look in the Yellow Pages under moving and storage companies, farm suppliers, gravel pits and commercial truck stops. There are several different kinds of scales. What's important is to find scales where you can weigh individual wheel positions in addition to the overall weight, and the axle weights. Remember, I said earlier it's quite possible to weigh an axle and be within the Gross Axle Weight Rating, but you can exceed the tire rating on one axle end or the other. Call the number where the scales are located and ask them if it is possible to weigh your RV in these configurations.

The next step is to weigh everything! The day you head to the scales have the RV fully loaded for travel. If you tow a vehicle or trailer behind the motorhome take the loaded vehicle with you. If you are weighing a travel trailer or 5th wheel, have the trailer and the tow vehicle loaded as if you were leaving on a camping trip. Be sure to include all passengers, cargo, food, clothing, fuel, water, and propane. Water, fuel and propane alone can exceed 750 pounds.

> **Note:** To download a free printable copy of a detailed guide with worksheets to take along on how to weigh your travel trailer or motorhome go to **www.bridgestonetrucktires.com**

Before you go to the scales, identify the Gross Vehicle Weight Rating (GVWR), Gross Axle Weight Rating (GAWR) for each axle, and the information about the correct tire and rim sizes. You also need to know the recommended cold tire inflation pressures for all vehicles and/or trailers you are going to weigh. Get this information from the Federal Data plate and RVIA Data plates we discussed earlier. **Follow the steps in the charts in Chapter 10 that pertain to your configuration and fill in the blanks.**

> **Note:** If any overload condition exists it must be resolved immediately!

In some cases it might be possible to redistribute the weight and then weigh it again. If the overload condition still exists you'll need to remove some weight from the RV.

Load Capacity

Just like the axles your tires and wheels have load ratings too. The maximum ratings are molded into the side of the tires. Keep in mind these are maximum ratings. The sidewall of the tire shows the maximum load and the minimum inflation pressure for that load. Never set the inflation pressures below the recommendations you find on the vehicle manufacturers placard and do not exceed the maximum inflation

Mark J. Polk

pressure ratings found on the tires sidewall. Make sure you know the load and inflation pressure for your wheels too. Many times these ratings are stamped on the inside of the wheel. If not, your dealer should be able to help find out what they are. Never exceed the maximum load or inflation pressure ratings of your wheels.

The actual permissible load for a tire depends on the tire size and load range. The maximum load amount is molded into the sidewall of the tire. You could increase your load capacity by changing to a higher load rated tire of the same size at a higher pressure, but keep in mind you still must not exceed the gross axle weight rating of the vehicle and you can't exceed the maximum tire inflation for the wheels. It's also possible in some cases to increase tire load capacity by increasing the inflation pressure in your tires, but you cannot exceed the maximum pressure specified for that tire.

> **Note**: Consult your tire dealer for load and inflation tables.

It's also important that you use the same inflation pressure on both ends of each axle. If you weigh the RV and axle end loads differ enough that the tables specify different inflation pressures for each axle end, the axle is out of balance and you need to redistribute the load. If for some reason you cannot redistribute the load you must inflate the tires on both ends to the pressure required for the axle end with the heavier load.

> **Never** operate your vehicle with tires inflated to less pressure than required for the load.
> **Never** operate your vehicle with tires inflated to less pressure than specified on the vehicle placard, no matter what the load.
> **Never** inflate your tires above the maximum pressure shown on the tire sidewalls

Tire Failure

This would be a good time to discuss some of the leading causes of premature tire failure?

➢ Overloading the tires
➢ Under inflated tires
➢ Ozone and UV rays
➢ Age of the tires
➢ Rotating tires

The tires on your RV are the most vulnerable component affected by overloading the RV. There are numerous reasons for this. First and foremost is when the tires are not inflated properly for the load. Failure to maintain correct tire pressure can result in fast tread wear, uneven wear, poor handling, and excessive heat build up, which can lead to tire failure. Another problem is, when you weigh your RV the total weight of the axles may be within the axles weight rating but it may be overloaded on one side of the axle or the other. This is a common problem with RVs and many times the cause is poor weight distribution and/or improper loading of the RV. When this happens the tire or tires on the end of the axle that is overloaded are subject to tire failure. When a tire fails many RVers contribute it to a defect in the tire, but that is rarely the reason. The only way to avoid this is to weigh each axle end separately to determine if a tire overload condition exists. The maximum load on each axle end is half the GAWR for that axle. If an axle end has dual tires, the load on each tire is half the load on the axle end.

> **Note:** Never exceed the maximum tire load rating that is molded into the tires sidewall along with the inflation pressure for that load.

Another leading cause of tire failure is under inflated tires. The load rating for a tire is only accurate if the tire is properly inflated. Under inflated tires cause extreme heat build up that leads to tire failure. The appearance of the tire can look normal but the internal damage is not visible and the tire can fail at any time without warning. If you find any tire twenty percent or more below the correct inflation pressure have it

Mark J. Polk

removed, demounted and inspected. Driving on a tire that is twenty percent or more under inflated can cause serious, permanent damage to the tire that may not be visible. Tires with internal damage from under inflation can fail catastrophically without warning.

Tires can lose up to two pounds of air pressure per month. If you don't check your tires for three or four months they could be seriously under inflated. Ideally you should check tire inflation, and adjust it if required, everyday that you move or drive your RV. If you can't get into the habit of doing it on a daily basis you need to make it a point to check all tires weekly at a minimum when you're traveling. You always want to check the tires when they are cold, meaning that you don't drive or move the RV before checking inflation pressure.

Note: Never check tire inflation pressure when the tires are hot. You'll get a higher pressure reading, and if you let some air out they'll be under inflated when they are cold.

Tire Inflation

The only way to correctly measure the inflation pressure in your tires is with a quality inflation pressure gauge. Using your boot, or a hammer is not a quality pressure gauge, and don't ever depend on your eyes to check tire inflation. There can be as much as 20 PSI difference between tires that look the same. You need to invest in an accurate inflation pressure gauge. You should get one with a double, angled foot. This makes it much easier to check the outer tire of a dual set.

Wipe off the valve stem before you remove the valve cap. The valve stem caps should be metal with an inner rubber gasket. A good cap will provide a seal even when the valve doesn't. Plastic caps may not provide a good seal at higher inflation pressures used on RV tires. Check all of your tires and adjust the pressure according to the manufacturer's recommendation. Never set the inflation pressures below the recommendations you find on the vehicle manufacturers placard and do not exceed the maximum inflation pressure ratings found on the tires sidewall. Over inflated tires are more likely to be cut, punctured or broken by sudden impact if they hit an obstacle, like a pothole at high speeds.

If you have dual wheels you'll want to add extension hoses to the valve stems to make the job of checking tire inflation easier. It can be nearly impossible to check the inner dual without extension hoses. The best extension hoses will have stainless steel reinforcement and external braiding for long trouble-free life. Make sure the ends of the hoses are securely attached to the wheels. If you add extension hoses you need to replace the rubber valve stems with all steel valve stems. The added weight of the extension hoses can cause rubber stems to leak air resulting in under inflation.

Tire Maintenance
Ozone in the air and UV rays from the sun shorten the life of your tires. It's not uncommon to see RV tires with low mileage and plenty of tread that are ruined by the damaging effects of ozone and UV rays. Ozone in the air causes tires to dry rot and deteriorate. UV rays from the sun make it happen quicker. This is especially true of the tires sidewall. Inspect your tires for checking or cracks in the sidewalls. If you notice any damage, have the tires inspected by a professional. There are basically two ways to protect your tires from these elements. Keep the tires covered with covers that will block out the sunlight when not in use. For long-term storage remove the tires and store them in a cool dry place away from the sunlight, and away from grease, oil, and fuel. I also recommend that you place something like a piece of wood between the ground and the tires. Be sure that whatever you use is larger then the footprint of the tire. No portion of the tire should hang over the edge of the tire block. This can cause internal damage to the tire.

The age of your tires is another factor that contributes to tire failure. All tires manufactured in the United States have a DOT number. The DOT number can be on the inside or outside sidewalls. The last three or four digits in the DOT number identify how old the tire is. Older tires used three digits. The first two identify the week of the year that the tire was built and the third identifies the year. Newer tires use four digits.

Mark J. Polk

Again the first two digits are the week of the year and the last two identify the year. For example, 1006 is the 10th week of the year, and 06 is the year 2006. If you question the age of your tires, especially on a used RV and you can't find the DOT number, have them inspected by a qualified tire center. Tires over seven years old should be replaced.

Have you ever owned a vehicle and neglected to have the tires rotated and one day you suddenly notice that the front tires are wore out but the rear tires look fine? I'm sure that this has happened to most of us until we learned the valuable and expensive lesson of not rotating our tires. If one tire shows signs of wear faster than another tire it may be a signal that something other than normal tire wear is happening and you should have it checked. But if it's just normal tire wear you can even out the wear and extend the life of your tires by having the tires rotated on a regular basis. Talk to your tire dealer about proper tire rotation intervals.

Occasionally washing your tires with soap and water is OK, but anything beyond that can actually shorten the life of your tires. Sidewall rubber contains antioxidants and anti-ozone's that are designed to work their way to the surface of the rubber to protect it. Washing tires excessively removes these protective compounds and can age tires prematurely. The same is true of most tire dressing designed to make your tires shine.

Always keep in mind that weighing your RV is a snapshot in time. Weights can and do change according to how you load and distribute the weight in your RV and on many other factors. You should get in the practice of weighing your RV periodically to stay within all weight ratings.

Tire failure can be extremely dangerous, and can cause extensive damage to your RV. There are no guarantees, but by practicing good tire maintenance and weighing your RV, you can feel much safer and secure that the weakest link will do its job while you're out exploring in your RV.

Chapter 10

Weighing your RV

Portions of this chapter are excerpts, courtesy of the Recreation Vehicle Safety & Education Foundation (RVSEF) & Bridgestone/Firestone North American Tire.

Understanding RV weight issues can be confusing. I want to assist you in making your RV travel safer by understanding and managing your vehicle weights. Remember, getting to your favorite destination safely is half the fun.

Weighing your RV can be the difference between a safe, enjoyable trip and a costly, disastrous trip. The Recreation Vehicle Safety & Education Foundation (RVSEF) has weighed over 10,000 motorhomes and trailers in conjunction with RV events. The results are a real eye opener. Nearly a quarter of the RVs weighed had loads that exceeded the capacity of the tires on the vehicles. On average, these RVs were overloaded by over 900 pounds based on manufacturer specifications. In a separate survey conducted by Bridgestone/Firestone, 4 out of 5 RVs had at least one under inflated tire, a third of which were dangerously under inflated and at risk of failure. Most of the weight was on the rear. 40% of all rear tires were overloaded. Improper weight distribution resulted in 28% of all motorhomes being out of balance by 400 pounds or more from one axle end to the other.

With multiple slide out rooms, amenities like washers and dryers, holding tank capacities and the ample amount of storage space available on modern RVs it's easy to see why so many RVs are overloaded. Add this to the fact that many RVs are already close to capacity when they leave the factory and the problem is magnified. The purpose of this section is to improve consumer awareness and safety on a topic that is

Mark J. Polk

confusing and many times not even brought up. Overloaded RVs are extremely dangerous. **That's the bottom line!**

Our goal with this section is to inform you on how to avoid becoming a statistic in relationship to overloaded RVs. It will answer your questions about weights and walk you through the proper steps to ensure that you don't exceed any of the manufacturers' weight ratings. Always keep in mind that weighing your RV is a snapshot in time. Weights can and do change according to how you load and distribute the weight in your RV and based on many other factors. You should get in the practice of weighing your RV periodically to stay within all weight ratings. Whenever an overload condition exists resolve the problem before using your RV.

Why Should I Weigh My Motorhome?

Driving or towing an overloaded RV is a leading cause for RV accidents. The suspension system, tires, wheels, brakes, axles, and the RV itself all have weight ratings. Weight ratings are established by the manufacturer and are based on the weakest link in the chain. When you exceed a weight rating, you are overloading one or more components on the RV, and risk wearing the component out prematurely or complete failure of the component.

I mentioned earlier the Gross Vehicle Weight Rating (GVWR) is one of the most crucial safety factors of your RV. The GVWR is the maximum allowable weight of the vehicle when fully loaded for travel including, all passengers, all cargo, fluids and fuel. The GVWR for the RV is based on the Gross Axle Weight Ratings (GAWR). The GAWR is the maximum allowable weight that can be loaded on each axle of the RV. The GAWR is based on the lowest weight rating of the other components in the system like suspension components, brakes, wheels, and tires.

The tires on your RV are the most vulnerable component affected by overloading the RV. There are numerous reasons for this. First and foremost is when the tires are not inflated properly for the load. Failure to maintain correct tire pressure can result in fast tread wear, uneven wear, poor handling, and excessive heat build up, which can lead to tire failure. Another problem is when you weigh your RV the total weight of the axles may be within the axles weight rating but it may be overloaded on one side of the axle or the other. For example, let's say you have an axle that is rated for 6,000 pounds. When we weigh the RV the weight on that particular axle is 5,950 pounds. We are with in the weight rating for the axle, but when we weigh each axle end separately we discover that one end weighs 3,400 pounds and the other end weighs 2550 pounds. We are still within the 6,000 pound axle weight rating, but the tires are rated for 3,000 at 80 PSI. This means the axle end that weighs 3,400 pounds is overloading the tire by 400 pounds, even if the inflation pressure is correct.

This is a common problem with RVs and many times the cause is poor weight distribution and/or improper loading of the RV. When this happens the tire or tires on the end of the axle that is overloaded are subject to tire failure. The only way to avoid this is to weigh each axle end separately to determine if a tire overload condition exists.

Why Should I Weigh My Travel Trailer or 5th Wheel?

The concern for weighing a travel trailer or 5th wheel is doubled. You need to ensure that the trailer and the tow vehicle are both within their weight ratings. We can take this one step further because you also need to be sure that the combined weight of the fully loaded trailer and the fully loaded tow vehicle does not exceed the Gross Combined Weight Rating (GCWR) of your tow vehicle.

The GCWR is the maximum allowable weight of the fully loaded trailer and fully loaded tow vehicle combined. This can be a bit complicated so I will try to explain it the easiest way I can. The tow vehicle and the trailer both have a GVWR. Let's start with the tow vehicle. Let's say we have a tow vehicle that has a tow rating of 7,900 pounds, a GVWR of 8,800 pounds and a GCWR of 14,000 pounds. We take our tow vehicle to the scales fully loaded with passengers, cargo, and a full tank of fuel and it weighs 7,105 pounds. This leaves us 1,695 pounds below our GVWR. If we are towing a travel trailer we would need to add the amount of the trailers hitch weight or tongue weight to make sure we are still within our tow vehicles GVWR. In this particular case we would probably be okay. But, if we are towing a 5th wheel the hitch weight or pin weight can be extremely heavy. With a 5th wheel you not only want to make sure you are still within the GVWR, but the GAWR too.

Now, the interesting thing is we started with a tow rating of 7,900 pounds, but we have to account for the weight of the passengers, cargo and anything else we loaded in the tow vehicle. Any weight we add to the tow vehicle decreases the tow rating by that amount. In our example when we subtract the weight of the passengers, cargo, and the additional 50-gallon fuel tank our tow rating goes from 7,900 pounds to 6,895 pounds. This is a significant difference from what we thought we could tow.

Now let's look at our trailer. The GVWR of a travel trailer or 5th wheel is the combined maximum weight rating of every axle on the trailer plus the hitch weight. The data plate on the outside of the trailer gives you the Gross Vehicle Weight Rating (GVWR). This is not the actual weight of the trailer; it is the maximum amount of weight that the trailers axles, brakes, tires and other components can support. The trailer might weigh 5,000 pounds, but the GVWR may be 7,000 pounds. This means that you could potentially add 2,000 pounds of weight to the trailer, if it is distributed properly, before you reach the GVWR. You need to consider how much weight you will add to the trailer when you're calculating the weight. You never want to tow a trailer that exceeds the GVWR. The components on the trailer are not designed to exceed the GVWR and it can be extremely dangerous.

Any manufacturer that is a member of the Recreation Vehicle Industry Association (RVIA) is required to have an additional weight label inside the trailer that will give you more information. Look for it on the back of a cabinet or closet door. It will provide information on the Gross Vehicle Weight Rating (GVWR), the Unloaded Vehicle Weight (UVW) or Dry Weight (DW), which it is commonly referred to, the weight of the fresh water tank and LP gas when full, and the Cargo Carrying Capacity (CCC) for the trailer. The UVW is the actual weight of the trailer when it left the factory. You also want to find out if this weight includes options on the trailer. When a dealer orders a trailer they list the options they want on it. These options include, but are not limited to, the roof air conditioner, awnings, stabilizer jacks, and a spare tire. You can see how quickly weight can add up on the trailer. Be careful when you look at the weights in the manufacturers brochures. These weights are for the base model trailer without options, and depending on what they consider to be options the weight can change drastically.

Let's say we selected a trailer that has a dry weight of 5,750 pounds. With aftermarket accessories, cargo, full fresh water tank and propane the actual weight of the trailer is 6,725 pounds. This only leaves us with 170 pounds before we exceed our tow vehicle rating, and if we add the weight of the fully loaded tow vehicle (7,105) and the weight of the fully loaded trailer (6,725) we are only 170 pounds away from exceeding our tow vehicles GCWR. One easy method to follow is to add the GVWR of the trailer and the GVWR of the tow vehicle; if the total is more than the GCWR of the tow vehicle it is probably a poor match.

These examples illustrate how quickly weights can add up and put us in a dangerous situation. The only way to know for sure if you are within all weight ratings is to have the tow vehicle and trailer weighed. You should never tow a trailer that is pushing the limit on the manufacturers tow rating or a combined weight that is pushing the tow vehicle GCWR. Remember these are maximum ratings and should never be exceeded.

Remember to include all of these factors in your weight calculations:
- ➢ Add the UVW of the trailer; make sure that it includes all options.
- ➢ Add the weight of any aftermarket accessories like a battery or satellite dish.
- ➢ Add the weight of any cargo you put in the trailer.

- ➤ Add the weight of water and LP gas that will be on the trailer. Water weighs 8.3 pounds per gallon. LP gas weighs 4.2 pounds per gallon.
- ➤ Add the weight of all passengers in the tow vehicle.
- ➤ Add the weight of any cargo in the tow vehicle.
- ➤ Add the weight of any after market equipment added to the vehicle.

More Reasons to Weigh Your RV!

- ➤ Safety, Safety, Safety
- ➤ Most importantly overloading your RV puts you, your passengers and other people in harms way.
- ➤ Overloading is the number one cause of RV related accidents.
- ➤ Overloading can lead to premature transmission failure.
- ➤ Overloading can lead to rapid vehicle suspension system wear or component failure to include: springs, shock absorbers, brakes and tires.
- ➤ Overloading can result in reduced handling capability.
- ➤ Overloading can result in steering problems.
- ➤ Overloading increases the RVs stopping distance and if serious overload conditions exist, the brakes can fail completely.
- ➤ Overloading causes rapid tire wear, irregular tire wear and finally tire failure.
- ➤ Overloading increases fuel consumption.
- ➤ Overloading can lead to untimely, dangerous breakdowns.
- ➤ Overloading can result in costly repairs.
- ➤ Overloading is both unsafe and illegal

How to Weigh Your RV

The first step is to find scales where you can weigh your RV. This shouldn't be a problem; you can look in the Yellow Pages under moving and storage companies, gravel pits and commercial truck stops. There are several different kinds of scales. What is important is to find scales where

you can weigh individual wheel positions in addition to the overall weight, and the axle weights. Remember, we said earlier it is quite possible to weigh an axle and be within the Gross Axle Weight Rating, but you can exceed the tire rating on one axle end or the other. Call the number where the scales are located and ask them if it is possible to weigh your RV in these configurations.

The next step is to weigh everything! The day you head to the scales have the RV fully loaded for travel. If you tow a vehicle or trailer behind the motorhome take the loaded vehicle with you. If you are weighing a travel trailer or 5th wheel, have the trailer and the tow vehicle loaded as if you were leaving on a camping trip. Be sure to include all passengers, cargo, food, clothing, fuel, water, and propane.

The actual process of weighing your RV is not that difficult. It may take a little time at the scales, but it is well worth it knowing that you're traveling safely within all of the manufacturer's weight ratings. **Follow the steps in the enclosed charts that pertain to your configuration and fill in the blanks.**

Note: To download a free printable copy of a detailed guide, with worksheets to take along, on how to weigh your travel trailer or motorhome go to **www.bridgestonetrucktires.com**

Caution: If any overload condition exists it must be resolved immediately.

In some cases it might be possible to redistribute the weight and then weigh it again. If the overload condition still exists you will need to remove some weight from the RV.

Mark J. Polk

Pulling Vehicle: Individual Axle & Gross Vehicle Weights

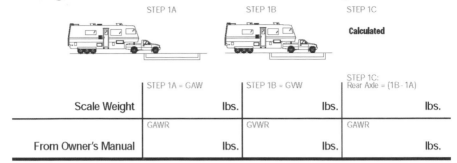

	STEP 1A	STEP 1B	STEP 1C
	STEP 1A = GAW	STEP 1B = GVW	STEP 1C: Rear Axle = (1B - 1A)
Scale Weight	lbs.	lbs.	lbs.
	GAWR	GVWR	GAWR
From Owner's Manual	lbs.	lbs.	lbs.

Pulling Vehicle: Individual Wheel Position Weights

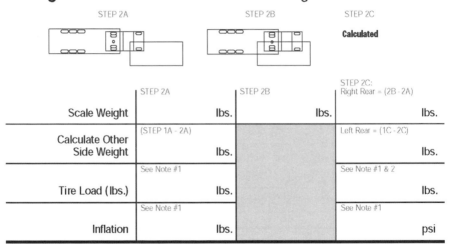

	STEP 2A	STEP 2B	STEP 2C: Right Rear = (2B - 2A)
	STEP 2A	STEP 2B	
Scale Weight	lbs.	lbs.	lbs.
Calculate Other Side Weight	(STEP 1A - 2A) lbs.		Left Rear = (1C - 2C) lbs.
Tire Load (lbs.)	See Note #1 lbs.		See Note #1 & 2 lbs.
Inflation	See Note #1 lbs.		See Note #1 psi

Travel Trailer: Individual Axle & Gross Vehicle Weights

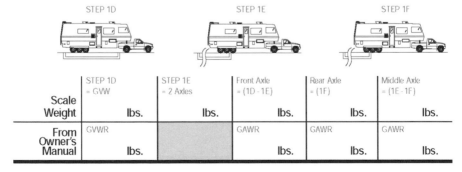

	STEP 1D	STEP 1E	Front Axle	Rear Axle	Middle Axle
Scale Weight	STEP 1D = GVW lbs.	STEP 1E = 2 Axles lbs.	Front Axle = (1D - 1E) lbs.	Rear Axle = (1F) lbs.	Middle Axle = (1E - 1F) lbs.
From Owner's Manual	GVWR lbs.		GAWR lbs.	GAWR lbs.	GAWR lbs.

Courtesy of RVSEF **www.rvsafety.org**

Travel Trailer: Individual Wheel Position Weights

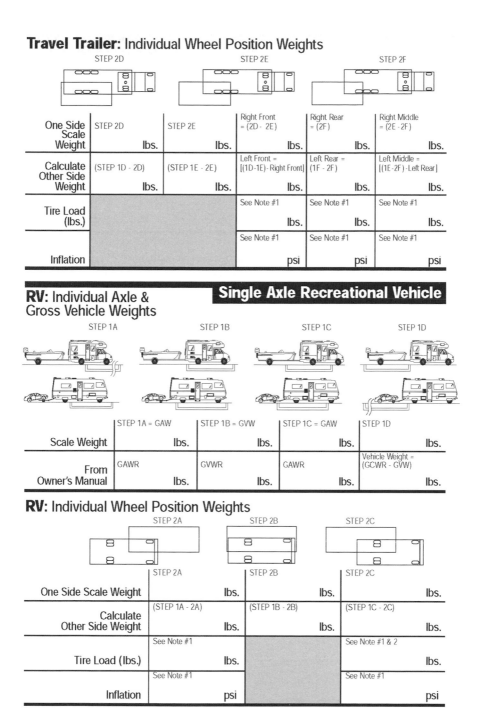

	STEP 2D	STEP 2E	Right Front = (2D - 2E)	Right Rear = (2F)	Right Middle = (2E - 2F)
One Side Scale Weight	STEP 2D ___ lbs.	STEP 2E ___ lbs.	___ lbs.	___ lbs.	___ lbs.
Calculate Other Side Weight	(STEP 1D - 2D) ___ lbs.	(STEP 1E - 2E) ___ lbs.	Left Front = [(1D-1E)- Right Front] ___ lbs.	Left Rear = (1F - 2F) ___ lbs.	Left Middle = [(1E-2F)-Left Rear] ___ lbs.
Tire Load (lbs.)			See Note #1 ___ lbs.	See Note #1 ___ lbs.	See Note #1 ___ lbs.
Inflation			See Note #1 ___ psi	See Note #1 ___ psi	See Note #1 ___ psi

RV: Individual Axle & Gross Vehicle Weights — Single Axle Recreational Vehicle

	STEP 1A = GAW	STEP 1B = GVW	STEP 1C = GAW	STEP 1D
Scale Weight	___ lbs.	___ lbs.	___ lbs.	___ lbs.
From Owner's Manual	GAWR ___ lbs.	GVWR ___ lbs.	GAWR ___ lbs.	Vehicle Weight = (GCWR - GVW) ___ lbs.

RV: Individual Wheel Position Weights

	STEP 2A	STEP 2B	STEP 2C
One Side Scale Weight	STEP 2A ___ lbs.	STEP 2B ___ lbs.	STEP 2C ___ lbs.
Calculate Other Side Weight	(STEP 1A - 2A) ___ lbs.	(STEP 1B - 2B) ___ lbs.	(STEP 1C - 2C) ___ lbs.
Tire Load (lbs.)	See Note #1 ___ lbs.		See Note #1 & 2 ___ lbs.
Inflation	See Note #1 ___ psi		See Note #1 ___ psi

Courtesy of RVSEF **www.rvsafety.org**

Mark J. Polk

RV: Individual Axle & Gross Vehicle Weights

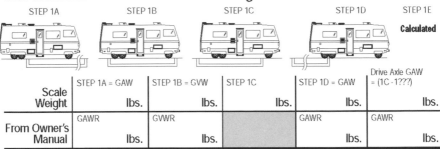

	STEP 1A	STEP 1B	STEP 1C	STEP 1D	STEP 1E Calculated
Scale Weight	STEP 1A = GAW lbs.	STEP 1B = GVW lbs.	STEP 1C lbs.	STEP 1D = GAW lbs.	Drive Axle GAW = (1C - 1???) lbs.
From Owner's Manual	GAWR lbs.	GVWR lbs.		GAWR lbs.	GAWR lbs.

NOTE: Should your tandem axle recreational vehicle be pulling a travel trailer, please see "Weighing Your Single Axle Recreational Vehicle," STEP 1D page 3.

RV: Individual Wheel Position Weights

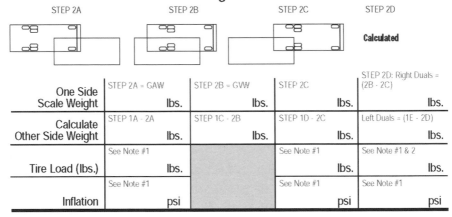

	STEP 2A	STEP 2B	STEP 2C	STEP 2D Calculated
One Side Scale Weight	STEP 2A = GAW lbs.	STEP 2B = GVW lbs.	STEP 2C lbs.	STEP 2D: Right Duals = (2B - 2C) lbs.
Calculate Other Side Weight	STEP 1A - 2A lbs.	STEP 1C - 2B lbs.	STEP 1D - 2C lbs.	Left Duals = (1E - 2D) lbs.
Tire Load (lbs.)	See Note #1 lbs.		See Note #1 lbs.	See Note #1 & 2 lbs.
Inflation	See Note #1 psi		See Note #1 psi	See Note #1 psi

CAUTION

Individual wheel position weights MUST NOT exceed the maximum tire load capacity. Maximum tire load capacity can only be achieved utilizing the maximum allowable psi as listed on the sidewall of the tire.

[1] From the tire manufacturer's load and inflation tables or the sidewall of the tires mounted on the vehicle.

[2] If vehicle has duals, read dual capacity from tire and multiply by 2 (two) to obtain dual assembly load carrying capacity.

For more information/additional assistance, contact your tire dealer.

Courtesy of RVSEF **www.rvsafety.org**

Chapter 11

Getting there Safely

Forty thousand people in the United States die each year on the road! This would be a good time to discuss getting to your RV travel destination safely. Getting there can be half the fun, as the saying goes, if you take a few precautions to make your trip safe.

Trip Planning

The first step is to plan the trip you are taking. Travel guides, magazines, state tourism boards and Internet sites offer valuable information to help you plan your trip. Route your trip on a map or from an Internet trip planning website. Always keep an atlas or maps in the RV or tow vehicle. Driving a motorhome or pulling a trailer can be stressful, especially if you don't know the route you will be traveling. Using a GPS system can make traveling much less stressful.

I am including this short checklist to assist you in planning your RV trips.

> ➢ Route your trip on a map or from an Internet trip planning website.
>
> ➢ Plan your itinerary to include what campgrounds you will be staying at.
>
> ➢ Give a family member or friend a copy of your itinerary and contact information.
>
> ➢ Make campground reservations in advance, especially during the busy travel season. Limit your traveling to 350 miles a day or less. Not only will your trip be more enjoyable, but this will allow

plenty of time to get set-up at the campground before it gets dark outside.

➤ Make sure your emergency roadside service is up to date. If you don't have one you should get one prior to leaving on your trip.

➤ Conduct pre-trip checklists for your RV.

➤ Check and refill any medications you will need.

➤ Be sure you have your calling card, credit cards, ATM card, checkbook and cell phone.

➤ Check the weather conditions for where you will be traveling each day. Take a weather radio receiver with you. Don't travel in bad weather or during high winds.

➤ Take your address book and stamps.

➤ Take emergency contact numbers.

➤ Take a spare set of eyeglasses or reading glasses.

➤ Take a spare set of keys.

➤ Make sure you have all your owner's manuals for the RV & warranty information.

➤ If you're under a doctor's care take along a copy of your medical records.

➤ Make a list of all medications you are taking and keep it in your wallet or other safe place for quick reference.

➤ Take passports (only if necessary) and check the expiration dates.

➤ Double check that everything is loaded in the RV.

Pre-Trip Checks

Do you know what two of the most common repairs made on RV's are? They are repairs to the steps and the TV antenna. Damage to RV steps and TV antennas occur frequently and can be costly to repair. The main reason for these frequent repairs is because you forget to do a walk around of the unit before leaving on a trip or leaving the campground. The good news is both of these common repairs can be avoided by following a simple "Pre-Trip Checklist" before heading out in your RV. Simple checks like checking your tires, lights, hitch work and other items

all contribute to a safer, stress free trip. You should make these checks everyday before traveling.

Let's start with the outside of the RV

- ➤ Check and adjust the air pressure in all tires. Always check the tires when they are cold, before traveling more than one mile.
- ➤ Check the lug nuts on the wheels. Discoloration and stains around lug nuts indicate they may be loose.
- ➤ Make sure all items in the storage compartments are secure. Lock all outside compartments.
- ➤ Check the bike rack and bikes for secure mounting if applicable.
- ➤ Make sure the power cord, water hose, and the sewer hose are disconnected and properly stored.
- ➤ Make sure all slide outs are in and slide out travel locks are securely in place.
- ➤ Make sure the TV antenna and/or satellite are down and stowed in the proper position for traveling.
- ➤ Check the awning. Make sure that it is securely stored and all travel locks and knobs are tight and latched.
- ➤ Raise all stabilizer jacks or hydraulic leveling jacks.
- ➤ Look under the RV for any indications of leaks (motorized) or anything out of the ordinary.
- ➤ Stow or retract the steps.
- ➤ Fill the fresh water holding tank with enough potable water to get to your destination.
- ➤ Check and secure the cap on the sewer outlet.
- ➤ Turn all LP gas appliances off and turn the gas supply off at the tank or bottles.
- ➤ Double check all hitchwork on towable RV's and on vehicles being towed behind motorhomes.
- ➤ Check all fluid levels for motorized RV's and tow vehicles.
- ➤ Remove and store wheel chocks and any type of leveling blocks.
- ➤ Check all running lights, turn signals, brake lights and headlights on the RV and tow vehicle.

Mark J. Polk

- ➢ Check for an up to date inspection or emission sticker and license plates.
- ➢ Check trailer brakes for proper operation.
- ➢ **Make one last walk around, on the outside of the RV, and check for anything you may have overlooked.**

Don't forget about the inside of your RV

- ➢ Walk through the entire RV and secure all loose items that could move, fall or get damaged while traveling.
- ➢ Turn off all appliances gas & electric. Turn off all pilot lights.
- ➢ Close all roof vents.
- ➢ Close all doors, drawers and cabinets.
- ➢ Check for anything in the refrigerator that could spill. Lock the refrigerator and freezer doors.
- ➢ Turn off the 12-volt water pump.
- ➢ Close the range top cover.
- ➢ Turn off all 12-volt lights and accessories that could drain the auxiliary battery. Don't forget the TV antenna booster.
- ➢ Close the windows and secure blinds.
- ➢ Secure any large items such as TVs and computers that might move or fall while traveling.
- ➢ All weight in the RV should be distributed evenly.
- ➢ Adjust your mirrors and seat and hit the road.

RV Travel Security

For one minute, try to think the way a criminal would think. If you were at a rest stop looking for your next target or victim, what would you look for? Let's pretend for a moment that you were going to target a vehicle. Which would be more appealing, a car whose owner stopped for a quick bathroom break or an expensive looking Type A motorhome, whose owners are out walking their dogs? I don't have the mind of a criminal but this is an easy choice. That expensive looking RV probably has expensive contents inside like, jewelry, cameras, or a laptop computer.

Okay, we have come to the conclusion that we, the RVers, are the prime target for the criminal mind, so we need to understand what we can do to protect ourselves and our personal belongings when traveling in our RV.

Don't stay overnight at a rest stop. Rest stops attract criminals. If you stop at a rest stop it should only be for a short break and then back on the road. Lock the RV and take turns using the facilities, always leaving someone in or close to the RV. Always be on the look out for anything or anyone that looks suspicious. Keep your cell phone handy in case you need it and don't ever open the door for anyone unless you know who is knocking.

Rest stops aren't the only place you need to be concerned about. Every time you stop to refuel there are certain precautions you need to take. It's easy to be vulnerable to a thief at a gas station or a truck stop. I have a bad habit of leaving my wallet on the console of our motorhome. The door isn't locked and your spouse is taking advantage of the time to walk the dogs. This is how quick it can happen. Get in the habit of locking the doors whenever you or someone else is not physically in the RV.

Most robberies occur at night and most travel related robberies occur at rest stops, gas stations, convenience stores and ATM machines. Try to schedule most of your stops during daylight hours, and whenever you stop be aware of your surroundings. If something doesn't look right leave.

Wal-Mart or other parking lots where you might stop to get a few hours of sleep can present security problems too. You should always park in a well lit area and the entry door of the RV should be facing where most of the activity is. A thief prefers to work where it is dark and where it is least likely to draw any attention. Close your curtains or blinds so it's not possible for someone to look inside. Don't open the door for anybody unless you know who it is. If it's a security guard ask for identification before you open the door.

As much as we would like to believe that campgrounds are 100% safe and secure don't let you guard down. You don't need to be paranoid, just use some common sense. Don't leave expensive equipment lying around

Mark J. Polk

unsecured. Vehicle tow bars, hitches, bicycles and other items need to be under lock and key.

Keep any valuables inside the RV secured and out of sight. It's a good idea to purchase a small fire proof safe to store valuables and important paperwork in. The safe might protect your valuables from the hazards of a fire but it will still need to be stored in a secure, out of the way place, inside the RV.

Always lock the RV when you're not physically at the campsite. Do not store valuable equipment in outside storage compartments. Believe it or not, a vast majority of RV's use the same exact key as yours for outside storage compartments. If you store valuables, like golf clubs, fishing gear or tools in the outside compartments you may want to have the storage compartment locks changed.

Before you leave on a trip make sure your Emergency Roadside Service Plan is current. If you breakdown on the road try to pull off in as safe a place as possible and call for help immediately. Stay with the RV until help arrives.

It's unfortunate that we live in a day and age where we need to take these added measures to protect ourselves. I don't want you to feel like everybody you meet during your travels is a thief or has bad intentions. Just use common sense and be aware of what is going on around you.

> Plan your trip, travel safe and smart and enjoy your RV experiences. Remember, getting there is half the fun!

On the Road
In a recent study these dates, ranked in order, were identified as the ten deadliest days of the year to drive. Mark these on your calendar and stay put on these dates. One more day at the campground or getting to your destination one day later can't hurt you, but driving on these dates could do much worse. As you can see most of the dates are close to, or on a major holiday. The reason for the August dates is because August is the busiest traveled month of the year.

1) July 4
2) July 3
3) December 23
4) August 3
5) January 1
6) August 6
7) August 4
8) August 12
9) July 2
10) September 2

Relax, and take your time. Whenever I'm towing a trailer or driving a motorhome I apply these three guidelines:

➤ Drive at a safe speed for the traffic and road conditions.
➤ Always stay alert, know what is going on around you.
➤ Anticipate driving situations before they happen.

Take plenty of breaks when you're traveling. Stopping, stretching out and taking brief walks can revitalize you. Do not rush to get to your vacation destination. Driving too fast and for long periods of time can result in fatigue and falling asleep at the wheel. If you feel tired you should pull over and rest or change drivers. It's a good idea to switch drivers every few hours. Keep a window cracked open to help you stay alert, and only eat light meals when you stop to eat.

Avoid driving or pulling your RV during bad weather and high winds. Because of the size and mass of RV's it can be extremely dangerous to travel during periods of high winds. It's better to get to your destination one day later, than to risk traveling in bad weather.

Limit your driving time to 5 or 6 hours a day (300 to 350 miles). Not only will you be more alert, but you will arrive at the campground with plenty of day light to get set up and settled in before it gets dark outside. This gives you a chance to unwind and get rested for another day of travel, and to enjoy some of the amenities the campground has to offer.

Always leave plenty of room between you and the vehicle in front of you. RV's are much heavier than your automobile and require a longer braking distance to come to a stop. This alone will prevent accidents, especially during emergency braking. Driving at a safe speed also lowers your braking distance. Always use a supplemental braking system on the vehicle you are towing.

Cell phones are nice to have for emergencies, but they can distract the driver. Do not use a cell phone if you are driving. If you must make a call, have someone that is not driving do it for you.

Never drink and drive!

Safe Driving Tips

> **Note:** Some of these tips apply to pulling a travel trailer, some apply to driving a motorhome and some apply to both.

> ➤ Don't speed. Driving at a moderate speed will put less stress and strain on the drive train components of your tow vehicle. It will also reduce the likelihood of the trailer becoming unstable and starting to sway.
> ➤ Monitor the gauges on the tow vehicle or motorhome instrument panel. If a gauge does not read in the normal range pull over as soon as it is safe, and call for help.
> ➤ Drive defensively! Stay alert and monitor what is going on around you at all times. Use your mirrors. For increased visibility, purchase some convex mirrors that you can stick on your side view mirrors. These mirrors are inexpensive and are available in auto parts stores. They come in different sizes and will improve your visibility a great deal, especially along the sides of the RV and in blind spots. If you're pulling a trailer it may be necessary to add mirror extensions so you can see along the sides of the trailer. The mirrors on your tow vehicle can be your best friend when you're towing a trailer. When you use your mirrors you will

know when a transfer truck is passing, and you can anticipate the need for a slight steering correction when the trucks air pressure causes the trailer to move. When you pass a vehicle, and can see the vehicles front tires on the road surface behind the trailer, it is safe to indicate and pull back in the other lane.

➢ Use the proper gear for driving conditions. If the transmission continues to shift in and out of overdrive you need to turn the overdrive off. Reducing gears can help to slow the trailer or motorhome down when descending inclines and give you the additional power you may need when ascending inclines.

Note: Read the tow vehicle owner's manual for proper gear selection when towing.

➢ Try to avoid sudden stops. Stopping to quickly can cause a trailer to slide and possibly jackknife.

➢ Try to avoid quick, harsh steering movements if possible. This can cause a trailer to become unstable and increase the possibility of trailer sway.

➢ Slow down on loose road surfaces, such as gravel, and when the roads are slippery and wet.

➢ When towing a trailer or a vehicle behind a motorhome you need to make wider turns than you are accustomed to. Remember the pivot point for the trailer is its axles. Watch for tail swing and exercise caution when turning on narrow streets and maneuvering around fuel stations.

➢ When maneuvering around the campground, watch for tail swing, low branches and utility hook ups.

Mark J. Polk

Controlling Sway

We have mentioned sway several times already. Sway becomes an automatic factor with travel trailers simply because of how the trailer is hitched to the tow vehicle. The good news is that even though the potential for trailer sway is there, it can be controlled. Let's look at some of the causes for trailer sway.

➤ First and foremost poor trailer design contributes to trailer sway. When there is too much weight behind the trailers axles causing the tongue weight to be less than 10% of the trailers weight it has a natural tendency to sway.
➤ Incorrect tire inflation.
➤ Improper weight distribution hitch adjustments.
➤ No sway control on the trailer.
➤ Crosswinds
➤ A transfer truck passing from the rear of the trailer.
➤ Descending inclines
➤ Towing speeds and hitch weight
➤ Tow vehicle not properly matched for the trailer.
➤ Improper loading, overloading and poor weight distribution.

Most of these causes for trailer sway have quick and easy fixes. When I was an RV sales manager I always asked the drivers that delivered the trailers how the trailer pulled. It was amazing that trailers built by certain manufacturers always handled good and others always handled poorly. But you must always take into account that the majority of these drivers seldom used any form of sway control. The point I'm trying to make is, before you purchase a travel trailer, do your homework on the manufacturer. A poorly designed trailer will never handle well. Find a trailer with a tongue weight that is 10 to 15 percent of the trailers weight and match it with a tow vehicle that is capable of handling the load.

So it is safe to say that with a **well designed trailer, the proper tow vehicle, correct tire pressure, hitch adjustments, sway control and a properly loaded trailer** we can control a great deal of potential trailer sway. That narrows the potential for sway down to what you could encounter at any given time, even with a stable trailer, strong crosswinds, transfer trucks passing from the rear, bad driving conditions and descending steep inclines. Any one of these conditions will tend to push the trailer and tow vehicle sideways, but with the proper sway control you can make normal steering corrections.

Should the trailer become unstable and attempted steering corrections don't control it you can use the manual override on the brake control to regain control of the trailer. Slide the lever over slowly and allow the trailer brakes to engage and the sway control to put the trailer back on a straight course. If trailer sway becomes severe, reduce your speed gradually, avoid using the vehicle brakes if possible and manually apply more trailer brakes.

Braking

The brakes on the tow vehicle and trailer are a critical element to safe towing. Always check the operation of the brake controller and trailer brakes before leaving on a trip.

> ➢ Have your trailer brakes, bearings and other components inspected at least once annually by a professional.

> ➢ Allow more distance for stopping then you are accustomed to. Do not follow other vehicles too closely.

> ➢ Do not use the tow vehicles brakes to control excessive trailer sway. This will usually make it worse. Manually apply the trailer brakes to regain control.

> ➢ When descending a steep incline, if it feels like the trailer is pushing the tow vehicle, reduce speed, down shift to a lower gear and use the manual override on the brake control to slow the trailer. Heavy use of the tow vehicle brakes can cause them to overheat and begin to fade.

> ➢ Always be prepared to slow down and avoid sudden stops.

Mark J. Polk

Passing Vehicles

➤ Allow more time for acceleration when planning to pass somebody. It may be necessary to shift out of overdrive for increased acceleration.

➤ Only attempt to pass a vehicle on a level road surface. **Never attempt passing on steep upgrades or downgrades.**

➤ When passing a vehicle or changing lanes, signal in advance and double check mirrors for oncoming traffic.

➤ When completing a pass, look in your mirror, if you can see the vehicles front tires on the road surface behind the trailer it is safe to signal and pull back in that lane.

➤ When passing, or being passed, anticipate the need to make steering corrections due to the air pressure created by other vehicles.

➤ Always be cautious of the road shoulder when passing. If the trailer gets on the shoulder it can jackknife or cause you to loose control.

Upgrades and Downgrades

Some vehicles have transmission tow modes. Consult your owner's manual for the proper gears to use on your tow vehicle when towing a trailer.

➤ Downshift on downgrades to lessen the braking action required. Reduce your speed. Remember that trailer sway is more likely to occur when descending inclines.

➤ Downshift on upgrades for increased acceleration and power.

➤ On steep or long downgrades, reduce gears and avoid prolonged brake use on the tow vehicle. The brakes can easily overheat. Use the vehicle brakes in intervals.

➤ If the trailer becomes unstable when descending an incline and the trailer starts to sway, reduce your speed, avoid using the vehicle brakes, and manually activate the trailer brakes to regain control.

➤ On steep or long upgrades monitor all of the gauges on the tow vehicle instrument panel. If gauges do not read in the normal range, or the vehicle starts to overheat, pull over as soon as you safely can and call for help.

Maximizing Fuel Economy

Now we're going to discuss something near and dear to every RV owner. How you can improve your fuel economy? The cost of gasoline is steadily rising and it is safe to say that it probably won't to go down in the future. It takes a while, but as with everything else you eventually accept the fact that higher fuel prices are here to stay. I for one am not going to let sky rocketing fuel prices change my plans for using and enjoying our RV. So, with that said and a motorhome that averages 7 to 8 miles to a gallon I am forced to find ways to save on fuel rather than waiting and hoping that fuel prices will go down. After a little research I was surprised to learn how easy it can be to improve our fuel economy. Whether you're towing a trailer or driving a motorhome there are many ways to improve fuel economy. By performing some simple maintenance procedures and changing our driving habits a little we can save a significant amount of fuel.

One shocking discovery I made was that for each 5mph you go over 60mph is equivalent to paying 10 cents more per gallon. So if you're traveling down the Interstate at 75 mph add 30 cents to the price on the pump!

Reductions in Fuel Economy

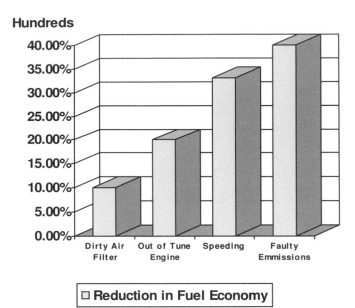

Hundreds

40.00%	
35.00%	
30.00%	
25.00%	
20.00%	
15.00%	
10.00%	
5.00%	
0.00%	Dirty Air Filter · Out of Tune Engine · Speeding · Faulty Emmissions

☐ **Reduction in Fuel Economy**

So How Can We Improve Our Fuel Economy?

➢ Talk to other RVers that have a motorhome or tow vehicle and trailer similar to yours. Compare gas mileage. If there is a significant difference compare notes and try to determine what makes the difference.

➢ Something as simple as a clean air filter can improve your fuel economy up to 10%.

➢ Checking and adjusting your tire pressure to the proper pressure can increase fuel economy by 3%, not to mention preventing premature tire wear and failures or blowouts caused by over or under-inflated tires. Tires can look normal when they are seriously under-inflated. Use a quality air pressure gauge and check your tires when they're cold, before traveling more than one mile.

➢ Excessive idling wastes fuel. If you're going to be sitting still for more than a couple of minutes shut the engine off.

- Using overdrive whenever you can saves fuel by decreasing the engines speed.
- Using the cruise control whenever possible saves fuel because it keeps the vehicle at a constant speed rather than variable speeds. This applies when you are driving on a relatively flat surface. Keep in mind the over 60 mph rule applies here too.
- Keeping the vehicle tuned up and in top running condition saves fuel. A poorly tuned engine can lower fuel economy by 10 to 20%.
- Poor emissions and/or a faulty oxygen sensor can cause a 40% reduction in fuel economy. Can you believe that? A 40% reduction.
- Following the recommended service and maintenance schedules will save you fuel.
- Using the recommended grade of motor oil will increase fuel economy by 1 to 2%.
- Using synthetic oils will increase fuel economy by 2 or more percent.
- Speeding and rapid acceleration reduces fuel economy anywhere from 5 to 33% depending on your individual driving habits.
- Added weight that you don't need reduces fuel economy significantly. We're all guilty of this one!
- Only using the dash air conditioner when it is absolutely necessary will save a significant amount of fuel.
- Use regular gas unless your owner's manual specifies a higher octane gas. You're just throwing money away when you pay the extra money for premium fuel.

Note: Do you know how many miles you get to a gallon of gas? Here's how to find out. Fill the fuel tank and write down the odometer reading. The next time you stop for gas fill the tank again. Now divide the miles you traveled between fill-ups by the amount of gas you bought the second time you filled up. This is how many miles you are getting to a gallon of gas.

Mark J. Polk

Chapter 12

Backing Up, the Big Dilemma

If you're going to tow a trailer the day will come when you have to back it up. From the time we are children we're programmed to do everything forward. You learn to crawl, walk and run going forwards not backwards. For the most part when we drive a vehicle we are going forward, and when we did learn to back a vehicle it was not that difficult. It's like if some one tells you to turn left or turn right, you know if you turn left the vehicle will go to the left. Even when you're backing the vehicle, if you want it to back to the left you turn the steering wheel to the left. It's almost natural; you look over your shoulder, turn the steering wheel and back the direction you want to go. **Not so with a trailer.** First of all you can't look over your shoulder; all you will see is the front of the trailer. Second of all, if you turn the steering wheel to the left the trailer is going to go to the right. The secret to backing a trailer is to learn a technique that does not require you to go against your natural instincts. When you're not confused about turning in the opposite direction you want to go it is much easier to back a trailer.

I want to offer a couple of different options on how to back a trailer and I feel confident that you'll find one that will work for you. But, regardless of how good the method is for learning to back a trailer, the only way you will become proficient at it is to practice, practice and practice some more. It's like learning to ride a bicycle, almost everybody falls a few times but with practice you quickly get proficient at it.

Pull Through Sites

Most campgrounds that you go to offer what are referred to as pull through sites. This means that you can pull in and out of the site without having to back up the trailer. You can often call ahead and reserve pull through sites. Or you can go miles and miles out of your way to find a campground that has pull through sites. You can attempt to do everything possible to avoid having to back the trailer. But what happens if you don't enter that gas station just right and you have to back up, or somebody's vehicle is blocking your pull through site. Wouldn't it be easier if you just learned to back the trailer? There would be much less stress involved if you didn't have to worry about it during your entire vacation.

Can I Learn to Back a Trailer?

I am convinced that anybody can learn to back up a trailer. I will admit that some people just have a knack for it. It just seems to be easy. But for other people it is much more difficult. I feel that it is all about learning a technique that works for you. Take for example a natural born artist. They can paint a beautiful picture as though it were nothing. But somebody without that natural ability is embarrassed to even try. Now what if we went to the store and bought a paint-by-numbers painting. If you follow the directions you end up with a beautiful painting. You simply found a technique to accomplish something you didn't think you could do.

Shorter versus Longer

Would it be easier to back a shorter trailer than a longer trailer? You would think so but that's not the case. If you don't believe me take a garden tractor with a small trailer attached to it and try backing it up. You can look over your shoulder and see everything you are doing but it is still difficult to back it up. A shorter trailer reacts much quicker to steering movements than a longer trailer. This is because the trailers axles are the pivot point and on a shorter trailer the axles are closer to the hitch ball mount on the tow vehicle. If you're backing a pop-up or short travel trailer it will require slower reactions and movements in the steering wheel than a longer trailer will.

Mirrors

Before we get started on backing techniques there are a couple of things we should discuss. One topic is mirrors. Again, some people have the natural ability to back a trailer by simply using the mirrors on the tow vehicle. On the other hand, some people with the natural ability to back a trailer find it difficult to do when using mirrors. I know this sounds strange but it's true. They feel that mirrors don't show you what the trailer is actually doing, especially when you're backing and a turn is required. The trick to backing without mirrors is to back in so the trailer turns towards the left side (driver's side) of the vehicle. This way you can look out the window over your shoulder and see what the trailer is doing. Backing from the right side (passenger side) is the blind side. It is much more difficult and dangerous to back from the right side. If you notice almost every campground you stop at is designed to allow you to back into the site from the driver's side. Using mirrors or not using mirrors is up to you, but whenever possible you should have a spotter to assist you when backing.

Spotters

The most important help you can have when backing a trailer is a spotter. They can watch what is happening behind you, in your blind spots and let you know what corrections need to be made. When you have a spotter you both need to agree on a set of rules. What I mean by this is where will the spotter be located, how will you communicate with each other, and who is telling whom what to do. Rule number one is, when you use a spotter whatever happens is the spotter's responsiblity. They are your eyes and the driver should do exactly what the spotter tells them to do. Rule number two is, use only one spotter. If you use two spotters I guarantee you they will both be telling you to do something different. You should develop hand signals that you both understand. How will you start, stop, turn left, turn right and know when to pull forward. The spotter needs to be in your view at all times.

> **Caution:** Never continue to back a trailer when you cannot see your spotter.

Eventually the day will come that you have to back a trailer without assistance. This can be done but it requires that you take extra precautions. Before you back the trailer you need to inspect the area behind and around where you will be backing. Let's take a campground site, you have a picnic table, BBQ grill, trees with low branches, water, electric and sewer hook ups and you need to position the trailer so you can use your awning. This can be a lot to watch for when you're on your own. So let's get started on how we can do this.

Backing Techniques

I personally have two techniques that I prefer. I call them assisted and unassisted. The assisted technique should be used whenever possible. This is the technique I used when I was the sales manager at an RV dealership. I have total and complete faith in this technique when it is followed properly. If you ever attended an RV show you know what I mean. You are allocated a certain amount of space and in an effort to show as many units as possible you had to back the trailers in within inches of the walls, campers and other obstacles. I have organized many RV shows and never so much as scratched a bumper.

Assisted Technique

The assisted technique implies what it says, that you have a spotter to assist you. It is quite simple. **The golden rule is for the driver to do exactly what the spotter tells you to do.** You may want to discuss who will drive and who will spot, because with this technique the spotter is responsible for putting the trailer where you want it. The first step is to establish hand signals that you both understand and agree on. Once this is done do a thorough inspection of the area you are backing into. It is important that you check the area immediately behind the trailer because

Mark J. Polk

for this technique to work effectively the spotter has to stand in front of the tow vehicle. Now you place an object (small orange traffic cones work well) on both sides of the site where you want the back of the trailer to stop at. The spotter will stand in front of the tow vehicle, in clear view of the driver, and can slowly walk from right to left checking blind spots and watching for the back of the trailer to reach the cones.

> **Caution:** You need to stop occasionally and look behind the trailer. **Small children and pets** can wander behind the trailer without you seeing them.

The reason this technique is so effective is because neither the spotter nor the driver has to think about doing the opposite when backing the trailer. The first step is for the driver to roll the windows down and turn the radio off. The driver leaves their hand on the top of the steering wheel like you're accustomed to and because the spotter is in front of the vehicle they simply tell the driver to turn the steering wheel in the direction they want the back of the trailer to go. So, if the spotter wants the trailer to go to the right they tell the driver to turn to the right. The driver slowly turns and backs in the direction the spotter tells them to. Nobody has to think about it, the driver just does what the spotter says to do.

The key to driving is **slowly turning and backing** in the direction the spotter tells you to. The two biggest mistakes made are turning the steering wheel too much and holding it in the turned position to long. If either of these mistakes occurs the result is that it will require greater correction to get straightened out, and if you continue to back while holding the wheel in that position too long the tow vehicle and trailer can jackknife. It will require some practice. The spotter will need to learn that once the trailer is into the turn its time to go the opposite direction to bring the tow vehicle and trailer back in line.

Do not be concerned if you have to stop, pull forward and start again. This will happen more than once during the early stages. Try it, and with practice I guarantee that before you know it you'll be backing like pros.

If you have always used mirrors for backing, or you prefer to use mirrors the spotter will be located behind the trailer. You need to keep the spotter in your mirrors at all times and remember in this case you turn the steering wheel in the opposite direction that the spotter is pointing in.

Unassisted Technique

The assisted technique is the preferred method, but you need to be prepared in the event that you have to back a trailer without assistance. If the backing maneuver is more than just backing in a straight line, and a turn is required, try to always back from the left side (drivers side). Backing from the left will allow you to see where the trailer is going. Backing from the right side (passenger's side) is your blind side and it is nearly impossible to tell where the trailer is going.

Earlier we discussed that the reason it's difficult to back a trailer is because it is the opposite of everything we have been taught. Fortunately there is a way to back a trailer unassisted without having to work against our natural instincts. This may sound a bit confusing at first, but if you think about it, it makes sense and the good thing is it works.

It is extremely important that you inspect the area behind and around where you will be backing. Look for any obstacles that may be in the way to include low hanging tree branches, picnic tables and utility hook-ups. You need to stop occasionally and inspect the area immediately behind the trailer.

Caution: If children are present in the area ask somebody to watch behind the trailer.

It is a good idea to place some orange traffic cones along the path you want the trailer to follow when you're backing. If you decide it's not necessary to mark a path you do need to place some type of object in your view where you want the back of the trailer to stop.

In the assisted method we kept our hand on the top of the steering wheel and did exactly what the spotter told us to do. In the unassisted method we place our hand on the bottom of the steering wheel in the center. Now if you want the back of the trailer to go to your left you slowly turn the wheel to your left as you back. To go to your right slowly turn the wheel to your right as you back. It's that easy. By placing your hand at the bottom of the steering wheel you don't have to confuse yourself with turning it in the opposite direction. Remember the two biggest mistakes are turning the steering wheel too much and holding it in the turned position too long. If either of these mistakes happen it may be necessary to pull forward and start over. It may also be necessary to stop, get out and check your progress, especially if you're backing from the right. Take your trailer to a large open area where you can practice and before long you'll be showing off at the campground.

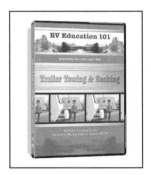

Our Trailer Towing Weights Hitchwork & Backing DVD demonstrates both of these backing techniques. See the RV Education 101 order form at back of book.

Chapter 13

Towing Behind a Motorhome

In the world of RV's a "Dinghy" or a "Toad" are terms used for the vehicle you are towing behind your motorhome. Making the decision to purchase a motorhome will eventually require more decisions, one of them being, will you tow a vehicle behind the motorhome.

If you haven't made the decision to tow, or not to tow when you initially purchased your RV, you will probably decide soon after venturing out the first couple times with the RV. When you arrive at your destination and hook the RV up, you might discover that you need to run to the local grocery store, or you want to go do some sight seeing. You will probably wish you had a small, economical vehicle along with you. It's convenient to tow a vehicle behind your motorhome and it's not that difficult once you learn how.

One problem is when you're not aware of what options are available. The thought of towing a vehicle can seem confusing, almost overwhelming. Another problem is not taking the time to learn how to properly tow a dinghy. I have seen many accidents just waiting to happen with motorhomes towing vehicles. This is because of various reasons like the tow vehicle exceeding weight limits, tow bars not properly set up, no braking system on the towed vehicle, towing vehicles without the proper modifications and much more.

That's the purpose and goal of this section, to help you learn how to properly tow a dinghy, and to assist you in making the right decisions to meet your particular towing needs. For the sake of a better word we will

Mark J. Polk

use the word "dinghy" to refer to the towed vehicle throughout this section.

Why Tow a Dinghy?

A motorhome offers us the freedom to explore the open road. We can go where we want when we want. But what happens when we arrive at a destination where we plan to stay put for a day, a week or a month? How do we explore the area, or take a quick trip to the grocery store? Well, we have our bikes with us right! Bikes are nice and we even get some much needed exercise, but are they really practical for touring the surrounding area or taking a day trip? Probably not, so what do we do? One option is to disconnect everything from the motorhome and take it. What a pain this can be just for a loaf of bread. Another option is to tow a vehicle behind the motorhome. Now when we need a loaf of bread or want to take a day trip we have our transportation readily available. This makes much more sense, but just how do we do this?

What are My Towing Options?

You basically have three options when it comes to towing a vehicle behind your motorhome. You can tow the vehicle with all four wheels up, with two wheels up, or with all four wheels down. In recent years towing with all four wheels down, using a tow bar, has become more popular, with more automobile manufacturers building vehicles that can be towed without modifications.

It's important that you understand all of the options available to you and that you take the time to research what method is best suited for you. There are many things to consider like the overall cost involved with the method you choose, weights, aesthetics, supplemental brakes, difficulty in hooking up and unhooking, vehicle modifications, warranty and more. My goal is to assist you in making an informed decision on which method is best suited for your particular needs. Let's look at some pros and cons for the three different options.

Four Wheels Up, (Car Hauler)

What this means is you use a car hauler/trailer to transport your vehicle. This is not always the most practical method for towing a vehicle, but based on your circumstances it might be the best choice for you. It's one sure way to avoid any concern and costly damage to your towed vehicle transmission and to avoid mileage from accumulating on the odometer. Let's take a look.

Pros	Four Wheels Up Cons
If you can't tow your vehicle with all four wheels down without costly modifications.	A car hauler can be a costly method to tow your vehicle.
If you're towing a classic automobile, antique car, race car, or want the flexibility to tow more than one vehicle.	With the additional weight of the car hauler you might exceed one or more of the RV's weight ratings.
If there isn't a base plate or tow brackets available for the vehicle you want to tow.	It might be difficult to find space to store the trailer at campgrounds.
Saves wear and tear on the towed vehicle	It can decrease maneuverability.

Two Wheels Up, (Tow Dolly)

Tow dollies are two wheeled trailers used to transport the vehicle you are towing with the drive wheels off of the ground. The tow dolly coupler connects to the ball mount on the motorhome and then you drive the towed vehicle up the tow dolly ramps so the drive wheels are on the dolly. You secure the towed vehicle using tie-down straps or chains. Tow dollies are intended for front wheel drive vehicles. Many RV consumers feel that a tow dolly offers convenience and is an affordable choice when compared to the equipment required to tow a vehicle with all four wheel down. In many cases tow dollies are already equipped with brakes, saving you money for a supplemental brake system and they are already wired for lights. There is not a great deal of maintenance required other than repacking the wheel bearings as required, having the brakes inspected and maintaining the tires and lights. Let's look at some pros and cons and you can decide if a tow dolly is the right choice for you.

Mark J. Polk

Pros	Tow Dolly	Cons
If you can't tow your vehicle with all four wheels down without costly modifications.		You cannot back up with a tow dolly.
If you want the flexibility of towing more than one vehicle.		With the additional weight of the tow dolly you might exceed one or more of the RV's weight ratings.
If a base plate or tow brackets are not available for the vehicle you want to tow.		It might be difficult to find space to store the tow dolly at campgrounds.
Saves wear and tear on your vehicle.		Hooking up & unhooking is more difficult.

Four Wheels Down, (Tow Bar)

I mentioned earlier this method for towing your vehicle is becoming the RV consumer's favorite choice in many cases. The ease of hitching and unhitching, not having to deal with a trailer and the fact that more vehicles are being built that can be towed this way all contribute to why this method is gaining in popularity. You be the judge.

Pros	Four Wheels Down	Cons
If you already own a vehicle that can be towed with all four wheels down.		You can only tow one vehicle without the expense of another base plate.
Easier to hook up and unhook than a tow dolly or car trailer.		Additional expense for a supplemental brake system.
You don't have to worry about where you can store the tow dolly or trailer.		The additional expense for the base plate or towing brackets and wiring for lights
The tow bar easily stores either on the rear of the motorhome or front of the tow vehicle.		Additional expense if your vehicle requires modifications to tow with all four wheels on the ground.

What Vehicles Can I Tow With Four Wheels Down?

Before you make the decision to tow a vehicle with all four wheels down you need to do your homework. There are some manufacturer approved vehicles that can be towed without any modifications to the drive-train or transmission, but there are a lot more that will require some type of modification to tow it with all four wheels on the ground. There are many factors involved such as automatic transmissions, two wheel drive vehicles, four wheel drive vehicles, the type of transfer case and more.

Most vehicles with an automatic transmission cannot be towed with all four wheels down unless it is a four wheel drive, and even then it requires a transfer case that can be shifted into neutral. Front wheel drive vehicles with manual transmissions and most four wheel drive vehicles with a manual transfer case are among the best choices for towing with all four wheels down. Even if you have a vehicle that can be towed with all four wheels down it's quite possible that it will have towing speed and/or mileage restrictions. So where do we start?

Check with the Vehicle Manufacturer

Start by reading your vehicle owner's manual to determine if the vehicle can be towed without any drive-train modifications. If the vehicle is approved by the manufacturer to be towed with all four wheels down the owner's manual will provide specific instructions on the proper procedures to use when towing. If the manual does not provide **specific instructions** on whether or not it can be towed with all four wheels down, or if you're unclear about any towing restrictions check with the vehicle manufacturer. Don't hesitate to contact the vehicle manufacturer to get specific information about towing a vehicle. Your vehicle warranty could be voided from damage caused by towing a vehicle and not following the manufacturer's guidelines. Do not rely on what a vehicle salesperson tells you. Almost all vehicles approved to be towed with all four wheels down will include this information in the vehicle owner's manual.

Follow all Special Instructions

If you don't already have a vehicle to tow, a good resource to check on what vehicles can be towed with all four wheels down is at **www.motorhomemagazine.com**. As a service to its readers each year they publish a "Dinghy Towing Guide." Keep in mind that this is only a guide. It is **your responsibility** to make absolutely sure the vehicle you

Mark J. Polk

are considering can be towed with all four wheels down, with no drive-train modifications, before you make a purchase or actually tow the vehicle. Information in the guide is subject to change at any time! Always check the vehicle by year model. Just because you could tow a certain model with all four wheels down one year doesn't mean every year model of that vehicle can be towed with all four wheels down.

> **Note:** The vehicle manufacturer is the final authority.

This guide includes manufacturer approved vehicles for towing without modifications that can be towed at speeds of at least 55 MPH and for distances of at least 200 miles without special procedures. Pay particular attention to any speed or distance restrictions that could ultimately affect your vehicle warranty. Also, pay attention to the restrictions and special instructions listed in the footnotes. The guide lists other valuable information like vehicle curb weights, fuel economy and base retail prices. Keep in mind the lighter the vehicle, the better it is. It is easy to exceed a motorhomes receiver weight rating and the Gross Combined Weight Rating (GCWR). Note also that some models listed in their four wheel drive version can be towed without modifications, but their two wheel drive version of the same model can not be towed with four wheels down.

Be sure and follow any special towing instructions or procedures found in the vehicle owner's manual. You might be required to remove a certain fuse before you tow the vehicle or to stop towing after so many miles and start the vehicle to allow drive train components to be lubricated.

> **Note:** Following any and all special instructions can save you money and protect the vehicle warranty.

Vehicle Modifications

There are many reasons why some vehicles are not approved by the manufacturer to be towed with all four wheels down. It may be that the vehicle will not track or follow the motorhome properly, or maybe a component in the drive-train could be damaged, and sometimes it is because of liability and warranty concerns. Another reason is the expense involved for a manufacturer to test and approve vehicles for towing with all four wheels down.

The good news is, in many cases where vehicles are not approved by the manufacturer to be towed with all four wheels down; they can still be towed in this method by adding some type of aftermarket accessory. The most common problem is, when the engine is not running components in the drive-train that require lubrication are not being lubricated. Towing a vehicle like this can result in thousands of dollars worth of damage, and/or possibly overheat and catch on fire.

There are specialty aftermarket products and modifications available such as drive shaft disconnects and/or transmission lube pumps that can be added so a vehicle is mechanically capable of being towed without damaging the drive-train.

> Remco, the towing experts, **www.remcotowing.com** offers a product line that adapts to approximately 80% of the vehicles in today's market.

> ➤ The **Remco drive shaft coupling** prevents automatic transmission damage to your rear wheel drive vehicle. This is basically a mechanical clutch that is installed into the rear portion of the vehicle drive shaft. The coupling has a control cable so you can engage for driving and disengage for towing right from the driver's seat. No mileage accumulates on the odometer when the coupling is disengaged.

> ➤ The **Remco lube pump** prevents transmission damage to your front wheel drive vehicle. Automatic transmissions are lubricated by an engine driven transmission fluid pump, which means when you are towing the vehicle with the engine off the transmission is not being lubricated. The Remco lube pump was developed to provide a reliable lubrication system for the tow vehicle transmission when you're towing.

Mark J. Polk

> The **Remco axle lock** disconnects the automatic transmission for towing a front wheel drive vehicle. The axle lock makes it possible to tow many of today's front wheel drive vehicles with automatic transmissions and it's easy to engage and disengage.

> **Note:** Contact the aftermarket product manufacturer to check on details pertaining to towing specific vehicles.

If for some reason the vehicle you want to tow falls in the 20% that cannot be modified for towing, for whatever reason, you still have the option of possibly using a tow dolly or a car trailer. All vehicles can be towed on a car trailer, as long as you don't exceed weight ratings, and most front wheel drive vehicles can be towed with a tow dolly. This would be a good time to discuss some weight issues.

Weight Issues

Driving or towing with an overloaded RV and dinghy combination is a leading cause for RV accidents. Weight ratings are established by the manufacturer and are based on the weakest link in the chain. When you exceed a weight rating you are overloading one or more components on the RV and risk wearing the component out prematurely or complete failure of the component. You never want to exceed any weight ratings. Let's take a look at what weight ratings concern us as it pertains to towing a dinghy.

Motorhome Tow Ratings

One of the first steps is to find out how much weight the motorhome itself is rated to tow, but possibly more important is to find out how much the hitch receiver on the motorhome is rated to tow. For the sake of an example let's say your motorhome is rated to tow 6,500 pounds. Now go and look at the label on the hitch receiver, on the back of the motorhome, to see what it is rated for. Many of the older gasoline powered motorhomes came equipped with receivers rated for 3,500 pounds and many of the newer gasoline powered motorhomes are rated to tow 5,000 pounds. **What this means is, regardless of what the motorhome is rated to tow you can not exceed the hitch receiver rating.** This is mainly due to the frame rail extensions on the motorhome chassis. When a manufacturer builds a motorhome they extend the chassis frame rails of the truck chassis to accommodate the length of the motorhome. This is usually accomplished by welding the extended frame rails to the existing chassis. This added length can compromise the amount of weight the motorhome can safely tow so they use a hitch receiver rated at less weight to limit the amount of weight you can tow. At a minimum the hitch receiver must be rated to tow the Gross Vehicle Weight Rating (GVWR) of the vehicle you are towing.

Great strides have been made in recent years especially between Ford and Workhorse gasoline powered motorhome chassis'. They have both increased the Gross Vehicle Weight Ratings (GVWR) and the Gross Combined Weight Ratings (GCWR) of their chassis'.

Tow ratings for diesel chassis' can range anywhere from 10,000 pounds to 15,000 pounds and therefore tow ratings are not much of a concern. The thing you will need to keep in mind here is that a diesel chassis might be able to tow 10,000 pounds but chances are the tow bar and other hitch components are probably rated for much less weight. The majority of tow bars manufactured are rated to tow 5,000 pounds; some companies do manufacturer tow bars that are rated for heavier applications. Be sure and check towing and hitch components for maximum weight ratings.

Hitch Receiver Classifications

I mentioned a moment ago the hitch receiver on the back of the motorhome is rated to tow a certain amount of weight. There is usually a label affixed to the receiver to let you know the maximum rated weight you can tow.

> **Note:** The lighter the vehicle being towed the better. It will put less strain on the motorhomes drive train components, brakes, and the motorhome will handle better.

Mark J. Polk

Hitch Ball and Ball Mount

I also mentioned that every component on your RV has a weight rating, so do all of the components used to hitch the vehicle to the motorhome. In addition to the hitch receiver weight rating the hitch ball and ball mount you use also have maximum weight ratings that they are capable of handling. Hitch balls have three basic measurements, the ball diameter, the shank diameter and the shank length. Ball diameter sizes come in 1 7/8", 2" and 2 5/16". The ball size must be the right size for the coupler on the tow bar, tow dolly or trailer you are towing, and be rated to tow the vehicles Gross Vehicle Weight Rating (GVWR.) The hitch ball base and shank play a major role in the hitch balls weight rating. The ball mount is the removable portion of the hitch that slides into the hitch receiver and must be rated for the amount of weight you are towing.

Tow Bars & Safety Cables

Most of the tow bars manufactured are rated to tow up to 5,000 pounds, but there are some tow bars designed for heavier applications with up to 10,000 pound ratings. If you haven't already purchased a tow bar make sure you check the rating of the tow bar you are considering. You also need to take the fully loaded vehicle you are towing to a set of scales and have it weighed to make sure the vehicle doesn't exceed the tow bar or any other hitch component weight rating. You can look in the Yellow Pages under moving and storage companies, gravel pits and commercial truck stops to locate a set of scales. Remember, you never want to exceed any weight rating.

All states and Provinces require the use of safety chains or cables when you are towing a vehicle. Each component of the safety chain or cable system must be rated for the amount of weight you are towing. This includes the hooks, links, and the location where the chains or cables attach to the motorhome and to the towed vehicle.

Gross Combined Weight Rating (GCWR)

Another important weight consideration in addition to the hitch receiver is the motorhomes Gross Combined Weight Rating (GCWR). Look for the manufacturers GCWR on the RVIA weight label or in the chassis manual or in the motorhome manual. This is the combined weight of the fully loaded motorhome and the fully loaded tow vehicle when weighed together. The hitch receiver on the motorhome might be rated for 5,000 pounds, but when the motorhome is fully loaded for travel you may only have 3,000 pounds, or less, before you exceed the GCWR. This is especially true on older motorhomes and this is also why it is extremely important to have the motorhome and the towed vehicle weighed together. I once had a customer that assumed their tow vehicle only weighed 3,500 pounds, but when I sent them to the scales it actually weighed over 5,000 pounds. You cannot exceed the GCWR. This is the maximum weight the motorhomes components can safely handle. Remember, you never want to exceed any weight rating.

Types of Tow Bars

Now that we have a better understanding of what we can tow and some of the weight limitations this would probably be a good time to discuss the different types of tow bars that are available to the RV consumer. Tow bars like everything else have come a long way in recent years. They are lighter, yet stronger and most are self aligning making it much easier to hook up and they are self-storing. There are three basic groups that tow bars fall in.

1) A rigid tow bar
2) A self-aligning vehicle mounted tow bar
3) A self-aligning motorhome mounted tow bar.

Self-aligning tow bars afford you the convenience and ease of hooking the vehicle up by yourself and they easily store on the vehicle or the motorhome. Let's take a look at what each type has to offer to help make your buying decision a little easier.

Mark J. Polk

Rigid Tow Bars

We'll start with the most basic type. Rigid tow bars do not collapse, or self-align. They are one solid piece and require precise alignment between the tow bar coupler and the hitch ball when you are hooking up. It really requires two people to hook this type of tow bar up because

there is no adjustment. In most cases a rigid tow bar is removed from the vehicle when you're not using it. They are the least expensive type and are great if you don't tow very often or if you are on a limited budget.

Self- aligning Car Mounted Tow Bars

Car mounted tow bars were the first self-aligning tow bars to be introduced to the RV consumer. They made the job of hooking the towed vehicle to the motorhome much easier, and when you weren't using the tow bar it would simply

Courtesy of Roadmaster,Inc.
www.roadmasterinc.com

fold away on the front of the vehicle for easy storage. There was no more heavy lifting involved or struggling to make connections. Over time, these car mounted tow bars were improved making them even easier to use. If you prefer to remove it when not in use, most are simple to remove. If you choose to leave it on you need to take precautions that it doesn't get stolen or damaged in an accident.

Self-aligning Motorhome Mounted Tow Bars

Motorhome mounted tow bars were first introduced to the RV consumer in the mid 90's. Since that time they have become the RV consumer's choice in tow bars. They are somewhat lighter and easier to use than a car mounted tow bar, and

Courtesy of Blue Ox
www.blueox.us

they are easy to secure on the rear of the motorhome. Some of these tow bars eliminate the need for a drop ball mount and the ball coupler is replaced by a swivel joint. Manufacturers continue to advance in tow bar technology every day.

What else do I need to Tow with Four Wheels Down

Having the right vehicle to tow, the right tow bar to tow with and being within all of the weight ratings is a good start, but this is only part of the equation to safely towing a dinghy. You will need some additional equipment like a base plate or tow brackets, safety cables, a light kit and some type of supplemental braking system. Let's see what else we need and why we need it.

Base Plates & Tow Brackets

We talked briefly about the different ways a tow bar attaches to the motorhome, but how do we attach the tow bar to the vehicle we are towing? You need to have a base plate or towing brackets installed on the vehicle so you can attach the tow bar. The base plates are custom designed to fit a particular vehicle. They bolt to the frame of the vehicle and some require additional drilling and possibly modifying the front of the vehicle or the bumper. Manufacturers like Blue Ox, **www.blueox.us** and Roadmaster, Inc. **www.roadmasterinc.com** are designing high tech brackets that are nearly impossible to see, keeping the aesthetics of the vehicle appealing to the eye.

I mentioned earlier that nearly 80% of the cars in today's market can be modified for towing with all four wheels down. This means that base plates and towing brackets have to be made for all of these vehicles. Keep in mind that just because there might be a base plate or towing brackets for a particular vehicle doesn't mean the vehicle can be towed trouble free with all four wheels down. Always remember to do your homework first. On the other hand if a base plate or towing brackets are not available for a particular vehicle this probably does mean it cannot be towed with all four wheels down. In a case like this you will need to look into the possibility of using a tow dolly or car trailer.

Mark J. Polk

Safety Cables or Chains

I briefly touched on safety cables when we were talking about weight ratings. States and Provinces require safety cables or safety chains, rated for the weight of the load, in the event the vehicle is separated from the motorhome.

One end of the cables are attached to the receiver on the motorhome, and the other end to a permanent fixture on the tow vehicle, normally the base plate or tow bracket. The cables are crossed, "X" to form a saddle that would prevent the coupler from contacting the road surface in the event of a separation. The cables need to be long enough to allow for full turns but not so long that they drag on the ground.

Light System or Light Kit

It's obvious that part of a safe towing system would include brake lights, taillights and turn signals on the vehicle being towed. There are basically two options when it comes to lights. You can use some type of aftermarket light bar or magnetic lights that you temporarily attach to the dinghy when you are towing. This might be an option for somebody that doesn't tow that often. The light bar would have to be removed and stored when you're not using it.

The other option is to wire the vehicle lights directly to the motorhome trailer wiring harness plug. Manufacturers like Blue Ox™ and Roadmaster™ offer after market wiring kits designed just for this. These kits include all of the necessary components to wire the vehicle and to protect the vehicle electrical system from electrical feedback that can damage sensitive electronic components. If you don't feel comfortable doing the wiring yourself take it to your local RV dealer or authorized service center.

Supplemental Brake Systems

The brakes on a motorhome are designed by the vehicle manufacturer to stop the weight of that particular vehicle, not the additional weight being towed behind it. This additional weight adds a substantial increase to the distance required to stop safely. In many situations the brakes on a motorhome are already working at the maximum capability. When you add to that a towed vehicle without brakes, you are asking for trouble. Some chassis manufacturers state that towing weight in excess of 1,500 pounds requires an independent braking system and a break away system.

Most U.S. States and Canadian Provinces have their own laws on the requirement for brakes on a towed trailer. The word **trailer** also applies to a **vehicle** being towed behind a motorhome. These laws are normally based on the amount of weight being towed. One problem with this is that it might be legal to tow a 2,000 pound trailer with no brakes in the state where you live, but as soon as you cross the state line of a bordering state it is illegal to tow the same trailer without brakes. Add to this your insurance company may not cover you in the event of an accident involving a trailer with no braking system. Again, the most important reason is for your safety and the safety of others.

Braking Laws

Safety is not the only reason to get a braking system. In many states it's the law. If you are involved in an accident where a braking system is required and you don't have one, you could be sued. Braking laws vary in different states so check with your state on braking requirements. Many states and Canadian provinces require brakes for weights above 2,000 lbs.

If the current trend continues, almost all states will require braking systems within a few years. Breakaway systems are also required in many states. I highly recommend that you purchase a breakaway system along with your braking system.

Wear and Tear

A braking system can greatly reduce wear and tear to both your motorhome and vehicle brakes. A good braking system can also help to prevent possible brake failure due to brakes overheating on motorhomes. Most manufacturers of braking systems claim a reduced stopping distance by as much as 20% to 30% with the use of a braking system. This is achieved by the motorhome and the towed vehicle braking themselves and not the motorhome braking both, thus putting less strain on the motorhomes brakes, the hitch and the towing system.

Types of Supplemental Braking Systems

There are many different types of supplemental braking systems available on the market today. For the most part they can be put into the following categories: surge, hydraulic, air and vacuum. Within these types of supplemental brake systems there are several different sensing mechanisms used such as a mercury switch, proportional valve, pendulum, receiver slide, accelerometers, computer and the brake lights on the motorhome.

To go one step further there are many different ways these brake systems are activated including hydraulic, air, electric, inertia, vacuum and cable. Some of these systems are simple to install and use and some are much more complex. Some systems can be left in place once they are installed and others need to be removed and put back in place every time you tow. Keep in mind that these supplemental brake systems are not designed to make the motorhome stop any quicker; they are designed to help slow the towed vehicle down and to help decrease the stopping distance due to the increased weight of the towed vehicle. **Before you decide on a particular supplemental brake system there are several things to consider:**

➤ What type of braking system is most compatible with the type of motorhome you have?

➤ How often do you plan to tow?

➤ Do you want to tow the same vehicle all of the time, or will you be towing different vehicles?

➤ Are you going to do the installation yourself or have it done by somebody else?

➤ Is the system going to involve tampering with your vehicles brake system?

➤ What kind of warranty does the braking system offer?

I want to give you a brief overview on the types of supplemental brake systems available so you understand some of your options. I am not suggesting, recommending or promoting any particular brand or manufacturer, and you should talk to your RV dealer about which type of supplemental brake system would work best based on your needs.

Supplemental Surge Brake Systems

Surge brake systems operate when you apply the motorhome brakes and the momentum of the towed vehicle pushes (surges) toward the motorhome. In most cases a slide receiver is used to sense this movement and when the motorhome slows down the towed vehicle pushes on the slide receiver and a cable activates the towed vehicle brakes. These systems don't require modifications to the towed vehicle or motorhome brakes.

Supplemental Hydraulic & Air Brake Systems

These systems are activated when pressure is applied to the motorhome brakes causing a proportional amount of pressure to be applied to the towed vehicle brakes. Air is transmitted from the motorhome to the towed vehicle brake system either from the motorhome airbrake system or if it has hydraulic brakes from an air compressor usually mounted to the RV. These systems require tapping into the motorhome air and/or hydraulic systems.

Supplemental Vacuum Brake Systems

Some vacuum systems create its own vacuum and some use the vacuum system on the motorhome. Most of these systems use a vacuum assisted arm to pull down the towed vehicle brake pedal when a decrease of forward momentum is sensed. The vacuum system is also applied to the towed vehicle power assist unit.

Other Supplemental Brake Systems use a self-contained unit that temporarily attaches to the brake pedal in the towed vehicle. Most of these use an inertia sensor to detect a decrease in forward momentum.

Mark J. Polk

An air cylinder pushes an arm forward applying pressure to the towed vehicle brakes.

There are many effective supplemental brake systems on the market that are difficult to put in one particular category or another. Some use high-speed electric actuators to apply the towed vehicle brakes; some are cable driven by an electric solenoid, some are proportional and some aren't. **Talk to your RV dealer about which type is right for you.**

Break Away Systems

Breakaway systems are designed to stop the towed vehicle if it were to break away, or separate from the motorhome. Many states and provinces require this added measure of safety. Be sure and ask about a break away system when you purchase your supplemental brake system.

Tow Bar Set-up

Perhaps the most important thing to keep in mind when setting up the tow bar is to keep it as level as possible between the motorhome and the towed vehicle. What I mean by this is the receiver on the motorhome should be as close to the same height as the tow bar attachment points on the base plate of the tow vehicle. Blue Ox recommends that the receiver hitch of the motorhome should never be more than 4 inches higher than the base plate attachment points. They go on to say that 4 inches or less keeps the tow bar level with the ground or slightly angled up towards the RV from the car.

> **Caution:** The tow bar should never be angled UP towards the car from the RV.

The reason for this is simple. If you have to stop quickly or make a panic stop and the distance is greater than 4 inches out of level, the tow bar coupler could disconnect from ball mount due to the angle and force from the braking action. There are many other factors involved that contribute to the RV and towed vehicle set up, but keeping the towing system as level as possible is crucial.

Drop Receivers

So how do we get a level towing system when the distance between the motorhome receiver and the tow bar attachment points is greater than 4 inches? It's easy; you purchase a drop receiver to keep the tow bar level. Drop receivers are available in 2-inch to 10-inch drops. If the base plate is higher than the receiver hitch on the motorhome the drop receiver can be inverted.

Courtesy of Blue Ox
www.blueox.us

On the Road Inspection Checklist

A good habit to get into when you are towing a dinghy, tow dolly or trailer is to inspect the hitch work, vehicle or trailer every time you stop, whether it's to re-fuel or to spend the night somewhere.

Every time you stop you should check:

➢ The tow bar coupler, base plate and all hardware for secure mounting.

➢ Check for any loose nuts or bolts and check all pins and clips for secure mounting. Have any damaged component in the towing system repaired before using it.

➢ Check that the safety cables are still properly attached.

➢ Check that the break away cable and light cord are properly attached.

➢ Check for any tires loosing air on the towed vehicle and/or trailer.

➢ Every morning before you leave use a quality tire inflation gauge to check the tire pressure on both the motorhome and the towed vehicle. Adjust the tire pressure according to the tire manufacturer specifications. Do not check tires when they are hot after traveling more than one mile. The readings are only accurate when the tires are cold, before traveling more than one mile.

Mark J. Polk

➤ Feel the wheels on the tow vehicle and/or trailer to see if they are hot to the touch. Wheels hot to the touch are an indication that there might be a problem with the brakes or wheel bearings.

➤ If you are towing a tow dolly check the towing straps on the vehicle wheels for secure mounting.

➤ Verify that all lights are operational.

➤ Do not continue to tow a vehicle or trailer until any defects in the towing system have been corrected.

Tow Bar Care & Maintenance

Tow bars and other components in the towing system wear out over time. They are subject to a great deal of physical abuse as they perform the function they were designed for. The good news is that by following some simple care and maintenance procedures you can get many years of reliable service from your tow bar and other towing components in the system.

For starters, keeping your tow bar clean will add to the life of the tow bar. It's natural for the tow bar to be exposed to road dirt and grime. Eventually the dirt and grime will lead to problems with the tow bar not operating properly or the tow bar leg latches to not latch properly. Clean and lubricate the tow bar in accordance with the manufacturer instructions.

I have mentioned it a couple of times already, but always inspect the nuts and bolts for tightness and secure mounting. Loose nuts and bolts allow certain components to move that aren't supposed to move which can lead to component failure. Inspect all locking pins for wear and proper operation. Replace any worn locking pins with new ones. Inspect the coupler for proper operation and any signs of wear. Use a cover to protect the tow bar when not in use.

Clean the safety cables and the light cord. Store these items in a storage bag when not in use. Inspect and clean other components of the towing system like the ball mount, hitch ball, base plate on the tow vehicle and the receiver on the motorhome.

Note: If you are in doubt about the condition of any component in the towing system have it inspected by a professional.

Tow Dolly

I mentioned earlier that tow dollies are two wheeled trailers used to transport the vehicle you are towing with the drive wheels off of the ground. Tow dollies make a good choice when the vehicle you're towing cannot be towed with all four wheels down or if the vehicle would require expensive modifications to tow with all four wheels down.

Selecting the Right Tow Dolly

Tow dollies are manufactured to accommodate a certain size vehicle. They must be able to handle the width and the weight of the towed vehicle. Like everything else we have discussed, tow dollies have maximum weight ratings too. When you purchase a tow dolly make sure that it is designed to support the weight and size of the towed vehicle. Some dollies are adjustable, meaning the same dolly can be set-up to tow different size vehicles, and others are made to tow just one size vehicle. Normally the width of the towed vehicle determines the size tow dolly you will need. Check with the tow dolly manufacturer before making a purchase.

Note: Matching the wrong vehicle and dolly can result in damage to the towed vehicle.

Some tow dollies come equipped with brakes and others do not. Check with State or Province laws and the motorhome chassis manufacturer about the requirement for a towed vehicle braking system, based on the amount of weight you will be towing, before you purchase a tow dolly.

Loading and Unloading the Tow Dolly

Before loading the vehicle unto the tow dolly make sure the tow dolly coupler is properly attached to the ball mount and that you are using the proper size hitch ball for the coupler. Use a safety pin or clip to secure

Mark J. Polk

the locked coupler. Attach the safety chains or cables making sure they are crossed, "X" to form a saddle that would prevent the coupler from contacting the road surface in the event of a separation. Plug the light cable in and check all of the lights for proper operation. Follow the tow dolly manufacturer instructions to determine the proper hitch height.

Note: Follow the tow dolly manufacturer's specific instructions for proper loading, unloading, and vehicle tie down procedures.

Tow Dolly Pre-Trip Checklist

Perform these checks before each travel day:

➢ Check and adjust tire pressure to manufacturer recommendations. Check inflation pressure when the tires are cold, before traveling more than one mile.

➢ Check wheel lug nuts. Tighten to manufacturer specifications.

➢ Check that wheel hubs and bearings are properly adjusted and lubricated. Follow the manufacturer instructions or have them checked by a repair facility.

➢ Check that all nuts and bolts are properly tightened.

➢ Do not use the dolly with any loose or damaged hardware.

➢ Check that the coupler is properly secured to the ball mount. **Note:** follow manufacturer instructions for adjusting coupler tightness.

➢ Check the safety chains for proper attachment.

➢ Check all lights for proper operation.

➢ Check that the tow vehicle is properly secured to the tow dolly. Follow manufacturer instructions for proper tie down procedures.

➢ Make sure the towed vehicle parking brake is released after it is properly secured to the dolly.

➢ Stop after 10 miles of travel to check the tie down straps. Re-adjust as required. Check every 100 miles afterwards at a minimum.

> Do not attempt to back the tow dolly!

Tow Dolly Towing Tips
> Perform all pre-trip checks before using the tow dolly.
> Make turns wider than you are accustomed to. Do not attempt to make sharp turns or U-turns. If you turn to sharply the vehicle you are towing can come in contact with the tow dolly fender causing damage to both the towed vehicle and the dolly.
> Do not attempt to back the loaded tow dolly. Backing can damage the tow dolly and the towed vehicle.
> Allow a safe following distance (at least two car lengths), and anticipate all stops.
> Do not speed, drive at a safe speed and keep in mind the dolly is wider than most vehicles towing it. Stay centered in your lane of traffic.
> If you experience excessive sway it may be caused by an improperly loaded tow dolly. Stop when it is safe, check and re-tighten the tie downs, or reload the vehicle. Check tie down straps every 100 miles at a minimum.
> The towed vehicle should always be facing forward on the dolly. A towed vehicle loaded from the rear can contribute to trailer sway.
> Never allow any passengers to ride in the towed vehicle.

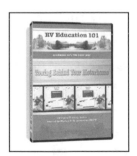

Our Towing Behind your Motorhome DVD covers this information in depth. See the RV Education 101 order form at back of book.

Chapter 14

RV Preventive Maintenance

Types of Maintenance

It doesn't matter whether you own a pop-up or a diesel pusher, when you made the decision to purchase an RV it was a major investment. Like any other major investment there are certain things we must do to protect our investment so we can enjoy it. Your RV needs to be maintained just like your house and automobiles need to be maintained. There are three basic types of maintenance for your RV: preventive maintenance, scheduled maintenance and emergency maintenance.

Preventive maintenance is maintenance you perform on your RV before a problem exists. These checks are designed to prevent or identify potential problems that could lead to mechanical breakdown, malfunction or failure of a component or system on your RV. Preventive maintenance consists of cleaning, inspecting, lubricating, adjusting and servicing your RV.

Scheduled maintenance or routine maintenance is performed in intervals normally based on time, mileage or hours. Scheduled maintenance is designed to keep your RV in top operating condition and prevent untimely breakdowns and repairs. It is absolutely essential that you read your owner's manual and warranty information in regards to who is responsible for what when it comes to scheduled maintenance. Scheduled maintenance that is required by the manufacturer and not performed can void your warranty.

Emergency maintenance is maintenance and/or repairs required when you least expect it due to component, system or mechanical failure.

The lack of preventive maintenance and/or scheduled maintenance will eventually result in emergency maintenance. If you don't check the air pressure in your tires (preventive maintenance) the under-inflated tire over heats and prematurely fails resulting in emergency maintenance.

An RV is larger and heavier than your automobile and its not just the chassis you need to be concerned about, it's your entire house sitting on top of the chassis. The good news is the average RV owner can perform the required RV care and maintenance and prevent untimely break downs and costly repairs (emergency maintenance).

Start your preventive maintenance program with these checks and over time add some of your own checks and without even realizing it you will be identifying and preventing potential problems before they exist.

> **Note:** If you don't feel comfortable performing your own maintenance find a reputable RV service center to do it for you.

> **Note:** Always check your owner's manual for routine and scheduled maintenance intervals. Service your vehicle as recommended by the chassis and RV manufacturer.

RV Chassis Checklist

> **Check all fluid levels**

Check the engine oil, transmission, power steering, brakes and windshield washer fluid. Adjust levels as required. Change fluid and filters In Accordance With (IAW) your vehicle owner's manual recommended intervals. When checking the transmission fluid consult your owner's manual for proper instructions. A low fluid level indicates a leak and must be investigated further. If the transmission fluid has a burnt smell it needs to be replaced. Follow your owner's manual for the proper types of fluids to use.

Mark J. Polk

➢ **Check the air filter**

A clean air filter helps your engine perform better and improves fuel economy. Replace the air filter IAW scheduled maintenance intervals, or when you see it is dirty.

➢ **Check for any leaks**

Look under the RV and or the tow vehicle for any indications of leaks. Locate the source of the leak and have it repaired. Transmission fluid leaks contacting hot areas like exhaust system components contribute to vehicle fires.

➢ **Chassis lubrication**

Have the chassis lubricated IAW manufacturers recommended intervals.

➢ **Check radiator coolant**

Check the level, condition & concentration of anti-freeze. Antifreeze not only protects the engine in cold temperatures, it helps the engine run cooler in hot temperatures. For best results coolant should be flushed and replaced every couple of years. Do not drain or flush coolant directly on the ground.

Caution: Never remove a radiator cap when the engine is hot!

➢ **Check radiator hoses & clamps**

Look for worn, cracked, brittle or soft spots in the hoses. Replace as required.

➢ **Check heater hoses & clamps**

Look for worn, cracked, or soft spots in the hoses. Replace as required.

➢ **Check all belts**

Look for signs of wear and for any cracks in the belts. Check the belts for proper tension. It's a good idea to take spare belts with you on your trip.

➢ **Check all lights**

Check all lights for proper operation prior to using your RV.

> **Check wiper blades**

Check your wiper blades for wear and/or poor operation. It's too late once it starts raining.

> **Check the starting battery**

Check the RV or tow vehicle starting battery state of charge, water level, cables and connections. If you're not familiar with working around lead acid batteries have them checked at an authorized service center.

> **Check the condition of your tires**

Look for uneven wear, cuts, poor tread depth and check for dry rot on the tire sidewalls. Check all tires for proper tire inflation with a quality tire inflation pressure gauge. Check the tire pressure before traveling each day and always check the tire pressure when the tires are cold, before traveling more than one mile. Adjust inflation pressure to the manufacturer's recommended pressure.

> **Start the engine and allow it to warm up**

Check all gauges for proper operation. Monitor your gauges while driving. If a gauge reads out of the normal range pull over as soon as it is safe and call for assistance.

> **Check the dash air for proper operation**

Whether you're pulling a pop-up a travel trailer or driving a motorhome, try to avoid using the dash air when the engine is under a strain, such as on an upgrade.

> **Check your emergency kit**

At a minimum it should include a flashlight, extra batteries, jumper cables, first aid kit, basic hand tools and warning devices.

Note: In addition to these checks if you have a pop-up or travel trailer the wheel bearings and brakes should be inspected at least once annually. Inspect any canvas for dry rot and tears; inspect all hitch work and the coupler for damage. Inspect the breakaway switch and pigtail for proper operation.

Mark J. Polk

RV Coach Checklist

➢ **Exterior of RV**

Maintaining the exterior of you RV contributes to extending the life of the RV and protecting your investment. If you let your RV go, without cleaning it for periods of time it can be very difficult to get that new look back.

➢ **Inspect roof and body seams**

Every seam on your RV and anywhere the manufacturer cut a hole in your RV has the potential to allow water in. Inspect your RV roof and all seams on a regular basis for potential water leaks. Consult with your RV dealer for sealants compatible with different types of materials.

➢ **Test the roof air conditioner(s)**

Clean or replace A/C filters. Clean filters will help the A/C work more efficiently.

➢ **Test the refrigerator in AC & LP gas mode**

Do not over pack the refrigerator, allow for air to circulate. Installing a thermostatically controlled refrigerator vent fan will improve the refrigerators efficiency.

➢ **Check the auxiliary battery(s)**

Check the auxiliary battery state of charge, water level, cables and connections. If you're not familiar with lead acid batteries have them checked by an authorized service center. If the RV is equipped with battery disconnect switches make sure they are in the off position when you're not using your RV to prevent battery drain.

➢ **Check operation of the generator under load**

Check generator engine oil & all filters. Service the generator as recommended by the manufacturer. Exercise the generator for a minimum of two hours monthly with at least a half rated load. Consult the generator owner's manual for load ratings.

> ## Check all appliances

Check all of the AC, DC and LP gas appliances for proper operation. It's a good idea to have your LP gas system checked by your authorized RV service center annually.

> ## Holding tanks

Thoroughly flush out the holding tanks every time you empty them. Use RV toilet paper and enzyme based holding tank chemicals. Many of our free dump stations are closing due to chemicals that are harmful to septic systems.

> ## 12-volt appliances and accessories

Check all 12-volt appliances and accessories for proper operation.

> ## Check & test all safety devices

Check fire extinguishers, smoke alarm, carbon monoxide and LP gas leak detectors before each trip. Replace batteries as required.

> ## Check the operation of the awning and inspect the awning fabric

Inspect your awning for proper operation. If you have your awning out when it's raining, lower one end to allow the rain to run off and prevent water from pooling on the fabric, which can cause extensive damage.

> ## Check electrical source

Prior to plugging your RV in to the campground electrical source check it with a digital test meter for proper voltage and polarity.

> ## Water system

When you return from a camping trip you should always drain the water out of the water system. Locate and open the low point water drains, drain the fresh water holding tank and the water heater tank. **Caution:** Never drain the water heater when the water is HOT or under pressure.

Inspecting Your RV for Water Damage

If there is a way to get in your RV, water will find it. Water leaks on an RV can cause extensive damage and can be extremely costly to repair. When I worked at an RV dealership I saw the damaging effects that water can cause to an RV time and time again. I learned the lesson the hard way. I appraised a unit that was being traded in and didn't identify the extensive water damage, which resulted in a thousand dollars worth of repairs. Hindsight is 20/20 and I quickly learned how to inspect for, and identify potential water damage on RVs. My recommendation is that you inspect for potential water leaks twice a year at a minimum, once in the fall and again in the spring.

Every seam on your RV and anywhere the manufacturer cut a hole in your RV has the potential to allow water in. To protect your investment and your wallet take the time to **REALLY** inspect all of these seams and sealants. Water damage on an RV is similar to progressive damage to a tire. The outside of the tire looks fine, but the internal damage, over a long period of time, causes the tire to fail without any warning. The outside of your RV looks fine but the internal damage caused by water over a long period of time can result in the entire roof, floor or wall rotting away without you knowing it. Here are a few things to look for during your inspections.

Safety first! Be extremely careful whenever you are working on your RV roof. You can be seriously injured from a fall. You have to get on the roof of your RV to properly clean and inspect it for any damage or potential water leaks. The first step is the ladder you use to get on the roof. If your RV does not have a ladder on the back to access the roof it probably is not designed to be walked on. In this situation it may be necessary to use a couple pieces of plywood or particle board to help distribute your weight. Many RV manufacturers have an option called roof rack and ladder ready. If the RV dealer orders this option the roof is built with a heavier roof decking. Even so you need to walk lightly when you're on the roof.

Inspection Checklist

➢ To stop a leak before it starts **thoroughly** inspect all roof and body seams. Consult with your RV dealer for sealants compatible with different types of materials.

➤ Look for any discoloration and feel for any soft spots on the ceiling around roof vents, air conditioners, TV antennas, plumbing vents, and any other openings that were cut in the roof.

➤ Look for any discoloration or wrinkles in the wallpaper, and feel for any soft spots on the walls around all windows, doors, vents, slide outs, or any other openings that were cut in the side walls.

➤ Identify the location of items like the water heater, furnace, outside shower, potable water fill and city water inlet on the outside of the RV and then access those areas from the inside of the RV and look for any indications of water damage around these openings.

➤ Open all overhead cabinets and look in the top corner where the walls meet the ceiling for any discoloration or feel for any soft spots. This would indicate a leak at the seam where the sidewall and the roof attach.

➤ Check in all outside storage compartments for any indications of water leaks or water damage.

➤ Check for any soft spots on the roof itself especially around the roof seams at the front and rear of the RV. Thoroughly inspect all sealants on the roof around every opening.

➤ Some Type C motorhomes are notorious for leaks in the cab over bed area. Look for any signs of discoloration and feel for soft spots. Reach under the mattress and feel for water.

➤ Look and feel on the outside of the RV for any signs of delaminating. Delaminating is caused by water getting between the exterior fiberglass and the sidewall. When this happens the exterior fiberglass separates from the sidewall of the RV. You can stand at the front or rear of the RV and look down the side for any noticeable ripples or what looks like a bubble. You can also press on the sidewalls. If you feel the exterior fiberglass move it is delaminating. Often times, delaminating starts around where an opening was made in the sidewall.

Don't just inspect your RV for water damage; **REALLY** inspect your RV for water damage. If you do this on a regular basis you can locate and

Mark J. Polk

repair the source of any water damage before it has a chance to do a great deal of damage.

Rubber Roof Care & Maintenance

One of the most neglected areas on your RV is the roof, out of sight out of mind. Rubber roofing on an RV is a great product, but like everything else without routine preventive maintenance it will not last as long as it could. First of all, there are different types of rubber roofs. Different manufacturers provide different instructions with their product. What we want to concentrate on is what applies to all rubber roofs used on RVs.

Caution: There are other types of RV roofing material used like fiberglass, aluminum and vinyl. Read your roof manufacturers instructions for proper cleaning and sealing techniques to prevent damage to your roof and possibly voiding your warranty.

Rubber roofs should be cleaned three to four times a year and depending on where you park or store your RV it may need to be cleaned more often.

Note: Regardless of the type of rubber roof you have **never** use any cleaners or conditioners that contain petroleum solvents, harsh abrasives, or citrus ingredients.

These types of cleaners can cause permanent damage to any rubber or vinyl surface. Most manufacturers of rubber roofs recommend you use a medium bristle brush and a non-abrasive cleaner. For light cleaning you can use warm water and a mild detergent like Dawn dish washing liquid. To clean, condition and protect the roof there are commercial cleaners and protectants designed just for rubber roofs. Hard to clean areas like stubborn stains caused by leaves, sap, mold or mildew may require a second treatment. Use caution to prevent the cleaners from getting on the sides of the RV. Always rinse the sides, front and back of your RV before rinsing the roof to prevent streaking or damage to the finish on your RV.

Cleaning the roof is only part of maintaining it. Every time you clean the roof, you need to inspect the sealants around all of the openings and the seams on the roof. Water will take the path of least resistance and if there is the smallest opening it will find it. You need to thoroughly inspect the roof sealants for potential leaks and reseal any areas of the roof seams and around openings where you suspect a leak. Check with your RV dealer for sealants that are compatible with your roofing material. A while ago I discovered a product called Eternabond™. You only need to use it one time and the area you're sealing is sealed forever. You can use it to permanently seal all the seams on your roof and it's great for repairing any damaged area like a rip or tear in the roof. Eternabond™ works on any type of RV roofing material and it's as easy to apply as a piece of tape. For more information you can go to their website at **www.eternabond.com**

RV Awning Use, Care & Maintenance

RV awnings are a great feature to have on your RV. There are different types of RV awnings and they serve different purposes. There are window and door awnings that provide shade over your RV windows or entry door. There are slide out awnings that protect the slide out roof from debris and water. And there are patio awnings that provide us with shade when we want to sit and enjoy the outdoors. The awnings on your RV will provide years of reliable trouble free operation, if you take the time to do a little preventive maintenance and cleaning.

The fabric used on awnings is made from vinyl or acrylic. Some awnings have an aluminum or vinyl wrap-around weather guard that protects the awning fabric when it's in the travel position. When you open the awning for the first time each year, or if it has been stored for a while, you will need to inspect the awning fabric for any signs of mildew or stains. Vinyl awnings will mildew. If the awning fabric is fairly clean, normal cleaning can be accomplished with a soft brush and mild soap and water. Do not use oil based or abrasive cleaners. Clean and thoroughly rinse both sides of the awning. For more difficult stains, or mildew, there are after market commercial cleaners made just for awning fabrics.

> **Note:** Carefully follow all of the awning and cleaner manufacturer directions.

Inspect the awning fabric for any tears or excessive wear. Do not store the awning when the fabric is wet. Allow it to dry completely on both sides before storing.

You can clean the awning hardware with the same cleaner you use to wash the RV. While the awning is out, inspect the awning hardware. The bottom awning brackets support most of the load from the awning. Check that the lag screws in the awning brackets are tight. Inspect the arm pivot holes for any enlarged holes or broken rivets in the handles. Check for a warped roller tube. If the roller tube is warped it will be noticeable when you roll the awning out. Inspect the end caps for secure mounting and broken rivets.

> **Caution:** Do not attempt to remove the awning end caps. Spring tension can result in serious injury.

Make sure the awning rail is securely mounted to the side of the RV. Have any damaged or broken parts repaired before using the awning. In addition to cleaning and inspecting your awning there are a few things to keep in mind when using the awning. Always lower one end of the awning to allow for water run off. The weight from water pooling on the awning fabric can cause extensive and costly damage. Wind gusts over 20 miles per hour can also cause extensive damage to the awning and to the RV. Never leave the awning out unattended. If everyone is leaving the campsite, store the awning in the travel position. When you go to bed, store the awning. Even when you are at the campsite, you should use awning tie downs to prevent any sudden damage caused by high wind gusts or a sudden storm. You have the option to position the awning arms straight down and stake them to the ground, but you will get better support if they're attached to the bottom awning brackets. Remember, it is much easier to prevent damage to your awning than it is to repair it.

RV Patio Awning Operation

There are several types of awnings and awning manufacturers. This checklist may not cover every item as it pertains to your awning. The purpose of this checklist is to give you a basic guide to follow when opening and storing your retractable patio awning. Use only the checks that apply to your particular awning.

> ➤ Most awnings have some type of travel locks about mid way up, on both main support awning arms. These locks assist in storing the awning to the side of the RV while traveling. Release these locking mechanisms.
> ➤ Behind both main awning arms, on the support arms there will be a knob that should be hand tight. Loosen both of these knobs.
> ➤ Look up at the end of the awning roller tube on the right hand side towards the front of the RV. You will see a small lever. This lever is what locks the roller tube to the side of the RV. Take your awning rod and with the hooked end reach up and pull the lever down to release the locking lever.
> ➤ Look up, around the middle of the roller tube, and you should see a loop for the awning strap. With the hook end of your awning rod reach up and hook the loop. Pull the awning strap down until you can reach it with your hand. The awning should release and pull freely from both ends. Continue pulling down on the strap until the awning fabric and tube are fully extended.
> ➤ Now, the inner support arms, where you loosened the knobs, should slide freely to the top of the main arms and lock into place. Do this on both ends. When they are locked in place, starting on either end, take one hand and pull down on the main awning arm until the awning fabric is taught. With your other

Mark J. Polk

hand reach up and hand tighten the knob. Repeat this on the other end.

➤ On the side of each main arm you will notice a lever. Starting on either end, take one hand and put it on the front of the main arm and take the lever with your other hand. Raise the main arm up to the height you want the awning at, using the lever to help lift it. When you lower the lever it will lock into the closest adjusting hole on the arm where you release it. Repeat this on the other end.

Caution: Do not get your fingers or hands close to any moving or sliding parts.

Reverse these procedures to retract the awning. Once the inner support arms are retracted you will need to release the awning lock lever to store the awning. If you are retracting the awning by yourself take your awning rod in one hand and with your other hand take the awning strap and slide it all the way down the right hand side of the awning tube to where the awning lock lever is located. You need to pull down on the awning strap, applying enough pressure to release the awning lock lever. **Caution: as soon as the lever is released the awning tube will begin to retract. These tubes have springs that are wound with tension.** Hold the strap securely and release the locking lever. Continue to hold the strap firmly and work it back to the middle of the awning tube by sliding it in the groove. When the awning strap is close to the middle of the tube slowly let the awning begin to retract by easing off the awning strap. Place the hook end of the awning rod into the loop of the strap and continue to retract the awning until it is in the stored position. Do not let go of the strap early. The awning can violently hit the side of the RV causing damage. Secure the travel locks on both main arms and hand tighten both knobs on the support arms.

Chapter 15

Winterizing & Storing Your RV

Winterizing your RV

When winter approaches it is a time to make some decisions. If you live in a climate where temperatures drop below freezing you need to protect your RV water system from getting damaged. Parking the RV for the winter will require some preventive measures so it will be ready to use next spring. You'll also be glad you did it when you don't have costly repair bills due to the damaging results of winter. Now the question is how do you prepare it for winter, and who will be doing it? If you're like me and you enjoy performing the routine maintenance on your RV, not to mention saving a few dollars, the "who" part is answered. As for the "how" part, I have taken a checklist from my "Checklists for RVers" e-book that I feel is the easiest and most effective way to winterize and store your RV. If you would like to actually see how to winterize your RV you can purchase our "Winterizing and Storing your RV" training DVD.

Note: See order form at back of book or **www.rveducation101.com**

Before you get started there are a few items you will need. These items can be found in most RV parts stores. Non-toxic RV antifreeze, the amount depends on the layout and length of your plumbing lines.

Two to three gallons will normally do. A water heater by-pass kit, if not already installed. A water pump converter kit or tubing to connect to the inlet side of the water pump and some basic hand tools to remove drain

Mark J. Polk

plugs. Now we can winterize the RV water system to protect it from freezing. Be sure to read your owners manuals for unit specific winterizing guidelines. Follow the steps below that apply to your RV:

➢ If you have any inline water filters remove and bypass them before starting.

➢ Drain the fresh water holding tank.

➢ Drain and flush the gray and black water holding tanks. Flush the black tank thoroughly or clean it using a wand.

➢ Lubricate the termination valves. Do not use petroleum products on any rubber components, including termination valves. Some holding tank chemicals have lubricating qualities already added.

➢ Drain the water heater tank. Remove the drain plug and open the pressure relief valve. Re-install the drain plug after it drains.

Caution: Never drain water heater when hot or under pressure

➢ Open all hot and cold faucets; don't forget the toilet valve and outside shower.

➢ Locate and open the low point water drain lines. There is one for the hot and cold water lines. Using the water pump will help force water out, but turn it off as soon as the system is drained.

➢ Recap all drains and close all faucets.

➢ By-pass the water heater. If you do not have a by-pass kit installed the water heater will fill up with antifreeze before it goes through the water lines, **wasting six gallons of antifreeze**.

➢ Install a water pump converter kit, or disconnect the inlet side of the water pump (the line coming from the fresh water holding tank) and connect tubing from the pump into a gallon of RV antifreeze.

➢ Turn the water pump on and pressurize the system. Starting with the closest faucet, slowly open the hot and then cold valves until antifreeze appears. Replace antifreeze container as required.

➢ Repeat on all faucets from the closest to farthest away. Don't forget the outside shower.

➢ Flush the toilet until antifreeze appears.

- Turn the water pump off and open a faucet to release the pressure. Go to the city water inlet, on the outside of the RV, and remove the small screen over the inlet. Push in on the valve with a small screwdriver until you see antifreeze. Replace the screen.
- Pour a cupful of antifreeze down each drain. Pour a few cups in the toilet and flush into the holding tank.
- If your water heater has an electric heating element make sure it is in the off position. This will protect the element if the unit is plugged in while being stored.
- Make sure all faucets are closed.
- Consult your owner's manuals for winterizing icemakers, washing machines and other appliances not covered.
- The unit is winterized.

De-Winterizing Checklist

Depending on how your unit was winterized it will need to be de-winterized. Follow this simple checklist to get your water system ready for camping season.

- If you used non-toxic RV antifreeze open all drains and drain the antifreeze from the system. If you do not have a bypass kit on the water heater, drain the antifreeze from the water heater.
- If you put any antifreeze in the fresh water tank be sure and drain it.
- Close the drains.
- Re-connect the outside shower hose if it was removed.
- To remove antifreeze from the 12-volt water pump, add water to the fresh water holding tank, turn the pump on and open all water faucets. Run water through the system and then turn the pump off.
- Take the water heater out of the bypass mode and hook your hose up to the city water inlet. Turn the water on and open all water faucets. **Run fresh water through the system for**

several minutes. Don't forget the outside shower if equipped.

➤ Flush the toilet.

➤ Check the entire water system for leaks.

➤ Fill and drain your black and gray holding tanks at least once.

➤ Inspect the termination valve and lubricate the valve handles.

➤ Treat the black tank with holding tank chemicals.

➤ Sanitize the water system.

➤ Re-install any water filter cartridges you removed for winterizing.

Storing Your RV

When temperatures drop we winterize our RVs so we won't have any problems with it next spring, but winterizing your RV is only part of preparing it to sit idle for several months. What needs to be done to really prepare your RV for several months of storage? Many of us don't think about it, but the storing portion is just as important as winterizing the water system.

When I produced our winterizing video, I included an entire section on properly storing the RV. It's important that we consider things like batteries, ventilation, the condition of sealants, mice, and fuel system protection just to mention a few. So, let's look at some things we should do in addition to winterizing our RV water system. The storage procedures are divided into two sections, the coach storage and the chassis storage. Follow the steps that apply to your RV.

Note: See order form at back of book or **www.rveducation101.com**

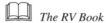

Coach Storage

➤ Store your unit under a covered area if possible. If not, avoid parking under trees or in areas where grass and weeds will grow.

➤ If you choose to buy a cover for the RV, be sure it is made of a breathable material. This will help in preventing mold and mildew. Do not use one of those "blue tarps" to cover your RV.

➤ Chock the wheels front and rear. Leave the parking brake off. If you're storing a pop-up angle the tongue downward to assist in snow and water run off.

➤ Inflate the tires to the manufacturer's recommended max cold pressure. Cover the tires to protect them from the harmful ultraviolet rays. Place something between the tires and the ground. Make sure whatever you use is larger than the actual foot print of the tire.

➤ If you do not remove the tires for long-term storage periodically move the vehicle to prevent flat spots on the tires.

➤ Close all of the window blinds to avoid sun exposure to the carpet, drapes and upholstery.

➤ Wash the exterior of the unit and clean the interior thoroughly.

➤ Make sure the awning fabric is clean and dry before storing.

➤ On a pop-up make absolutely sure the fabric is clean and dry before storing. This is a good time to check for tears, and repair the fabric.

➤ Inspect all roof seams, body seams and window sealant for cracks and openings. Water can get in the smallest openings so really inspect all sealants. Consult your dealer for sealants compatible with these materials.

➤ Service all locks with a graphite spray lubricant. Lubricate all hinges and moving parts with WD 40.

➤ Turn all LP gas appliances off. Turn the main LP gas supply valve off. If you're storing a pop-up or travel trailer make sure the LP gas regulator is covered.

Mark J. Polk

- Remove the fuse for the LP gas leak detector while the unit is in storage. This will prevent the batteries from discharging. Don't forget to replace it next spring.
- Insects are attracted to the odorant that is added to LP gas. To prevent mud daubers and wasps from building nests in and around your gas appliances, cover the refrigerator vent, furnace vent and the water heater vent.
- Inspect the underside of the unit thoroughly. Look for anywhere that mice or other rodents can get it, and seal as required.
- Strategically place mouse and ant traps in and around the unit. Avoid using mouse poison inside the RV.
- Remove all perishables and anything that can freeze.
- Leave doors, drawers and cabinets open.
- Remove all consumables that would attract mice and other rodents.
- Defrost the freezer compartment and clean the refrigerator. Leave the refrigerator doors open and place some baking soda inside to absorb odors.
- Clean the air conditioner filters, and cover the air conditioner.
- Turn off the main breaker and unplug all appliances.
- Remove dry cell batteries in clocks, flashlights and other items.
- The use of Maxx Air™ products will provide the airflow and ventilation required during storage while keeping the elements out.

Chassis Storage

- When you put your RV in storage it's a good idea to remove the batteries and put them in storage too. This is quite simple to do. When you're removing the batteries always remember to remove the negative terminal first. Clean the batteries with a 50/50 mixture of baking soda and water if necessary. Store the batteries in a cool dry place but not where they could freeze. Batteries in storage will loose their charge. Check the state of charge every month and charge batteries that are at or below 80% state of charge.

➤ Check and fill the water levels in all batteries that are not maintenance free. Check the electrolyte level and add distilled water if necessary.

➤ Charge all batteries as required. A discharged or partially charged battery will freeze much faster than a charged battery.

➤ Remove and clean all battery terminals and posts. Spray the terminals with terminal dressing to protect against corrosion.

➤ If you plan to start the unit while in storage, and to periodically plug the unit into shore power, leave the batteries in the unit. Plugging into shore power once a month, for about eight hours, will keep the coach batteries topped off.

➤ If you put the unit in long-term storage; remove and store the batteries where they will not freeze. In either case keep the batteries charged.

➤ During short-term storage, start the unit monthly and run it with the dash air on for at least 30 minutes.

➤ If you don't plan on starting the unit, or won't be able to start it, buy some fogging oil from a marine supply store to protect the cylinder walls. When the unit is parked where it will be stored, spray the fogging oil into the engine intake, downstream from the air filter with the engine at an idle. Complete the same steps on the generator. Follow the manufacturer's directions.

Caution: Do not use fogging oil in a diesel engine

Note: Fogging oil is used to protect the internal engine components and to prevent corrosion when the RV is in long term storage and the engine won't be started. It is commonly used in marine applications. Follow the manufacturer's directions.

Mark J. Polk

- Fill the fuel tank prior to storage and add a fuel stabilizer. Run the engine and the generator long enough for the stabilizer to get through the fuel system. Follow the manufacturer's directions.
- If the unit is not in long-term storage exercise the generator at least two hours each month with a 1/2 rated load. Consult your generator set owners manual for rated loads.
- Change the oil and oil filter on the engine and the generator prior to storage. Acids accumulate in used oil and can corrode engine bearings.
- Check the engine radiator for the proper concentration of antifreeze. Consult your owner's manual for the correct type of engine antifreeze. Drain, flush and refill the system every two to three years.
- Drain the windshield washer reservoir or add the appropriate antifreeze solution to prevent it from freezing.
- Perform a chassis lubrication prior to storage.

Now your RV is ready for storage and hopefully you won't experience any problems when you perform your spring maintenance checks next year.

Our Winterizing & Storing your RV DVD covers all of this information in depth. See the RV Education 101 order form at back of book.

Chapter 16

Spring Preparation

Your RV has been sitting idle over the winter. Now the early signs of spring are here and it's time to take it out of storage and prepare the coach and chassis for this years camping season. If you're like me, you want to have some type of logical sequence to follow rather then haphazardly checking the unit out. I made a simple checklist to use so that nothing is overlooked. I prefer to do the majority of spring preparation myself. If you're more comfortable having someone else do it you can schedule an appointment with a reputable RV service center to have it done.

Spring Preparation Checklist

➤ Depending on how your unit was winterized it will need to be de-winterized. If you used non-toxic RV antifreeze you need to run fresh water through the entire system until all traces of antifreeze are gone. To remove it from the 12-volt water pump add water to the fresh water-holding tank, turn the pump on and open all water faucets. When the antifreeze is out of the system turn the pump off and take the water heater out of the by-pass mode (if applicable). Re-install any water filter cartridges you removed for storage.

➤ At this point I like to sanitize the water system. Make sure all of the drains are closed and drain plugs are installed. Take a quarter cup of household bleach for every fifteen gallons of water your fresh water tank holds. Mix the bleach with water into a one-gallon container and pour it into the fresh water holding tank. Fill

251   Mark J. Polk

the fresh water holding tank completely full of water. Turn the water pump on and open all faucets, run water until you smell the bleach. Close the faucets and let it sit for at least twelve hours. Drain all of the water and re-fill the tank with fresh water. Turn the pump on and open all faucets until you no longer smell bleach. It may be necessary to repeat this process to eliminate all signs of the bleach.

➢ With the water system under pressure inspect for water leaks. Check the operation of the toilet.

➢ Wash the unit thoroughly. This is a good time to inspect the roof and body seams, and window sealants for cracking that would allow water to get in. Consult a dealer for sealants compatible with these materials.

➢ Inspect the operation of the awning and clean the awning fabric as required.

➢ Inspect the tires for signs of dry rot. Inflate all tires to the recommended COLD tire pressure.

➢ Lubricate all hinges and locks with spray lubricant.

➢ Remove any tape or protective covering you may have put over LP gas vents to keep insects and rodents out. Check any mousetraps you may have put out. Open all doors and compartments and check for rodent intrusion and water damage.

➢ Inspect and clean the interior.

➢ Plug in any appliances that you unplugged for storage and replace any dry cell batteries you may have removed. This is a good time to put new batteries in items like smoke alarms.

➢ Test the operation of the carbon monoxide alarm, LP gas leak detector and smoke alarm.

➢ Check the fire extinguisher. Be sure it is fully charged.

➢ Reset any breakers you may have turned off. If you removed any fuses for storage re-install them.

- Clean or replace air conditioner filters if it wasn't done prior to storage and remove any covers that were put over air conditioners.
- Open vents and windows and air the unit out.
- If you removed the coach and chassis batteries for storage install them. Whether they were removed or not check the electrolyte levels, clean the terminals and clamps, and check the charge level in all batteries. Recharge batteries as necessary.
- Check the operation of the electric steps if applicable. Lubricate step mechanism.
- Test the operation of the hydraulic jacks if applicable. Check hydraulic fluid level.
- Test the operation of the back up camera and monitor if applicable.
- If you didn't change the oil and filters in the generator prior to storage this is a good time to do it. Inspect the generator exhaust system for damage prior to starting. Start and run the generator for two hours with at least a half rated load on it. Consult the generators owner manual for load ratings.
- Turn the generator off and plug the unit into shore power. Turn the refrigerator on in the electric mode. Allow sufficient time to cool and check for proper operation.
- Check all 12-volt interior lights and accessories.
- Test the monitor panel for proper operation.
- Check the operation of slide outs if applicable.
- Check the remaining 120-volt appliances for proper operation.
- Test the Ground Fault Interrupter (GFI) for proper operation.
- Turn the refrigerator off, leave the doors open and allow sufficient time for it to get to room temperature so it can be checked in the gas mode.
- Before I use the LP gas system I have a leak test and gas operating pressure test preformed. A qualified technician with the proper equipment should do these tests.

- After this is accomplished turn the LP gas valve on and check the operation of all LP gas appliances. Be sure the water heater is full of water before testing the water heater. If a gas appliance is not operating properly have it inspected by a qualified technician. Insects are attracted to the odorant added to LP gas and build nests that can affect the appliance from operating properly.
- If your unit was in long-term storage and you didn't change the engine oil and filter prior to storage this would be a good time to do it.
- Check all fluid levels in the transmission, power steering, engine coolant, engine oil, windshield washer and brakes. Consult vehicle owner's manual.
- Start the engine and check for proper readings on all gauges. Check for proper operation of the dash air conditioner.
- Perform complete chassis lubrication if it wasn't done prior to storage.
- Check the condition of windshield wiper blades and replace them if necessary.
- Check the operation of all chassis lights.
- Make sure the vehicle emissions/inspection sticker is up to date.
- In addition to this if you have a pop-up or travel trailer the wheel bearings and brakes (if equipped) should be inspected at least once annually. Inspect any canvas for dry rot and tears; inspect all hitch work and the coupler for damage. Inspect the breakaway switch and pigtail for proper operation.

Summer Camping Tips

As summer approaches it not only means prime travel season is upon us, but so is the heat. If you ever walked inside an RV that is sitting in the direct sunlight on a hot summer day you know what I mean. Fortunately there are some things we can do to make our summer RV camping trips more pleasurable.

> ➤ Strategically park your RV to take advantage of any shade that is available, especially on the side where the refrigerator vent is located. Don't be afraid to ask for a shady site when you check in at the campground. This will not only help cool the RV down, but your refrigerator and roof A/C will work much more efficiently.

> ➤ You can also improve your air conditioners efficiency by keeping the A/C filters clean. In most cases you can wash the filters in warm soapy water, rinse thoroughly and allow them to dry before reinstalling. Another option is to clean the filters with a small hand held vacuum cleaner. I recommend you keep a new set on hand in the event the old filters have seen better days.

> ➤ Use your main awning and any window awnings to assist in cooling the RV down. In addition to the awnings use your window blinds or drapes to help keep the sun out and the cooler air in.

> ➤ Campground voltage can fluctuate, especially during the summer months when campers are running their A/C, placing a higher demand on campground electricity. You should monitor the voltage coming in to your RV with a digital voltmeter. If voltage drops below 105-volts or goes above 130-volts turn your appliances and electronic equipment off until proper voltage is restored.

> ➤ Install a thermostatically controlled refrigerator vent fan at the back of the refrigerator, or at the top of the roof vent, to assist with drafting the hot air away from the refrigerator. If you are mechanically inclined these fans are fairly easy to install, or you can have your RV dealer install one for you. Either way it's worth

Mark J. Polk

it. The fan removes the heat built up behind the refrigerator improving the refrigerators efficiency by up to 40%.

➢ Another ingredient to keeping your RV cool is proper ventilation. Proper ventilation helps prevent excess heat from building up in your RV. You can install Maxx Air vent covers, over the roof vents to allow for ventilation. They are inexpensive, easy to install and they let the fresh air in, even when it's raining, while the stale, musty air, smoke, cooking odors and heat escapes. I use a vent cover on each end of our RV to promote cross ventilation. To get more information on Maxx Air products you can visit their website at **www.maxxair.com**

➢ To help keep the inside of the RV cool try to avoid opening the door as much as possible and cook outside rather than inside whenever possible.

➢ Take a couple of small fans with you to help circulate the air. If for some reason you can't run the A/C you'll be glad you have them.

Chapter 17

Collection of RV Tips

In conclusion, I wanted to include some basic RV tips. When my youngest son, Tyler was about six years old he contributed some of his RV tips based on his many years of RV experience. **On the top of each page you will see one of Tyler's Tips too.**

> **Tyler's Tip**: Don't tuch any butuns unless mom or dad sez it's ok.

Tip # 1
Whenever you are using the TV antenna on your RV, hang the keys to the RV or tow vehicle on the TV antenna handle. This way you will never leave and forget the antenna was up. One of the most common repairs to RVs is a damaged TV antenna.

Tip # 2
To assist you with heating your RV during cold weather camping, and to save a significant amount of LP gas that your RV furnace uses, purchase a portable electric ceramic heater. They work extremely well and many models available on the market come equipped with thermostats.

Tip # 3
You never know the condition or quality of potable water at various campgrounds. Always use a water filtration system to filter the drinking water in your RV, or take bottled water with you for drinking water.

Mark J. Polk

> **Tyler's Tip:** Nevr strt the jenerator when the moterhome is plugd in to electrisiti.

Tip # 4

If you have a travel trailer and use a weight distribution hitch, once the dealer makes the proper adjustments, spray paint the link that you use for the proper amount of tension. This way you will always keep the spring bar tension adjusted properly.

Tip # 5

There are numerous electronic devices and equipment in your RV that can drain the coach battery when you're not using the RV. Some examples are; the TV antenna booster if left on, LP gas leak detectors, clocks in radios, or just leaving a 12-volt light on by accident. If your RV is not equipped with a battery disconnect switch you can purchase a battery disconnect, from an RV dealer, that can be installed directly on the battery post. When you aren't using the RV and you don't have any requirement for the coach battery you simply raise a lever and disconnect the battery.

Tip # 6

Whenever you return from a trip you need to drain the water from the water heater tank. This not only will prevent stale and musty water, but it will prevent costly damage that could occur if water were left in it and it froze causing it to expand and split the water heater tank. Removing the plastic plug to drain the water heater tank can be difficult and over time the plug corners will round off. A simple solution is to install a petcock, available at most RV dealerships, which will make draining the tank much easier. **Caution:** Never drain the water heater tank when it is hot or under pressure.

Tip # 7

Take updated photos of your pets with you on trips. If they should get lost you can use the pictures to assist in finding them.

 *The RV Book*

> **Tyler's Tip:** Be kareful in a slippri sleping bag. Yu can fall frm the top bonk bed in the midle of the nite.

Tip # 8

Never leave your RV awning out for any period of time when you are away from the campsite. A quick wind storm or thunder storm can result in expensive repair costs to the awning and the RV. If your awning is out and it begins to rain lower one end to allow the water to run off. Water can quickly pool up in the center of the awning fabric and the weight can damage the awning. If the wind begins to pick up at the campground put your awning in its stored position. Better safe than sorry.

Tip # 9

While driving in a motorhome it can cost less in fuel to run the generator with the roof air on than it costs to run the automotive dash air.

Tip # 10

After you unhitch your trailer at the campground remove the hitch head or trailer ball mount from the receiver and secure it if it doesn't have a locking mechanism. Not everyone at the campground is honest. It will also protect your shins and children from getting hurt when playing around it.

Tip # 11

Hire a lawn service company to maintain the outside of your home when you're going on extended camping trips. Stop your newspaper and mail or have a dependable neighbor collect it for you.

Tip # 12

Plan and prepare your meals at home before you go on a trip. Store them in freezer safe microwave able containers for quick and easy meals.

Tip # 13

Water pressure at campgrounds can be extremely high and cause damage to your RV plumbing system. Always use a water pressure regulator when you hook-up to the campground water supply. Always connect the water pressure regulator directly to the campground water source. This way you regulate the water pressure where it originates. I have seen instances where people hook the regulator to the city water inlet on the RV and the pressure causes the hose to swell up and rupture. It's also a good idea to turn the water supply off if you're going to be away from the campground for extended periods of time.

Tip # 14

Remember to remove travel locks from the slide out before attempting to put it out. Always check outside clearance for slide outs. Move seats and seat backs forward before putting slide outs in or out.

Tip # 15

Don't forget to retract the steps when it's time to leave. RV steps are a close second to TV antennas for the most common repairs on RVs.

Tip # 16

When making the water connection at the campground use a 90 degree elbow, available at RV parts stores, at the city water connection on the RV to keep the water hose from kinking.

Tip # 17

If you have dual wheels you will want to add extension hoses to the valve stems to make the job of checking tire inflation easier. A word of caution, if you add extension hoses you will want to replace the rubber valve stems with all steel valve stems. The added weight of the extension hoses can cause rubber stems to leak air resulting in under inflation.

Tip # 18

Tires and load range designations on tires have changed over the years. It used to be a 6-ply or 8-ply tire, and you knew the higher the number the stronger the tire. Now they use a letter to designate load range and tire strength. To help simplify this you can take the letter for the load range on the tire, determine what number it represents in the alphabet, and multiply that by two, to determine the strength of the tire. It sounds much more difficult than it is. If your tire is a load range "D" that is the 4th letter in the alphabet. 4 X 2 equals 8 so a load range "D" tire is equivalent to an 8-ply tire in strength.

Tip # 19

Always use a non-toxic, white RV drinking hose for your potable water connection at the campground. Take a black or green garden hose along for all other purposes such as cleaning the RV or flushing out holding tanks. You will always be able to distinguish the difference by the color of the hose.

Tip # 20

If you're traveling with pet's check with the campgrounds you plan to stay at in advance about kennels and boarding arrangements; if you are planning to take day trips or leave the campground for extended periods of time.

Tip # 21

Keep a current campground directory and call the campground you plan to stay at in advance to make reservations. This will assure you that you will get a site when you arrive.

Tip # 22

Always hide a spare set of keys to the RV and/or tow vehicle where you will have access to them in the event you lose your keys.

Mark J. Polk

Tip # 23

Always keep loose change on hand for Laundromats and toll roads. Don't forget the laundry detergent.

Tip # 24

When you leave on a trip, give a family member an itinerary of where you plan to be; or your cell phone number so they can contact you in case of an emergency. If you don't have a cell phone give the names and phone numbers of the campgrounds you will be staying at.

Tip # 25

When you check the condition of your battery using the monitor panel, make sure the RV is not plugged in to shore power. If it is, you will get a false reading (fully charged). To get a more accurate reading of the battery's condition check the monitor panel when the unit is not plugged in, and turn a couple of over head lights on to place a small load on the battery.

Tip # 26

Use only non-toxic RV antifreeze to winterize your RV. Never use automobile type antifreeze in RV water lines, it is extremely toxic.

Tip # 27

Before leaving on a trip always check the license plate and inspection/emission sticker on the RV to make sure they are current or won't expire while you are gone. Always make sure your RV insurance is current.

Tip # 28

The battery charger in the RV converter is only designed to keep the coach battery(s) topped off. It is not designed or capable of recharging a battery that is completely discharged.

Tip # 29

Show your children where the water heater and furnace vents are located and explain to them how hot they get. Keep children away from these vents, they can cause serious burns and injuries. Don't allow small children to turn any hot water faucets on. Hot water temperatures can be extremely high if not set properly.

Tip # 30

Having routine maintenance performed on your generator will assure you years of faithful service. Maintenance schedules are based on usage. Monitor the hour meter and refer to the owner's manual for routine and scheduled maintenance intervals.

Tip # 31

A water heater by-pass kit can save you six gallons of antifreeze when it's time to winterize your unit. You drain the water heater, put it in the by-pass mode and the antifreeze bypasses the tank and goes directly into the water lines.

Tip # 32

If you use a friction sway control always remove it before backing up to prevent damage to the friction sway bar.

Tip # 33

When you are packing items in your RV it is much easier if you use various sizes of see-through plastic containers. It is more organized and will prevent items from moving and falling while you travel. You can also look and see what is in each container without removing everything from the cabinet.

> **Tyler's Tip:** Nevr fil yur cup to the top wen travling. Dady hits bomps and yur drink flis out.

Tip # 34

LP gas is odorless, colorless and tasteless. It is odorless, but to assist you in detecting a leak when it is manufactured an odorant is added. If you are not familiar with the odor of LP gas, the next time you go to a qualified fill station ask them to let you smell it. Most people describe the smell as being similar to rotten eggs. Some people insist it has a garlic odor.

Tip # 35

Whenever you are determining the towing capacity of a vehicle make sure you know the rear axle ratio. It is quite possible to have the same type and size of vehicle with the same engine and tow ratings vary by several thousand pounds. The axle ratio is a comparison of how many times the drive shaft rotates versus the rear wheels. A 4.10:1 axle ratio means the drive shaft rotates 4.10 times for each rotation of the rear wheels. The higher the numeric value the better the vehicle will tow.

Tip # 36

If you're under a doctor's care, take a copy of your medical records with you when you go on a trip. Check and refill any prescription medication you will need while you are away.

Tip # 37

A tow vehicle that is four-wheel drive will have a lower tow rating than an identical vehicle that is two-wheel drive. The reason for this is the transfer case in the four-wheel drive vehicle adds additional weight to the vehicle, which lowers the tow rating by that amount. Keep in mind that any weight you add to the tow vehicle takes that same amount away from the tow rating.

> **Tyler's Tip:** Don't forgit yur flashlite. It gits vary darc out at nite.

Tip # 38

With your tow vehicle and trailer connected on a level surface stand back and look at it. If the lowest point is where the trailer tongue coupler sits on the ball mount you need to talk to your RV dealer about a weight distribution hitch. If you have a weight distribution hitch and it is still the lowest point between the tow vehicle and trailer the weight distribution hitch head and bars may need to be adjusted.

Tip # 39

When an RV manufacturer's brochure states that the bed in the RV is a queen size bed it is not the same dimensions as the queen size bed in your home. Do to limited space a queen size bed in an RV is either the actual width of a queen size bed or the actual length, but very seldom both. This is why your queen size sheets don't fit properly. If you want fitted sheets you'll probably need to have them custom made. This usually applies to other bed sizes in RVs as well.

Tip # 40

When stopping to refuel, select interstate exits that have several service stations. This will give you a better selection of fuel prices and where it will be easiest to maneuver with the RV. Watch out for tail swing!

Tip # 41

A quick and easy way to test your RV plumbing system for leaks is to turn the 12-volt water pump on when there is water in the fresh water holding tank. Once it pressurizes the system and turns off it should not come back on until you open a water faucet. If the pump does come on sporadically, even for short periods of time, water is leaking somewhere.

Mark J. Polk

> **Tyler's Tip:** Don't ty yur dog beehind yur bike and ride arond the kampgrnd.

Tip # 42

Print a detailed map and routes of your entire trip from an Internet trip planning service. It is a free service and it is a great help in tracking distance, routes, and exits that you need to be watching for especially in congested areas.

Tip # 43

Check the condition of your windshield wiper blades before you leave on a trip. This is one of those things we don't think about until the next time we need them.

Tip # 44

Know what the overall height of your RV is and constantly be aware of road clearances, gas stations, bridges, under passes and low hanging obstacles like overhead wires and tree branches. Post the height of your RV where it is easy to see to serve as a reminder.

Tip # 45

People using cell phones while they drive are at a much higher risk of being involved in an accident. The collision rate is equivalent to a drunk driver with a blood alcohol level of .10. Every RVer should have a cell phone with them, but avoid using it while driving and be alert for other drivers talking on a cell phone.

Tip # 46

Make sure your first aid kit or medicine cabinet includes items for bug bites, bee stings, swimmers ear, sunburns, upset stomachs, chapped lips, heartburn, rashes, sore throats, headaches, and fevers. Expect the unexpected; you might not have access to a store or pharmacy.

Epilogue

Well, if you got this far you must have finished "The RV Book." My goal with RV Education 101 and "The RV Book" is to help make all of your RV experiences safe, fun and stress free. We purchase RV's so we can travel to new destinations, relax and build lasting memories with our family and friends. We want to get away from work, the phone calls and other day-to-day hassles. RV's give us the freedom to go wherever we want, whenever we want. But, nothing will ruin a trip or a vacation quicker than not understanding how to properly use and maintain your RV.

Whether you own an RV now, or you are getting ready to purchase one in the future, I hope that reading "The RV Book" made you feel more comfortable about using an RV. I tried to touch on all aspects of RV ownership; from selecting the right RV to setting it up at your favorite campground. In an attempt to make your RV experiences even more enjoyable we offer a complete line of RV training videos. Sometimes it's easier to understand how things operate if we can visually see it, and you can watch it as many times as you want, or need to. I am including an order form at the back of the book with all of our current titles. You can go to **www.rveducation101.com** for more information about our company and our products.

Thanks for purchasing "The RV Book" and happy camping,

Mark J. Polk

Index

Mark J. Polk

rder Form

RV Education 101

To order by FAX, include credit card information and FAX to 910-484-8276

To order by mail, fill out form and send it, along with payment to:

RV Education 101
3969 Stedman Cedar Creek Road
Fayetteville, NC 28312
Phone 910-484-7615
www.rveducation101.com

✓ **Method of Payment**   Check_____ **Credit Card**_____

Name_____ Date_____

Address_____ City_____ State____ Zip_____

Phone_____

Credit Card Orders: Visa____ Master Card____ American Express____

Name on Card_____ Card #_____

Expiration Date_____ Signature_____ Date_____

Use this form to order DVDs. For VHS and book orders please call or use our website.

DVD Titles	✓ Quantity	Amount
Pop-up		
Travel Trailer/5th Wheel		
Type A Motorhome		
Type C MH Rental/Owner		
TT Towing & Backing		
Towing Behind a Motorhome		
Winterizing & Storing Your RV		
Recommended Essential Items		$5.95 each
RV Campground Basics		

S&H $4.95 1 item / $7.95 2 or more items   **S&H**_____

DVDs $24.95   **Total**_____

With us, camping really is
all fun and games.

**Great people.
Great camping.™**

Creating fun for RVers is serious business for the friendly and
helpful staff at KOA's 450 North American locations. Join us for
a great camping getaway and enjoy this special offer on your
next adventure. We'll be waiting to welcome you!

273   Mark J. Polk

Our 450 independently owned KOA locations have a whole lot to offer. Accommodations include a variety of RV sites, cabins, and tents. You'll enjoy unsurpassed guest service, spotless restrooms, convenience stores, pools and more. Many KOAs offer wireless Internet, full hookup, 50 amp pull-thru RV sites too. We look forward to making your RV adventures great.

Plan your trip and make reservations today at koa.com.

Please present this coupon upon check-in. Onetime use only. Valid Through 12/31/08. 10% off one stay, limit 4 days Kampsight® code: 101

Campground Instructions:

• This promotional Value Kard is valid for the FULL 10% Value Kard savings benefit.

• Please enter the code on the front of this card as the Value Kard number in Kampsight® to ensure the proper discount is given.

• This card is valid for onetime use only, for a maximum stay of four nights. Please collect the card from the camper at check-in and destroy.